The Adventure
of Language

The Adventure
of Language

Michael Girsdansky

Prentice-Hall, Inc., Englewood Cliffs, N.J.

Library of Congress Catalog Card Number: 63–10692

Printed in the United States of America
01397–T

PRENTICE-HALL INTERNATIONAL, INC.
London · Tokyo · Sydney · Paris

PRENTICE-HALL OF CANADA, LTD.

PRENTICE-HALL DE MEXICO, S.A.

To:

Cathy,
Karina
and
Paul Scott
in order of size.

Contents

linguistic and the scientific world-outlooks
. . . a world of process and change . . .

A constantly changing world . . . how
certain languages treat Change . . . everyday ideas in new ways of speech . . . odd
adjectives and prepositions . . . strange
singulars and plurals . . . does a language
make a world? . . . ideas of Time . . .
the many ways of seeing things . . .

The decline and fall of "whom" . . .
some imaginary sentences . . . the classical tradition . . . declension, word-order
and conjugation . . . categories of speech
in European tongues . . . verbs and the
logic of sentences in the West . . . how
logical are linguistics distinctions? . . .

CHAPTER 5

Styles of Language, high and low . . .
the growth of "the high tradition" . . .
levels of style and the fame of Rome . . .
horses in history . . . the natural way of
saying things . . . syntax and parataxis
. . . subordination and coordination of
sentences and their parts . . . complex
and compound sentences—and simple ones,

too . . . how other languages build up
their sentences . . .

The idea of "word" . . . how free are
words? . . . changes at the beginning—
Welsh . . . Hebrew rings changes on
vowels . . . 't is or is it? . . . two words
marry to make one . . . one word can be
a sentence—or vice versa . . . French,
German and English "words" . . . a tentative definition . . . examples and oddities . . . the merging of forms and how
hard it is sometimes to draw the line . . .

A deadly blunder in translation . . . types
of misunderstanding . . . peoples' names
for themselves . . . overlappings of meaning . . . how *not* to translate . . . Norman and Saxon . . . how to borrow a
word without knowing what it means . . .
wigs and wigmakers . . . the meanings of
virtue . . . geographical changes in Language . . . temporal changes in Language
. . . "nice" wasn't nice, once upon a time
. . . the story of "silly" . . . what happened to *christian* . . . puns and their
classification . . . French and the lowest
form of humor . . . we're all misunderstood . . .

CONTENTS

The sounding reed

"MAN is the weakest reed in the universe—but he is a thinking reed," said French philosopher Blaise Pascal. And he is a sounding reed as well. The breath of spirit blows across him; its sound is voice, and its shape is language.

Modulation of this vibrating column of air, trembling in the throat's moist tube of flesh, is Man's greatest invention: brighter than fire, and stronger than spears. For language, in the lost days of its beginnings, gave warmth and some answer to fear and loneliness. Even after the first fires had rattled into embers, there was the soft and halting sound of voices, and the caves and shabby encampments became for the first time something more than frightened huddling-places.

More than the gift of company, speech gave Man community, too. Weak as individuals, men learned to draw a new strength from the nerve and muscle of language: no saber-tooth or mastodon could stand for long against the *collective* might of those new and strange creatures whose purpose was bound together by the barks and yips their mouths could make.

That delicate thread of shaken air has been Man's badge—and burden—ever since. Even today, men who share a common tongue know themselves as somehow kin; though it is perhaps false knowledge, the feeling is still sincere. Confronted by the babblers of a foreign speech, the tribal man beneath the skin of each of us still bristles with suspicion, or snickers uneasily at an implication of the faintly outlandish or ridiculous. Why not? This is the long-lived remnant of an earlier day, in which the name of the home tribe meant "The Human Beings," or "The Speakers." Those Others—the aliens—were just as often "The Un-Men," "The Stutterers," or "The Mutes."

*   *

At least once in every man's lifetime, there comes the feeling that "none of this is real": the solidity of brick, the conventional cut of tie and trouser-cuff, the subject of conversation at the moment, even the shape of hill and river; all of these at one time or another seem to grow for a moment or two pale and distant. There have been many explanations of this feeling, but perhaps one which is as close to truth as any other is that, in such instance, we half see our surroundings as lesser creatures do—directly, without the tinted glasses of humanity. At such times language strikes us as irrelevant.

Suddenly, one of the props is knocked out from beneath the long taken-for-granted world of words and human understandings. The universe of words—a universe so much our second nature that we seldom think of it—melts away. It is then that we may feel how truly artificial, how man-made, are the sounds and rules of grammar which float like a thin film over that other and far older world of the hard, the tangible, the *real*.

And here then is Man, lost in the midst of that hard reality, presumptuously pasting his labels to the sequoia and the star, insisting that the universe be cut and shaped to the specifications of individual logics and the categories of particular modes of speech. There are many who would term this insufferable arrogance and call for greater humility on the part of That Prideful Animal.

I have come to see this presumptuousness in a different light.

Though there may be some great part of folly in Man's pride, I think of it as a folly to be respected. The idea of a forked bit of tissue balancing precariously upright while it judges—and christens—the universe is enough to stagger anyone with its incongruity. If this be arrogance, it is an arrogance worthy of awed respect.

For Man's first uncertain words brought a new thing into the world: awareness. With the creation of these patterned sounds, repeatable at will, the gigantic universe around became less important in one sense. No longer was it necessary for a given aspect of reality to be actually present; *now it could be talked about*, resurrected from absence and made vocally real. By means of Language, Man pulled himself up by his bootstraps long before he had boots.

And this new awareness of Man set him once and for all outside the framework of the "natural world"—a world which, before him, had not even known it was. Space and time, change and stasis, nearness and distance, were no longer qualities of a purely indifferent world, or scampering reflexes working blindly within the lower nerve-centers of mute beasts. They were reborn as *symbols*, patterns of electric charge dancing through the inconceivably complex network of Man's brain.

But something more than these neutral concepts came into the world together with speech: love and hope—love and hope which recognized themselves. And other, less pleasant, things, for there is always a price to be paid. Conscious hate and fear were born, too—and knowledge of death. Cast out from the Eden of unawareness, men knew Good and Evil. With the possibility of greatness came the unique opportunity to be corrupt, and only Man writes—or makes—tragedies. Wisdom and foresight can be bitter, for "of all creatures, only Man knows that he must die."

Yet, if to be human is to know pain and sorrow beyond that of other, simpler creatures, nonetheless Man has his lonely joys—and a chance at nobility. William Faulkner, in his speech accepting the Nobel Prize for Literature, voiced a concern lest, in the last days of a dying earth, when stars are growing dark and cold, and the very fabric of nature itself begins to ravel at the seams, the last sound of all will be that of the human voice, talking . . . talking . . .

*   *

Man is the weakest reed in the universe, but he is a thinking reed.

And he is a voiced reed, that creature who is human.

🖋 I

"Man became man"

"Thanks to Language, Man became Man."
—*Baron Friedrich von Humboldt* (1769–1859)

THE day is hot and oppressive; with a haze that dims the hills, turning the vague glimpses of them blue. Cicadas have been singing their rattling, buzzing song in the trees and the farmer's dog looks at the cattle in the field indifferently, his tongue lolling as he sprawls in the shade of the porch.

The farmer wipes the sweat from his brow with the back of his forearm, and turns to his son. "Hot day," he says. The boy nods agreement.

They toss hay from the top of the wagon into the upper loft of the barn, hour after hour. Slowly, though neither farmer nor son notice it, the cicadas slow their song till it dies away. Now, the air should be still, but for a few minutes more there is the uneasy twitter of birds. Strange, for it is not yet dusk. Or *is* it? The air is getting darker.

No. It is the middle of the afternoon; twilight is still a good way off. But blue-black clouds have been making their way slowly over the western horizon. Suddenly, a small quick breeze starts up: a strange, half-chilly breeze that turns up the undersides of the leaves, showing an unexpected flash of light green. The swallows that have been darting here and there begin to circle low over the lake, and the dog barks nervously once or twice. The cows moo softly.

Eventually even the human beings notice it. Something in the air tells them what it is, even before they look up from the hay. One of them—no matter which—says, "Looks like rain." The other nods. In half an hour the wagon and cattle are safely in the barn. Just as the man, the boy, and the dog are making their way into the farmhouse kitchen, the first heavy drops begin to fall through the sullen air.

*   *

Something like this scene has probably been a part of human experience ever since Man began to pen up cattle and tend them, to plant and to harvest. Even in those earlier days in which chance herb-gathering and hunting were the means of survival, equivalent words were doubtless spoken.

Words were spoken. That is the only part of this scene which is purely human, for in every other response it was the humans who were slow and backward. The birds sensed the coming storm, as did the cattle and the insects in the trees. The dog certainly knew of it far, far in advance, scents coming to him more strongly through the dampening air.

As well as simple awareness, there were sub-human messages among the animals. The cattle communicated a feeling of general unease to one another through their lowing; the birds with their low circlings and premature twilight-song expressed a knowledge of the foul weather to come; even the stilling of the cicadas' ratchet-like buzz was a kind of message-by-default. But though it is certain that information passed between these individuals of each kind before the rain began to fall, it is just as certain that it was not Language—even crude Language—that was used.

Only Man, so far as we know, has achieved true Speech. *Dozhd' eedyot, Es wird regnen, il pleuvra, rain's coming.* Only by men are these, or any other words, uttered, for Language is uniquely human.

Easy to say, but what are we saying? What *is* Language?

The first answer one is tempted to give is, "Words that mean something." But parrots can repeat certain words, even words in sequence; yet they are not human and their words not even a Language. Such words are a reflex evoked by highly particular situations in which the bird finds itself. In another sense, a computer—an electronic brain—could be designed even today which would respond to certain orders with audible or typed-out words or sentences.[1] Yet this is not Language as either the man in the street or the psychologist understand it.

What *is* it, then?

There have been hundreds of definitions offered over the centuries, but the following might serve as a rough approximation:

Language is a set of *arbitrary symbols* (words) which are placed in *orderly relationship* with one another according to conventions accepted and understood by the speakers, for the transmission of *messages*.

We will take a closer look at the key terms in this definition on the pages following.

Arbitrary symbols—Although we shall see later in this book (chapter 6) that "word" is an extremely difficult concept to make precise, for the moment let us accept it as understood. Even believing that we know what a word is, however, there are many who think of *a* word as *the* word.

There is the old joke about a man who invented an Italian pasta product and named it *spaghetti*. When asked why he had given it that name in particular, he answered, "Because it looks like spaghetti, it feels like spaghetti, and it tastes like spaghetti." The joke notwithstanding, there is no right or natural name for

---

[1] We are speaking of present-day computers in which this verbal response is by no means an example of true speech or writing. Eventually there might be developed machines which could employ Language in a sense analogous to Man's use of it; but that is something for the future (See chapter 15).

anything—except as the speakers of a particular language agree upon it; and then it is right and natural only for them.[2]

Let it be noted that:

the Greek	*hippos*
the Hebrew	*soos*
the (Classical) Latin	*equus*
the (Medieval) Latin	*caballus*
the Russian	*kon'* or *loshad'*
the German	*Rosz* or *Pferd*
the French	*cheval*

all equally represent that neighing, prancing, racing animal which nuzzles its master's pocket for a lump of sugar. All the words above are as definitely *horse* as the English term: no more, no less. For the horse has no real name of his own.

In contrast to this highly "unnatural" capriciousness in the varieties of human speech—where in unrelated languages like words for like things are rare exceptions—non-human animals have a "vocabulary" that is comparatively fixed. This is so even when they are brought up in isolation from others of their kind. But the variety of messages which they send is limited, and the messages themselves always characterized by *immediacy*. That is, the grunt, squeal, moo, whinny or whatever—together with any accompanying bodily gestures—signifies little more than invitation to action (flight, attack, courtship, etc.) or the expression of mood such as was sketched out at the beginning of the present chapter; and in either case, they are a response to a single, particular situation.

The function of non-human animal sounds might well be

---

[2] Partial exceptions to this are the onomatopoetic words: terms commonly accepted as being imitations of universal and non-human sounds or noises. But even here, the conventional factor within a given language plays an extremely strong role. A French cat does not *purr;* he goes *ron-ron.* A German door swinging closed does not *bang; bums* or *knapps* is the sound for it. And no self-respecting piece of Russian machinery would ever break with a *snap;* it is a case of going *tr'esk* or not breaking at all!

compared with the use of a code-book in war-time. An officer wishing to transmit a message looks up a sequence of numbers or letters which stands for an entire complex of information—thus, "12563" might represent "send up a company of reinforcements." In contrast, human speech shares something of the nature of a cypher. A given number or letter stands for a letter in the original language; "xlzmz nmz svb?" might stand for "where are you?" with x = w, l = h, z = e, m = r, and so forth.

It is this difference in the use of sounds which may lie at the heart of the distinction between animal pseudo-speech and human language. Seen in this light, the gamut of animal usage may be regarded as a vocabulary of *signs,* as contrasted with human *symbols.* These two terms are often used interchangeably, but it would be well at this point to draw a sharp distinction between them. Briefly:

The sign marks (i.e., acts as a token), while the symbol represents.

As a token, the sign may either be reflected back to the utterer (as in expressions of visceral mood) or turned outwards in hope of response. The cat revels in the pure sensuous joy of having its ear-jaw area rubbed by a friendly finger, and its purr of satisfaction is as much a part of itself as the happy twitch of its whiskers; insofar as the purr is not intended as encouragement to the well-meaning human being, the purr *is* the enjoyment, as much as is the happy groan of a man stretching after a long sleep. In a similar fashion, the back-yard serenades of Tom or Tabby *are* love and desire (or at least the outward and audible signs thereof), rather than symbols of amour. For it is the nature of a symbol that it stand for something else.

The symbol may be thought of as the psychological equivalent of legal tender, which draws its importance not from what it is, but from what it is accepted as meaning. Just as the primitive system of direct barter has largely given way to exchange of pieces of metal (or even paper, one step further removed), so too, the system of immediate signs has largely been supplanted

by a system of symbols which bear no direct and necessary relationship to the situation at hand.

The word "fire," used as it usually is as a symbol, stands for
an entire collection of sense-perceptions and remembered associations: the notions of heat and light and pain are bundled together in that one constellation of sound, as are an entire set of
abstractions concerning what happens when certain materials
are heated sufficiently or brought into contact with flame. A rise
in temperature, the cooking of food, the destruction of forests
are perhaps the most immediate connotations evoked, but the
thought of charring, oxidation, and even the abstract notion of
arson follow thereafter. Both a physical and a psychological world
of meaning are called up with the one word "fire"; by no stretch
of the imagination can such properties be attributed to a simple
sign. Through the abstractional nature which it possesses, the
symbol becomes a means of generating the outside world within
the confines of human understanding; it can, in fact, do even
more and create "realities" never seen on land or sea—such as
six-legged unicorns, polka dot mermaids, and the like.

But though a symbol is something more than a sign, it can be
used for that simpler purpose as well. For instance, the word
"fire!" shouted in a theater is definitely a sign—a warning signal—
no different in kind from the distress-cry of a hungry calf, or the
flick of a white-tail deer to warn of approaching hunters.

It would be a great gain in our knowledge of human behavior
if we could learn the way Language grew among those first
humans who wrought the miracle of Speech. Unfortunately we
do not have time-machines and we probably never shall. There
will be no trips into prehistory for us, to watch the birth of the
Word.[3]

[3] Early linguists developed a number of theories to account for the origin of
Language—and showed a good deal of imagination in naming them. The
"ding-dong" theory assumed that there was some necessary and logical connection between the sound of a word, and the thing referred to; this theory
has been pretty largely discarded as more languages have come under study
(see the remarks following the story of the man who named spaghetti, above).
The "poo-poo" doctrine ascribed primitive language to exclamations of surprise, fear, etc. "Bow-wow" linguists insisted that Language grew from the

Nevertheless, proud new parents have probably seen some-thing vaguely reminiscent of this process as they watch their offspring go about the business of making their feelings and wants known. If it is not the acquisition of Language by people, it is at least the growth of Language in a person. (But it will never help to answer the riddle of how the first men learned Speech when there was no one around to learn it from.)

At first, the infant (Latin *infans*, "unable to speak") has only the use of his lungs—generally more than equal to the task—from which he pours out a large quantity of raw, unmodulated, highly audible sound. Even here, however, it is not difficult to distinguish between the yell which means *bottle, fast!* and the petulant whine which equals *wet!* Neither of these, in turn, is likely to be confused with the air of pure contentment and satis-faction embodied in *goo*.

Such use of sound is perfectly comparable with the cries of so-called dumb beasts, which is not surprising since the baby is still working at learning to be human. It is, however, when Junior says his first words, that loving progenitors are likely to make the mistake of thinking that—at last!—there is one more speaker in the house. It is true that eventually Speech will come, but those first words are no more true Language than the first steps are a learning of how to do the fox-trot. Junior has gradu-ated from the hungry-calf to the talented-parrot stage; but still his words are signs, not symbols.

For the up-and-coming young member of the human race, "bottle" is a sign fitted within a particular context; it may be a pointer equalling "I've seen that before! I know what that is!" or—more likely—"Dinner-time." In the same way, "doggie," fol-

---

imitation of natural sounds (onomatopoeia). All such theories (there are others, also intriguingly nicknamed) show at least the ingenuity of the originator, and one of them (or a combination of several) may even be correct. Unfortunately we shall never know; they are all unprovable. However, they were at least improvements over suggestions put forth earlier—such as the thesis which made Swedish the language of God in the garden of Eden; Danish the language spoken by Adam; and French the language used by the Serpent. (Needless to say, this theory was the work of a Swede in the 1600's—when relations between Sweden and France were not always perfectly cordial.)

lowed by a squeal of absolute joy, is toddler shorthand for "Oh boy! I can hardly wait to pet that!" (Followed by a wail instead of a squeal, of course, it means the precise opposite: "Mama, get me away from here!" Much hinges on the child, the situation, and—often—the dog.)

Eventually there comes that moment when the threshold is truly crossed, not in a single bound but by degrees, and the child may be said truly to Speak. Gradually "bottle" comes to stand simply for a glass container; the cluster of sounds is no longer a mere token of hunger, surprise, or recognition occurring within the small body at some fixed moment in time. So too, "doggie" grows to become a label affixed to all those nice (or nasty) creatures who can run faster than the child, have lots of hair all over, and can growl or lick. At this point, "bottle" and "doggie" can honestly be described as symbols, and the child's use of words as Language.

Then, of course, comes the problem of how to put these separate clusters of sounds together, so as to convey ideas which are a good deal more complicated . . .

Orderly relationships—Captain Jenkins of Her Majesty's 13th Horse Marines (Motorized) saluted crisply, and delivered his report: "They're a simple, childlike people, sir. Trusting and extremely friendly. The language itself is absurdly easy to learn —just a few hundred words—one-syllabled grunts, really—thrown together any old fashion . . ."

This is a parody, of course, but something like it has been part of the mythology of adventure fiction and true-life "journals of exploration" for at least the last 200 years, ever since the opening-up of America, Africa, and Australia. Sometimes the natives *aren't* friendly (in which case, read "childish" for "childlike" and add something about "unpredictable treacherousness"), but at least the language is always simple: a matter of "ugh!" "how!" or something equally moronic, and of course invariably "thrown together any old fashion."

A very comforting description to European supremicists. Unfortunately it doesn't happen to be true.

The implicit assumptions of this particular cliché are fairly easy to trace: The natives use spears. We use jellied gasoline. Therefore they are primitive. Children are also primitive little beasts. Therefore the natives are like children. Children don't speak very well. Therefore natives don't speak very well—and their language is a funny sort of baby talk. Q.E.D.

In line with this string of propositions, such dialogue as "Me Tarzan—you Jane," and "Treaty of Great White Father no good" is supposed to reveal a simplemindedness both in the speaker and in his native tongue. Leaving the idiocy of the logic to one side, it is a simple matter of fact that *"simple" peoples rarely speak "simple" languages.*[4] And as for the notion that the words of the natives' language can be thrown together any which way, all that need be said is that no language known is indifferent to the arrangement of the constituent parts of its statements.[5]

Messages—"My name is Ozymandias, King of Kings. Look on my works ye mighty, and despair." These were the words graven into the base of the statue standing forlorn and ignored in the midst of a great desert. But until someone—the "I" of the poem— saw that time-etched mass of stone, *there was no message.* It had died with the last man who (knowing the language) had walked past the image of his king, in the streets of that forgotten city a thousand years before.

Though this should be obvious on the face of it, it is mentioned because many people, even today, do not quite believe it.

[4] As we shall see in the differences between Latin and its modern Romance descendants, in the stripped-down logic of Chinese, and in the story of English itself, there is some evidence that the tendency is—within historical times at least—for languages to grow *simpler* with the passage of time, rather than more complex. Endings wither away, exceptional plural forms become rarer, irregular verbs drop from common usage or are regularized. But simple or complicated, "advanced" or "primitive"—no language yet encountered has proved to be without its own very definite and rigorous laws of logic and grammar—even if there has never existed a word for either of these two ideas in the language involved.

[5] This is true even of such primitive languages as Greek and Latin, in which endings attached to words permit rather more freedom of word-order than is possible in English. It is, of course, even truer of such advanced tongues as Malay and Chinese.

The idea that if we only speak slowly (or loudly) enough, foreigners will somehow understand us; our naïve certainty (usually below the level of consciousness) that our own tongue is somehow the "right" language; even the notion that a statement gains in trustworthiness upon appearance in cold print—all of these attitudes testify in some sense to a blithe disregard of the fact that it takes two to make a message—sender and recipient.

For a *message,* in most general terms, is only a collection of symbols transferred from one point to another. (The two points do not necessarily have to be separate in space: a letter or phonograph record may be left to posterity. When re-read or re-played, the message traverses the gap of time.) Even in the act of talking to ourselves we play two roles, one after the other. This can be seen in our habit of frequently speaking so in the second person: "You really made a fool of yourself that time, John my boy!" says John to himself. Additional proof that we always conceive of some listener to our statements lies in the fact that when we *do* use the "I" in self-conversation—as in "Oh, why did I do that?"—the remark is aimed at an imaginary audience around us, or at "our better self."

We might expect as much, for Man comes from notably gregarious stock. A night spent in the tropic rain-forests listening to our not-so-distant cousins, the monkeys, will show that togetherness must have been practiced for a good portion of the time we spent in the branches of our family tree. But the precise change that brought about true Speech . . . who can say what it was? Perhaps a sudden and obscure mutation, a change in the brain of some man-like creature a million years ago. Whatever it was, it was something which passed down to the cute and possibly furry offspring.

We shall never be certain exactly how Man became human; even a lucky fossil discovery will never show the subtleties of brain structure which made possible the gift of Speech. But such an ability, the gift of symbols and symbolism, must have been of use to spread so widely. It must have occurred among creatures accustomed to spending time with one another, and possibly creatures who looked for company because they were not quite sure of themselves and were afraid.

Aristotle called man a social animal. It is certainly significant that solitary, un-social animals (such as bears) lack even that pseudo-language of signs possessed by creatures who live in herds or flocks (bees, deer, etc.). (The exception being the limited "language" such hermit animals use in courtship—the only situation in which these loners deal willingly with their own kind.)

So it was from Man's social nature that Language grew, and helped to bring him even closer to his fellows. And this may have been more necessary than most of us realize, since pre-Man was probably not too well adapted to life in the raw—too recently down from the trees to feel at home on the ground, somewhat too heavy for comfort in the tree-tops. But however humble its origins, Language became something far greater than the first hesitant users of it could ever have imagined.

But no matter what he intended to say, and no matter what the sound he made, that first speaker's first word was "Adam." For what he said, though he never guessed it, was, "I am Man."

2

Dancer, dancing, and the dance

Oh, Chestnut tree, great-rooted blossomer,
Are you the leaf, the blossom or the bole?
O body swayed to music, O brightening glance,
How can we know the dancer from the dance?

—William Butler Yeats, *Among School Children*

AND this is Eden: the most lovely garden in the world; a garden that *is* the world, in fact. In that garden is Surprise, for in Eden everything is wonderful because all of it is new. If we ever bother to think of it, it must seem likely that the newborn child sees his brand-new toy, the World, as just such a place—a paradise of *things*.

When the knot of discomfort we adults have come to call *hunger* begins to make itself felt in the small belly, an immense and comforting bulk moves childward, there are soothing sounds, and then the happiness of milk . . .

There is the hugeness of bars surrounding the crib. To an infant eye, untrained in perspective, they doubtless seem to reach up to the unimaginably distant ceiling.

There will be the occasional confrontation with another thing —a thing somewhat like the soother and milk-giver—less adept at handling diapers, possessing scratchy cheeks, and with no easily-discernible purpose in the scheme of things.

Later, there may be dogs, cats, or goldfish—parakeets, even—
but the names for these things will come more slowly, after the
easy sounds of *mommy* and *daddy*.

. . . There will certainly be a first encounter with that blue
kind of ceiling almost always up there when there is an outing.
Often, puffy white things will be pasted to it. And both the
white and the blue will always be just out of reach . . .

For there will be reaching, of course. Later, crawling. Walking
after that. As time goes on, there will be the scraping of knees,
sliding down jungle-gyms, and riding on merry-go-rounds. Lick-
ing ice-cream cones, gobbling frankfurters, and swilling soda-pop
will follow soon enough. (These last will generally be preludes
to the holding of stomachs and howlings of discomfort.)

No, these young lives will never be dull ones. They never
have been. There is always action, and lots of it. But before the
action—so we think, we who can never remember our own first
learnings—come the Things.

*   *

It would be comforting to know that such is the natural course
of events: a nice, neat, and natural distinction between the doer
and the done on the one hand, and the doing on the other. It
would be pleasant to think that the Nouns and Verbs of the
classroom are inevitable reflections of What Really Is. The
dancer and his dancing—so our parts-of-speech minds run—
should be treated as creatures alien to one another. Such a sharp
split is after all certainly traditional with us, and tradition should
be of some weight in gauging the proprieties.

Unfortunately, this tradition is a limited one; one which
reached its fullest flowering in particular places, at certain times.
It is not universal. However, for better or worse, it has been *our*
tradition—the second nature of Europe and her children.

This compartmentalization of the universe into two principal
categories of actors and actions is more than a mere issue of

abstract philosophy, a question of pure logic. Such a division in the world of our ideas has (and has had) very practical implications in such widely separate fields as engineering and psychology.

This bifurcated view of reality comes to us in many guises: Mind versus Matter, Soul purer than Body, Energy as contrasted with Matter. Often the underlying distinction is thought of as being that of a solid, corporeal, and integral *something* as opposed to an immaterial and active *process*.

However, this two-principle outlook may assume other aspects as well. The half-deliberate, concrete regarding of Good and Evil as opposed essences (rather than actions) is perhaps an offshoot of a persistent "thingishness" in the languages and thought of Europe, at the expense of an activist philosophy. (As we shall see later on, there are peoples who do not draw the doer-doing distinction; and even some who see "doing" as basic, the "doer," the "done," and the "done-to," as secondary ideas.) When one of these two categories does take on a verb-like coloring, it is usually Evil. This can be seen in the common tendency to regard Perfection as a *state to be achieved* (or hoped for), while Imperfection is often regarded as that which interferes, upsets, or otherwise works actively to spoil the Ideal.

According to a widely-revered philosophic tradition of the West—the school of thought usually associated with the name of Plato—the notions of Good, Truth, and Beauty are more than notions: they are *things*. Seen in the light of such philosophic realism, it is not merely ships, shoes, and sealing-wax which should be regarded as thing-ish—in fact they take a decidedly secondary place—but a host of other concepts which most of us today would think of as qualities, properties, or abstractions.

Though few of us today are Platonists, much of our thought—and certainly much of our language—is still committed to a world outlook which sees the universe as primarily a collection of objects undergoing activity. This point of view is far from inevitable: some peoples refuse to distinguish in their languages between between object and activity (Verb vs. Noun); others conceive of action as primary (the Verb being the basic unit). Though it may seem strange to us, it is perfectly possible to view the world as a set of processes which "solidify" themselves only temporarily in "things."

If this reversed (to our way of thinking) idea of the universe is possible, why did the languages of Europe take the opposite path? Have we Westerners somehow achieved the heights of logic? Are all other, differing philosophies (and language systems) illogical, foolish, perverse?[1]

The evolution of this thing-dominated outlook may quite possibly depend on the history and nature of our Western languages. If so, it would explain the survival of over-simplifications in the face of proof that Nature is, in fact, not so simple as we would like. Scientists and philosophers (as well as men-in-the-street) do learn one language or another as their native tongue, after all. And from what linguistics has managed to unearth, it seems quite likely that each of the tongues of mankind has certain unspoken assumptions built into it regarding the nature of the world around us.

That we think of certain ideas as "natural" or "logical" may conceivably stem from the fact that we have ancestors who spoke certain languages. We do not owe the mainstream of philosophic or scientific thought in the West to the Chinese Mencius or the Amerind (American Indian) Sekwoya.[2] The traditions of our inquiry, the theorizings which are ancestral to our brand of logic, the notions we have of what is common sense: all these are the products of a small part of the ancient world—that part which lies cozily round the Mid-land (Mediterranean) Sea. The very

---

[1] If the reader does think these other interpretations of reality are necessarily nonsensical, it should be pointed out in passing that atomic scientists would probably not agree. The solidity of a chair or table, seen under high enough magnification, dissolves into a swarm of particles dashing madly hither and yon. And even these particles are not microscopic billiard balls, all densely compact; they are themselves vibrations. P.S.: It is not considered cricket to ask *what* is (or are) vibrating. Physicists will look unhappy when you do. The question, they will tell you, is "a meaningless noise."

[2] Immortalized as a type of redwood tree under a slightly different spelling.

name of that oversized lake gives our arrogance away, for it is near the middle of nothing except our pride.

The very beginnings of what we consider Reason were established there, in the rather kindly climate found over that warm arm of the Atlantic which even today looms far larger in our minds than it does on the map. And the men who made these beginnings spoke a common tongue—or at least tongues which sprang from a common source.[3] The men who later built upon these foundations were bound by the same common ancestry of speech—often unsuspected till recently: even tongues at first glance so alien to one another as Spanish, English, Russian, and Armenian, bear a distant kinship to Greek and Latin. And all can trace their lineage back to that language lost in the dust of close to 10,000 years ago. In a real sense, all Europeans are linguistic cousins, some close, some distant.[4] We all speak dialects of a common speech. Small wonder that the Western World agrees about much concerning the nature of Reality. Our ancestral language drew a hard-and-fast distinction we still observe: the distinction between the Dancer and the Dancing.

*   *

Western tongues (as a legacy from their remote common ancestor) have always been predisposed toward seeing the universe as a museum of exhibits—things, with sharply defined edges. As an appropriate reflection, the Noun stands inviolable, excluding everything which lies beyond the borders of its definition.

Corresponding to this exclusiveness is the logical "law of thought" known as the Law of the Excluded Middle: "A thing is either A or not-A; it cannot be both; it cannot be neither." The equivalent of this in everyday language would be: "If an animal is a horse, it cannot be some other animal; if it is some

---

[3] See chapter 9 for a discussion of Indo-European.
[4] Except for Hungarians, Finns, Estonians, and Basques (that mysterious people whose language is spoken in the Pyrénées of France and Spain).

other animal, it cannot be a horse; and no animal can be neither a horse nor some animal—it must be one or the other."

This law of thought makes very good sense. It *is* common sense, in fact. Until we begin to think about mules. What is that beastie, according to the Law of the Excluded Middle? It is neither one thing nor the other; it is both. It violates the neatly-drawn categories of *horse* and *not-horse*. It would be consoling if we could abolish it as a contradiction in terms; but it stands there stubbornly all the same—head down, mean-looking, and uttering an occasional bray to prove the point of its existence.

There is a reason for this, of course. Simply stated, it comes down to this: the universe is too large, subtle, and complicated to fit neatly into any of our logical or linguistic pigeonholes without bulging somewhere at the seams. The Indo-European scheme, with its sharply drawn distinction between thing-nouns and action-verbs, is no more objectionable than any other. But it does bulge. And it is not the only possible scheme.

Though no particular world outlook has a monopoly on Truth-with-a-capital-T, some viewpoints are more appropriate to given times, places, and circumstances than are others. In the early days of scientific and philosophical speculation, it was quite probably fortunate that Greek and Latin divided reality into a number of sharply distinguished categories.[5] Too much thoughtfulness—too early—can be stultifying. If the ancient world had had a real idea of the complexities of the universe, its rather simple little theories and diagrams might never have been developed. A picture of the solar system in which little points of light revolve round our earth, each set in a film of crystal which moves it, may be a false picture—but it is a starting point. Better that than nothing at all; and given the unaided human eye before the day of telescopes, and given natural perspective, the heliocentric theory was the most plausible assumption.

[5] The view implies that linguistic habits have encouraged particular directions of thought and discovery. It is only fair to point out that new discoveries and schools of thought can generate words—and often new logical categories, as well. The specialized meaning of the word *function,* as well as the concept expressed, are the products of a revolution in mathematical thinking.

If, somehow, the ancient Greek had learned that what surrounded him was an immensity of space in which planets were
worlds, and stars alien suns huger than our own, he might well
have thrown up his hands in despair. There were no tools, there
was no technology to produce the tools, which could investigate
and make sense of such a universe. Better for him—and for us—a
cozy little cosmos not completely beyond a man's ability to deal
with.

But though our knowledge of the world has far surpassed that
of the ancient Greek or Roman, Western Language since then
has taken little notice of changing pictures of the universe.

This conservatism of language is most clearly seen in everyday
life with respect to matters of vocabulary. We still speak of
"water," for instance, as though it were a single substance, one
and indivisible, because the substance has been known time out
of mind, occurs in abundance, and there has been little reason in
normal life to take note of its compound nature. There has never
existed any temptation for the average man to think of water as
anything but a unity.

The chemist and physicist, however, deal with it in terms of
its structure and the reactions it undergoes. Their term—H_2O—
reflects a deeper insight into the nature of watery reality, an
insight of which everyday language takes no formal notice. The
same conservatism holds true for almost all the commonly encountered—yet complex—substances which we speak of famil-
iarly; our language treats each as though it were something
simple and unified. "Salt" ($NaCl$), "rust" (Fe_2O_3), and "vin-
egar" (dilute CH_3COOH) are merely the most commonplace
examples which come to mind.

It might be said that the "simplistic" names given in everyday
language are the result of original ignorance; chemical analysis
is comparatively recent, and the words for every common substance were created long before there was any dream of the
world's true complexity. This is doubtless a partial explanation,
but it *is* only partial. Bronze, for instance, has been known for
millennia as an alloy of copper and tin, yet even it has always

been known under a single, unitary name. "Aqua regia" ("royal water") is a phrase still used in chemistry (!) to describe the solution resulting from the combination of two distinctly different acids. Thus, even the sciences have survivals which fail to reflect the entities with which they deal.

This tendency toward "unitary" naming in everyday life can be seen at work when a modern compound or piece of gadgetry gains wide use or acceptance. No sooner does it achieve widespread recognition than it is promptly redubbed with a simpler title and thought of as a single "thing"—by everyone but the original scientists, who may be the only ones who really know what the truth of the matter is.

This process of re-naming can be in the interest of brevity, as when dichlorodiphenyltrichloroethane is re-christened DDT. But just as often there seems to be another force at work (one might almost call it a Platonic feeling, when we recall that philosopher's "thingifying"). There appears to be a belief that a nicely compact name makes a concept, compound, device, or whatever, more *real* than does a mere descriptive phrase. "Calcium sulphate" and "Plaster of Paris" have precisely the same number of syllables, yet even today when its composition is well-known, the former name is never used outside a laboratory. "Carborundum," similarly, is the everyday term; "silicon carbide" is technical. Yet the scientific name is only one syllable longer, and if anything, is perhaps a trifle easier to spell. But who save a technician would recognize it, even in this technical age?

The belief that a precise, unitary name lends a greater degree of realness to the object named may have something to do with another linguistic habit, closely allied to the one mentioned above: we constantly use different, unrelated words to describe what is essentially the same thing. "Mare" and "horse," "doe" and "stag," "ewe" and "ram," are examples from agriculture and the hunt—areas rich in such forms. But here at least we are aware that we draw verbal-sexual distinctions among what we recognize as single classes of animal life.

At a deeper level, one we are often unconscious of, the example of "water" can be used again. That this universal liquid could change its state under conditions of heat or cold can not have been a total secret from mankind, even in pre-scientific eras; yet "water vapor" or "solid water" still strike us as supremely unnatural ways to refer to *steam* or *ice*.

Yes, a separate name does make for more realness, psychologically. And in Language, psychology is much indeed. The use of words which isolate and separate may spring initially from ignorance, when different aspects of a single thing are markedly unlike upon superficial examination. And even where knowledge is *not* lacking, men do find it convenient to put verbally asunder what God has joined together. (The Arabic of the Bedouin contains hundreds of words for different ages, sizes, shapes, breeds and personalities of camel, and all that pertains to them—because his life centers on them. Just so, an American draftee soon learns the numerous parts of his M-1 by name, a good job-printer can rattle off type-faces by the score, and an equine paleodontologist can recite the names of every crest and trough in any tooth of any kind of horse that has ever been fossilized in the last 40 million years.)

There *is* a real gain in the labeling of reality with more and more terms, we must admit. Originally devised as a convenience in practical activity, the new words have often made advances possible that were undreamed of under older dispensations.[6] But it has been *new* words at each stage of historical progress which have made particular advances possible; not the clinging to older certainties and categories which, alas, do not happen to fit the facts.

If there is one characteristic which might fairly be attributed

---

[6] The chemical names and notation mentioned earlier above permitted the development of modern chemistry and nuclear physics; more than that, they may well have encouraged the successive advances made in these fields. The example of Arabic versus Roman numerals—though not normally thought of as a case in linguistics—is an interesting analogy. At first a convenient import from the East, whose simplicity made already-known calculations easier (try multiplying MCVII by DCCCXIII), the new system rapidly became the actual tool which made such operations as $\sqrt[3]{14^6}$ conceivable, much less possible.

to recent theories of Language, it is a certain kind of humility. As we shall soon see, the modern student of linguistics is a good deal less cocksure than his predecessors about the nature of even so simple a thing as a word, much less the "obvious" notions of universal logic which earlier scholars were so ready to posit of Greek, Latin, or their own particular languages.

This humility is not confined to professional philologists, however; to the extent that he depends on notation and terminology, it is also true of the scientist. (We have seen how nicely unitary names in chemistry have given way to descriptions, and much the same is true of the mathematician, the physicist, the biologist, etc.)

This loss of arrogance may also be seen in the often baffling— sometimes infuriating—verbal technique of avant-garde writing. The punctuation used in the poems of E. E. Cummings and the sentence structure of James Joyce are good evidence of an increasing sophistication (in the best sense of the word) regarding the nature and limitations of conventional diction and grammar. Cummings' odd arrangements of words and punctuation-marks are often attempts to avoid the drawback of *linearity* that characterizes both the written and the spoken tongue. Through these innovations he tries (sometimes successfully) to present the simultaneous occurrence of several events, although letters and sounds have the unpleasant habit of following one another in procession. In *Finnegans Wake,* Joyce devotes an entire chapter to the conjuring-up of "the riverness of a river" by means of free-association and even free-er sentences, since the wet and running reality of the Liffy is too great to be encompassed within the smug self-content of standard syntax.

*   *

This excursion into science and modernism was an attempt to emphasize the need felt—in widely diverse fields of human activity—to render Language more faithful to Reality. Whatever one's opinion of modern poetry, there can be little argument that chemistry, at least, has proved its changes in nomenclature justified. And the change has been a deep one. The substitution of "sodium chloride" for "salt" is more than the use of five highfalutin syllables in place of one garden-variety specimen; "sodium chloride"—and even more so, "NaCl"—at this level of usage is no longer a noun in the sense in which most people would think of it. It does not represent—and was not intended to represent—a "thing." Rather, "sodium chloride" is an attempt to depict, linguistically, a structural *relationship* (1 atom sodium: 1 atom chlorine). Insofar as this relating of one concept to another involves activity, it may have the implications of what we normally think of as a *verb*,[7] or at least of a participle.[8]

Even the coldly scientific structure of chemical nomenclature, however, was found to be something less than an ideal depiction of the world around us. True, compounds were discovered to be built up from simpler elements, and for a time these elements were thought to be truly elemental, i.e., irreducible to anything more basic. (The very word "atom" is Greek for "not cuttable.") With one atom of an element, and the linguistic apparatus which described it, Man had at last approached the true bedrock of the universe—such was the certainty of the late 19th Century.

. . . until a man named Max Planck, a woman named Marie Curie, and an element soon to be named "radium" . . .

The universe seemed truly to fall apart then. Beginning with the amazing behavior of this rarest of new elements, it was discovered that there were even smaller particles than the uncuttable atom. The very elements themselves were a maze of

[7] It might be worded "Sodium and chlorine saltform"; and be analogous to "The turkey roasts." A pseudo-scientific rewording of this latter might be "Turkey and drippings roastbird." Equivalent to "NaCl" would be something like "TuDr," which would stand as a symbol for the luscious-smelling promise of Thanksgiving browning in the oven—just as "NaCl" can represent the white crystals distributed over the surface of potato chips.

[8] "Salt-forming." Compare this with "turkey-roasting," or even "clam-baking."

complexities, each atom composed of small particles most of which proved to be tiny charges of electricity, and subsequent investigation has shown that even these smaller particles are not the ultimate in simplicity. Matter, the comforting solidity of everyday experience, has turned into a mist of immaterial vibrations flickering through an imaginary space of far more than our familiar three dimensions.

The good squat reassurance of the table on which the writer's typewriter sits turns out to be merely a collection of likelihoods. There is no guarantee that this table is here—merely an overwhelming probability that it is. Unlikely, granted—but the typewriter *might* slip through the wood which supports it, as though the table were no more than a cloud. For that matter, the writer's fingers might just as easily slip through the plastic keys of the machine upon which he pounds.

These discoveries marked the rise of atomic physics, and with the development of this new field, even the language of then-standard science became inadequate.[9]

Needless to say, if everyday language has not caught up even with the insights of 19th Century chemistry—which itself has been outpaced by the discoveries of the last 60 years—it has scarcely had time to reconcile itself to the bewildering world which today we know we live in.

Unfortunately, we do not happen to live in that neatly-partitioned world which the traditional ideas expressed by language would seem to suggest. Things and substances have proved to be illusions of our senses, rather than justifications of our grammar, and when our languages claim inherent respect on the grounds of reasonableness—they lie.

The lie, in one way, may be for the best. We speak with an easy simplicity of cabbages and kings, as though in fact they

[9] There has since been developed a new language in which such terms as "tensor," "hyperon," "exchange force," and the like play a vital role. But though we can pronounce these words, their contractions (similar to the "Na" and "Cl" of chemistry) are Greek, Hebrew and German *fraktur* letters; the "grammar" is mathematics—very advanced mathematics.

can be absolutely identified and located. As with the ancient Greek, our linguistically-conditioned ignorance is probably for the good: too much subtlety and accuracy in day-to-day encounters might well make ordinary, non-scientific communication impossible.

But let us at least exercise as much humility with regard to the common sense of Language as do the chemist and the modern poet. Unlike that foolish Swede who was certain of a Danish-speaking Adam, let us concede that God gave no priority to one language or to a particular "logical" set of grammatical categories. The world is much, much greater than our way of words with it. As J. B. S. Haldane—a great scientist—once said: "The universe is not only stranger than we suppose; it is stranger than we *can* suppose."

We find the discoveries of modern science, or the utterances of modern writing, strange, but much of this strangeness is due to our provincialism concerning Language—especially our own language.[10] Insofar as we Westerners conceive of the universe as a collection of simple "things" distinct in nature, yet taking part in "actions," we are certainly doing that universe an injustice. In some ways this is a legitimate view of reality, and the tongues of the West have always drawn a sharp line between the actor and the action (noun versus verb). Yet it is not the only view, nor do we have the right to call it necessarily the best.

Because the languages in common use do so falsify whatever reality may be, modern science has become largely a matter of mathematical formulation, and mathematics has become a language. Though it appears strange and forbidding to many of us, it has its own rules of order and logic of concept. It is a language which amply repays time spent in its study, but this book can make no pretense of teaching it. *That* tongue—a language of

[10] By "our own language," is understood any of the western tongues, since their speakers have, till recently, had a predominant role in shaping modern civilization. Any readers whose first language happens to be Mandarin or Hopi are just as provincial, but at least have the virtue of having been underdogs.

quantity and change, of pure abstraction and absolute consistency—as Kipling said, is another story.

*   *

Our Western tongues, all ultimately the descendants of one ancient speech (*Indo-European,* see chapter 9), stress a distinction between what they think of as "things," and what they conceive to be "acts." Though this is not the only way in which one may profitably picture the hugeness in which we exist, these tongues have perhaps been vehicles of the most fruitful discussion and the richest discovery. But if history had taken another turning somewhere and sometime in the past, other languages might well have been the carriers of a world-wide culture. What other modes of speech could have done, with the rather different assumptions they make as to our world, is a matter of speculation.

But perhaps not entirely speculation. There are other nations rising today. In the not-too-distant future we may see a Swahili-speaker at work in nuclear physics. There may even come a day —though unfortunately this is unlikely—when his specialty will be taught (and published) in that tongue, and in languages equally alien.

The world is changing. Until recently, the Chinese, the Hungarian, the Finn, and many another, was obliged to pass on his findings in one of the "advanced" languages: German, French, English, and the like. But there are learned journals today in Magyar, Finnish, Turkish, and a host of other, formerly outlander tongues. There is an excellent medical journal in Japanese.

We shall have to wait and see . . .

There *are* other ways of regarding the universe. In their own fashions, they too, play the world false—but each in different ways from ours. And just as our two eyes placed apart as they are, give us stereoptic vision with its sense of depth; so too a wildly different language with its other logic and set of assumptions may show us things we have never dreamed of.

*3

Action in action

ACCORDING to the pre-Platonic philosopher, Heraclitus, "No man steps into the same stream twice." Modern science has further learned that it is never the same man who steps into that changing stream, either. The shifting swirl of bubble and foam over the pebbles of the river bed is only slightly more unstable than the wader going through it. Man himself is a whirl-pool; the seven years in which traditionally each particle of the human body is exchanged for another is too long an estimate. Even bone —that arch-conservative of living tissues—is replaced in three years or less.

If Man, with his sense of continuing identity and, like all living things, stubbornness in the face of dissolution, is so fickle, it is only in keeping with the instability of the world around him. Though mountains wear down more slowly than men, even their rocky fabric is a cloud of dancing and unreliable vibrations.

Even in the promise of youth, life carries within itself the hint of dying. In the very act of bedding down in warm earth, the quickening seed is becoming something un-seed: corn or wheat, pine-tree or willow. The young bird still wet with the yolk from the egg is moving toward the final certainty of dead bone-and-feather in some autumn field. And the child trying to catch a sunbeam in the park has already begun the decades-long fall into age.

*　　*

The languages most familiar to us—those of Europe, by and large—note this fleetingness in the world via secondary categories only—not primary.[1] Adjectives such as "fickle," "transient," "fleeting," "changeable," and the like, take cognizance of the wavering nature of The Way Things Are, it is true. Most languages, furthermore, have an utterance more or less equivalent to our "become." Even the past and future tense of European tongues implicitly recognize the fact that what *was* does not necessarily abide, and that what *will be* has not yet come to pass; to this latter extent, one might admit that change is primary—though imperfectly so—to the languages of the West.[2]

However, there are other tongues, less familiar to the average

---

[1] *Primary* categories are those which are unavoidable in the language concerned, while *secondary* concepts remain at the discretion of the speaker. Thus, *tense* (indicating the time of an action) is a primary device in English, and the tongues of Europe generally. When using a verb, we must specify the time at which the action occurred: *I ran, I run, I shall run.* There is no form available to us which ignores the temporal element. By contrast, credibility is, with us, secondary. We may say, "The house is large," and leave it at that. If we feel an urgent need to do so, we can particularize: "The house is large, so I'm told," or "The house is large. I know—I've seen it with my own eyes." But there is nothing which forces these comments upon us, as compared with the mandatory nature of tense.

As we shall see, however, there *are* languages in which such notions as credibility are primary, conveyed not—as in the English-language examples above—by added clauses, but by the very forms of the basic statement itself. The speaker of such a language is as much forced to make explicit notions of trustworthiness as we are notions of time.

As we can see, the primary-secondary distinction depends upon the language involved; one man's necessity is the next man's option.

[2] "Imperfectly so," in that tense indicates change only by implication; its central function is the fixing of an act at a specified point in time. Although the Romance languages, for example, have a special past tense—the "imperfect"—which often expresses the idea of change or process (our "was going" in contrast to the simple "went"), this distinction as a primary category exists only in the past. Spanish is a partial exception in that it has a continuous form analogous to English, but it is far more restricted in application. The universal use of such extended forms, as in "I shall have been going," with their unmistakable connotations of transitional action, is uniquely ours.

American or European, which are even more concerned with the mutability of existence than ours. To enter the world of such languages, however, is a difficult task. It is not merely that words, or sounds, will be alien; something more is involved. The very shape of thought, and the image of the universe implied by that thought, will be strange and—to us—unnatural. It would be best to proceed by easy stages.

To make the transition a less jarring one, let us first consider modes of speech in which familiar ideas are expressed in unfamiliar garb; the lenses through which we peer out at reality may be strangely tinted, but at least the landscape will have something of its old accustomed shape. Afterwards, we may be able to sketch in that even stranger world: a world in which the very ideas themselves are alien . . . though by definition they will always be human.

*   *

We began this chapter with the idea of change, and how it is reflected in the languages of Man. "Change," however, is a far more difficult idea to explain than to understand intuitively. If pressed for a definition, most of us would probably associate the notion with alterations in quantity or quality posited of the object, situation, or whatever changed: the small family which has become larger; the homely girl who has turned pretty; the beautiful house which has sunk into a hovel.

In all such cases, the languages of the West would agree that what characterizes the noun is expressed in a part of speech known as an *adjective* (Latin for "thrown" or "added onto"). And since we conceive of these attributes exhibited by the adjective as varying in intensity, we use a series of graded forms—*comparison*—to make clear the amount of the attribute possessed by the object in question when measured against some other object also having similar properties: one girl may be pretty; another pretti*er;* and a third the pretti*est.*

If the reader were asked if an adjective should be called upon to do more than this, he would probably shrug his shoulders and ask *Why?*[3] It would be a legitimate question because, to our way of thinking, quantity/quality and comparative intensity are the two basic types of information conveyed by this particular part of speech.

A Japanese, however, would see the matter in a somewhat different light. To him, a rose that *is* beautiful is fundamentally different from one which *was,* or *will be.* We agree, but point out that the difference is conveyed by the *was, is,* or *will be* of the sentence. Not so to the Japanese, whose verbs are only vaguely interested in matters of time (i.e., tense is a secondary category) but are shaped to indicate respect, self-abnegation, and the way in which an action takes place. The "when" of a thing lies in the adjective itself. To the Japanese there can be *were-beautiful, are-beautiful,* and even (as possibilities implicit within the bud) *will-be-beautiful* roses.

This tense system of the Japanese adjective is a good example of a familiar idea expressed in a strange way. Another example, concerned with direction, time-sequence, and so forth, is the rather odd way—to us—in which some languages handle their prepositions. There are, for example, tongues in which the preposition does not exist at all; the equivalent particle is added after the word concerned, so that the one speaks of Hungarian or Hindustani *post*positions. (In such languages, one would literally say: "the house in," instead of "in the house.")

This system of postpositions, however, is simply a reversal of usage commonplace to us. There can be even stranger linguistic behavior. In Hebrew and the Celtic languages (to choose only two examples), the preposition may fuse with a following pronoun to form a single word. The Hebrew *l'* (pronounced roughly like the "l" in "bottle") is such a prepositional kernel, generating

---

[3] A reader whose native language is English, at any rate. In many another Western language, the adjective also helps to indicate both *number* and *case.* For a discussion of these categories, see the chapter following. Even so, the line of argument set forth in the text is the same.

an entire set of forms which convey the notion of "to" plus whatever pronoun is involved. Thus:

li — "to me"

lah — "to her"

lo — "to him"

lanu — "to us"

The Welsh counterparts of these forms would be *ataf*, *ati*, *ato*, and *atom*, respectively.

Furthermore, the Hebrew preposition when followed by a *noun* may often merge with it, frequently changing the initial sound of the noun in the process: *b'* (pronounced approximately as "buh") means—among other things—"within"; "bye-yeet" is the word for "house." "Within a house" is expressed by the single word "buh-vye-yeet," in which the initial "b" of the noun is changed to a "v," since Hebrew finds two identical consonants, one immediately after the other, an unpleasant combination (which would occur in the more regular form "buh-bye-yeet").

We have had a glimpse of how the familiar ideas of *time* and *word-relationship* can be expressed in strange ways indeed. One more example, and then we shall move into truly alien territory —in which the thoughts themselves are strange and foreign.

The concept of *number* is one which the Western World finds congenial indeed. Whether or not Americans are especially materialistic is open to argument, but few would deny that the distinction between a solitary dollar and one hundred of them is a matter of some importance. As Dickens' Mr. Micawber put it: "Annual income twenty pounds, annual expenditure nineteen nineteen six—result happiness. Annual income twenty pounds, annual expenditure twenty pounds ought and six—result misery."

English (and the other languages of Europe) mark the difference between singular and plural by the use of a sign (or signs) which modify the form of the noun which represents a single instance. In English and French (with a few exceptions) this

plural sign is *-s*; German (often) employs *-e* or *-en*; Italian usually changes a final *-o* to an *-i*, an *-a* to an *-e*. The smallest possible
modification of the singular form, of course, is no modification
at all, and it is of passing interest that each of the languages
mentioned above has certain words whose plural is the same as
the singular.[4]

The Malay-speaker is more carefree (or less greedy, perhaps)
when it comes to his language's question of *how many?* When
confronted by the problem of the One versus the Many, he has
at his disposal at least three solutions:

(1) *He can ignore the distinction entirely.* If there is no great
importance to plurality in a particular statement, the speaker of
Bahasa Indonesia (the official language) can use the simple
singular form, and let it go at that. (This is not quite comparable
to the aforementioned small class of European words with identical singulars and plurals. These latter can generally be shown
to have once had separate forms which then collapsed into one;
either that, or the present-day singular/plural was once a "collective" analogous to "wheat," "flour," "sugar," etc. Malay usage,
on the contrary, seems to stem honestly from a historical indifference to a formal plural.)

(2) *He can use a pluralizing word.* Just as we can make explicit the notion of 1 sheep + 1 sheep + 1 sheep . . . by the
use of special words, so can the Malay. Numerals, or the terms
equivalent to "several," "many," "a few," etc., can make plurality
unmistakable, and in such a case no change is made in the
noun. The associated word or words makes "more-than-one-hood"
clear.

(3) *He can repeat.* If the citizen of Indonesia wishes to avoid
devices (1) and (2), there are many occasions when he can
simply use the noun concerned *twice.* By convention, this repetition is often accepted as indicating general multiplicity, rather
than simply the existence of a pair. Thus, *orang* is Malay for

---

[4] Examples: English—(one) *sheep*, (many) *sheep*; German—(ein) *Arbeiter*,
(viele) *Arbeiter*; French—(le) *nez*, (les) *nez*; Italian—(la) *città*, (le) *città*.

"man."[5] When it is vital to stress the idea of "more than one man," but one wishes to avoid such statements as *nine men, several men,* or the like, *orang-orang* can serve as a non-specific (but unambiguous) plural.

This last device—repetition—is one totally unused in the West for the indication of plurality (save for certain varieties of baby-talk in which small children may use "horse-horse" to indicate the presence of more than one of those splendidly prancing animals). It is, however, common in many of the indigenous languages of Africa, a number of American Indian tongues, and widespread in Chinese—the vehicle of a notably ancient and civilized culture. Needless to say, there is no implication of child-ishness in such repetitional plurals in any of the languages which use them as a matter of course.

*   *

The notions of Time, of Relationship, of Plurality: all these are accepted with a large degree of common understanding throughout Europe and America.[6] Though the particular linguistic devices by which these familiar concepts are expressed may differ, we have seen in the last few pages how the general notions behind the various modes of expression are basically similar. Now it is time to move to stranger landscapes in which there are still other notions of reasonableness and common sense; notions which are no more a matter of conscious thought and decision than our everyday (but unspoken) assumptions as to the nature of *when, how,* and *how many.*

Whether many of the concepts of alien tongues are strange to us because our language fails to indicate them, or whether our language fails to indicate them because our ancestors never re-garded them as important, has been the subject of much—possibly fruitless—discussion and argument.

[5] Hence "orangutan," from *orang utan,* literally *man* (of the) *forest.*
[6] In America, accepted by the immigrants—that is, the non-Indian population.

Benjamin Whorf, one of the more original linguistic theorists of the 20th Century, was often inclined to stress the first possibility: that language shaped sensibility. According to such a view, a particular language shapes and channels a people's world outlook, and this, in turn, is then reinforced by the original bias of the language spoken. Once established, these categories of thought make it extremely difficult for the speakers of the language concerned to re-consider the matter and shape their concepts according to some other scheme.

The problem here, of course, is to judge which came first: the language (which limited thought to certain channels), or the world outlook (which shaped a speech in conformity with its categories). The earlier schools of thought on the nature of language were, by and large, proponents of the theory that thought shapes language; a belief which of course made it somewhat easier to consider one's own tongue (or some other, but deeply respected speech, e.g., Greek, Latin) as a naturally rational one which merely reflected a universal logic written into nature by imperishable Intelligence. It would be only fair to admit that this latter theory is still held in considerable esteem—especially by many teachers of one or more of the classical languages.

The Whorfian hypothesis—or at least some theory with points of similarity to it—is a good deal more popular with the modernists who have attempted to attack the problem of language as a phenomenon in its own right, divorced from the essentially literary associations of the Humanities. Cultural anthropologists, too, find it unlikely that one particular language has been singled out for favor as the unique vehicle of the True and Correct. No wonder, for it was one of their breed who might truly be said to have given linguistics its insight into unsuspected crannies of thought and behavior.

It was in the New World that light was first cast on the *differentness* of the worlds in which different languages are spoken. Franz Boas, a German-born anthropologist, was the first to study systematically the numerous tongues of the American Indian (*Amerind,* for short), and to insist on their validity. By

"validity," we mean only that Boas insisted on a study of Amerind languages on their own terms, without the bringing-in of
prior concepts drawn from the European family of tongues.

As he observed, as long ago as 1906:

The psychological foundation and morphological [structural] development of American languages are so peculiar that their study must
be a revelation to the student of Indo-European or Semitic languages.
Well-known problems which [have been] discussed for years appear
in new aspects, and broad points of view for discussion of linguistic
questions present themselves readily to the student who takes up the
types of language peculiar to our continent.

Thanks largely to Boas' energy and dedication, the first volume
of the *Handbook of American Indian Languages* was published
in 1911—a monumental text of 678 pages. In retrospect, perhaps
the most important section of all was his 80-page *Introduction*,
in which he set forth a number of observations which were to
revolutionize largely what we have since come to recognize as
Comparative Linguistics.

It is enough for our purposes, that we acknowledge one dominant theme of this essay: the concept of *arbitrary selection*.

Seen in hindsight, the notion may appear simple; but genius
has been defined as that rare ability to point out the obvious—
first. In essence, the concept of Arbitrary Selection is a tribute,
lovingly dwelt on, to the creative and flexible nature of Man.

According to this theory, the human animal is uniquely that
creature who selects from the vast realm of the possible a limited
number of elements, chooses to regard these as "real," *makes*
them real, and of them builds a world and a language.

It is at precisely this point that the good hard-headed, common-
sensical realist will ask: "Very well, granted that each people
chooses its own model of reality; which one is *true*?"

The only answer to such a question is—we do not know. And
furthermore, it is quite possible that there is no really real—or
almost real—picture of the universe embodied in any language
spoken by members of the human family.

In the previous chapter we spoke of the possibility that *things* might be the first items of experience which impressed themselves on the baby's consciousness. The precise phrase used was, "it must seem likely" that such is the case. But as we have seen, it is a case of this viewpoint being likely to *us*. It is our linguistic habits—the habits of Europe—which draw a hard-and-fast distinction between solidities ("things") on the one hand, and processes ("actions") on the other. It is our—Western—languages which have taken this maze of a universe and given to it one particular structure. But it is not the only structure possible. Others have done—and do—otherwise.[7]

The Hopi of the American Southwest, for example. In *his* world, Time is not what it is to us. Time—generally without our realizing it—is in our world something which can be cut, measured, parceled, and divided. To illustrate, consider such a sentence as: "It took five days for us to build the cabin." Although such a statement makes a number of implicit assumptions which do not relate to the nature of Time, let us consider only those which concern the clock and calendar.

In speaking of "five days," we are assuming, tacitly, that a day is a "thing," analogous to—say—an apple. The phrases, "five days," and "five apples" are grammatically identical, consisting of numeral + plural noun. But may we, in fact, treat these two sets of entities in like fashion?

Even assuming that an apple is a ponderable, clearly delimited "thing" (and as we saw in the preceding chapter, such a view of objects is a false one), can we speak of a unit of time as being in any real sense also a "thing"? We can, after all, envisage a row of apples, each one set up next to its fellows; but the same can be said of days only if we imagine a fictitious space in which units of time may be placed end to end.

In contrast to this itemization of time—wholly in keeping with

[7] So, what Baby really makes of the universe, before he learns some language or another, we can never know. Even the best of attempts to become as a little child must remain informed and sympathetic guesswork.

a view of it in which we pass through, or are passed by, successive packages (instants)—the Hopi thinks of Time as a *process*: an accretion or adding-on to an already extant reality. Thus, in Hopi, a speaker might say that a house was finished *by the fifth day*, since a day is not a "thing" which can be duplicated.

To use an image which the Hopi themselves would probably never think of: Hopi-Time is a single snowball rolling down the hill of "the world as it is." Using the same metaphor, Europe-Anglo-Time might be likened to a row of snowballs, each of the same size.

Carrying the analogy one step further, the passage of time in Hopi eyes would be the accumulation of snow to the rolling mass, the snowball growing ever larger. In contrast, non-Hopi Americans—at least non-Amerind Americans—would see time's progress as a collection of snowballs rolling in procession down the hill past the fixed point of "now."

To escape the fiction of snowballs, and come once again directly to the realities of Time: where *we* would think of 1 minute + 1 minute = 2 minutes; the Hopi would regard a unit of time—that fiction in which so many heartbeats thud softly, suns rise and fall, air turns warm or chill—as a fragment, one of many, merging into the huge mass of tradition and age which lend strength to the pueblos, and have lent it since the kachina-gods made Man and the World.

It is perhaps a concomitant of the Indo-European preoccupation with a split-level universe—one neatly partitioned into "things" and "actions"—that these languages so familiar to us have the concept of Time that they do. A system of tongues in which it is felt necessary to devote an entirely distinct grammatical category (the noun) to objects *per se*, is likely to pay a rather high degree of attention to them, as "things." (It is a fact that the societies of the West are, by and large, highly conscious of objects. They have evolved perhaps the most complex and abstract form of economic exchange—the Stock Market, which is a shadow of a shadow; and Western European culture has brought the art of measurement to a state of perfection never before approached.[8]

Now what most obviously distinguishes objects from units of time is a certain quality of tangibility, and with it, extension. Even at a low level of technology—from which all peoples begin—it is comparatively easy to measure the area of a field, or the dimensions of a cow. It is only relatively late in a culture, however—and in few cultures, at that—that anything like accurate measurement of time is achieved.

Thus it is understandable that a primitive group of people whose language had a high degree of thing-awareness might transfer its notions of space to the as-yet-vaguely-understood province of time; and this is, in fact, what the speakers of proto-European did. We have preserved this habitual confusion. "It has been a *long* time since I saw him *last*," "A *lot* of time has *gone by* since that happened," "The whole business is *over* and done *with*,"—*even* the past (originally "passed")—all of these have original implications of spatiality, or location.[9]

But in Hopi the set of words which relate to time have little in common with those words used to refer to space-implying movement. In fact, Time as a primary category is rather un-Hopi-an. The Hopi verb is not concerned with matters of *when*, but rather with matters of validity and manner. There is something that is perhaps reminiscent of our courtroom procedure, in the strong emphasis placed by the language on the reliability of a statement.

The following three forms—drawn from a far larger number— will give some idea of the Hopi approach to action:

[8] It is true that there are non-European societies fully as preoccupied with tangibles and possession as we: the Kwakiutl Indians of the Pacific coast are a good example—and they too have invented "money": copper sheets used in ritual demonstrations of wealth. Nevertheless, it may fairly be said that we have excelled in this department of human endeavor. Had a native American culture been so completely devoted to manipulation of physical objects as our immigrant one, the Amerinds might have equaled our technological development—weapons and all. In which case, Sekwoya XVI might be sitting today in the White Tepee on the banks of the Potomac.

[9] Compare the French *passé* which means both "Past" and "passed"; the German "Past" is expressed by *Vergangenheit*—"gone-by-hood."

wari

warikni

warikngwe

Any one of these forms may be used when there exists in the speaker's mind the notion of "running." These forms, however, are not tenses, for as we said, Time as a primary category is something of which Hopi is innocent. The three words above correspond in no way to "he ran," "he runs," and "he will run." Rather, they are *aspects* expressing attitude and manner.

Wari is a non-committal form which might be translated as "performance of running." Again, no assumption is made concerning the time of running.

Warikni indicates not the actor's place in time, but the speaker's expectation: "performance of running, most likely," gives something of its flavor in English. Insofar as it does carry the idea of expectation, this form may also carry overtones of futurity—since we usually expect that which is still to come. However, a Hopi-speaker interrupting another—a most unlikely event among such truly civilized people—might use this form to indicate that he had already caught the trend of narrative, and anticipated the statement which would follow.

Warikngwe, in contrast, indicates not the speaker's attitude, but rather the predictability of the action—the extent to which it partakes of legitimate and customary activity. (To express this concept, English is forced to resort to the rather foolish expedient of a universal present tense: the statement, "The earth circles the sun once each year" is intended to show the eternal truth of a natural phenomenon. There is no implication in this particular use of a present-form verb that last year, things were different!

This non-tense conjugation of verbs is characteristic of a number of Amerind tongues. Wintu, for instance, has a special form which indicates that the speaker is a direct eye-witness to the event in question, as well as a special form devoted to hearsay (or out-of-sight) activities. (It is interesting to note that the hearsay mode is used when a man speaks of events in which he was involved when delirious or drunk. He, presumably, is in no condition to vouch for their authenticity.)

A speaker of English—by this time thoroughly infuriated with the stubbornly un-right thinking of Amerinds with regard to matters chronological—may be asking himself whether there is any way the Noble Red Man can refer to the time of an action. There is, of course. Just as we can express through secondary, optional terms the notions that are primary in Amerind verbs, the Indian can use optional devices in his own tongue to make explicit that which European verbs must include.

We have already mentioned the use of an expectational form in Hopi to add the flavor of futurity. There is also a compound of two verbs which often does duty for our past tense—the *remember-construction*. This consists of the use of "era"—"performance of remembering"—followed by any other verb. Thus: "era wari," literally, "performance of remembering performance of running" is idiomatically the English "I remember the running." This construction is often used when the specific pastness of an event is to be stressed. Though this past tense joins past to present through the linkage of memory and not the flow of time as such, even so, there is comparatively little lost in translating this *remember-construction* by an English past-form.

*   *

An entire book in itself would be required to do justice to the thousand-and-one ways in which languages (strange to our ears and minds) have partitioned the universe. More than one book, really. *The Handbook of American Indian Languages* comprises four sturdy volumes, and is not complete. It deals only with the languages of North America; studies of Guarani, Nahuatl, and the myriad other tongues of Central and South America are not to be found in it.

When one leaves the confines of the New World, even wider

vistas present themselves. We shall be able to gain some insight into two of the great languages of the Orient later, but it would be foolish to pretend that anything like a fair appraisal can be made of the countless tongues of Mankind in a single volume.

Hopefully, this chapter has given some idea of the capriciousness of Man, and Man-reflected-in-Language. What we, from the lofty heights of industrial civilization, regard as natural and proper, another folk may see as incidental, relatively unimportant, to be stated explicitly if necessary—ignored otherwise.

Thus the Navaho conceives of the world of flying objects as bi-polar: one word for "bird," another for all other aerial life from astronauts to bumblebees. We smile at his simplicity, but he in turn may laugh at our poverty-stricken verbs, so poor in aspects for the expression of completion, repetition, duration, and the like.

Both of us are right—and wrong. Even within the closely-knit group of tongues common to Europe—and English is one—there are differences of emphasis and outlook. Beyond this family, the richness of human variety and idiosyncrasy have produced wonders of precision and omission truly strange to the mind raised solely within Western categories of language and thought.

Man is a creature wonderfully and fearfully made, says the Bible. And in another sense than that of Holy Writ, fear and wonder have indeed made him as he has moved through the destiny of being human. Yesterday it was caves, today it is cities; but we still huddle together in timid pride, agreeing to agree on the diverse kinds of universe we will accept as real.

None of these pictures of the world is real. They are all, in one way or another, lies. (There *is* a world, but who has seen it with a completely innocent eye—except the newborn baby?) The scientist with his cyclotron; the shaman, dancing himself into trances in aboriginal Siberia; the Plains Indian walking to meet the vision which gives him his name: each is wrong in his own way. And each has a part of the truth.

Things and actions, Time and aspect. Gender and logic. These are a few of the varied fictions by which men have made their words, their comforts, their senses of right, and their knowledges of fear. But when the words are torn away—half-truths though they be—Man is left very poor and very naked in a world stranger than any word or thought can catch.

4

All our relations . . .

GRAMMAR: the *preev* is in the putting . . .

Whom may not be quite so dead as the dodo, but it is certainly heading down the same road to extinction as traveled by that unlucky bird. Daily, *whom* meets a fate similar to that of the maladjusted wildfowl—trotting friendly and guileless from the safety of seclusion (in the classroom), only to meet sudden death on the lips of the passing crowd.

Within a few centuries, at the most, the *who/whom* distinction will doubtless be as much a matter of linguistic ancient history as the complexities of the *thae, thaem, thaes* forms of the Anglo-Saxon (Old English) definite article—and who save scholars even dreams that our language ever had more than one word for *the*? Highschool students, dutifully coping with some *Highlights of English Literature* a few centuries hence will probably find an asterisk next to the word, with the following entry at the bottom of the page: "*Whom:* obs. for *who;* used as object of verb, or when following a preposition."

When *whom* goes, the language will be a little poorer, though purists are likely to exaggerate its importance. In terms of the Anglo-Saxon example given above, English seems to have suffered no lasting damage from the reduction of numerous forms to our single *the*. In all honesty, *whom* has long outlived its usefulness, its unique functions having been assumed by increasingly regular word-order. *I know who you saw,* in spite of the winces of grammarians, is a perfectly clear and acceptable statement, in no danger of confusion with *I know who saw you.*

Whom also paid the price for sounding too much like its more popular brother, *who.* Marked differences in the sound of pairs of words (the German *wer/wen,* the French *qui/que,* the Russian *kto/kovo*) probably help to keep alive a sense of the two forms' distinct functions among other peoples. But a blurred *-m* added to a *who* is a feeble device—unlikely to be honored, respected, or even noticed. Faced with its own frailness of identity, as well as its superfluity when word-order became standardized, *whom* responded by turning its face to the wall. The "obs." placed before it in some future grammar will be merely the last rites.

Except in the archaicism of poetic diction—and even poetry is growing colloquial these days—English has reduced the problem of *who does what to who(m) or what* to a matter of word-arrangement, making use of a limited number of fixed patterns. Not only English, but many another language as well, has joined this march away from different forms among words toward a setting forth of patterns of words which do not themselves change.

This can most easily be seen if we examine a number of "ideal" sentences. The examples following will be based on English word-order. Similar patterns could be given from such languages as French, Hindi, Bulgarian; the patterns would differ from one tongue to another, but each language would be consistent within itself.

Nouns

glorp
snoog
brilsk

Verb

(to) preev

If we admit that the *glorp preevs the brilsk to the snoog,* we may not be sure of any details of the transaction; but we are something the wiser, nevertheless. Given the information in that first sentence, we can assert with confidence the truth of the following sentences:

(1) *The glorp preevs the snoog the brilsk.*
(2) *The brilsk is preeved* (or just possibly *preeven*) *to the snoog by the glorp.*
(3) *The snoog is preeved* (*preeven?*) *the brilsk by the glorp.*

Furthermore, the questions:

(4) *Does the glorp preev the brilsk to the snoog?*
(5) *Does the glorp preev the snoog the brilsk?*
(6) *Is the brilsk preeved* (*preeven*) *to the snoog by the glorp?*

and

(7) *Is the snoog preeved* (*preeven*) *to the brilsk by the glorp?* will be answered with the word "Yes."

More than that: it will also be true that *glorps preev snoogs the brilsk* (if *brilsk* is a collective like *milk* or *sugar*; otherwise, *glorps preev snoogs the brilsks*). There will be little difficulty in ascertaining the one-or-manyness of the characters in this little drama.

Throughout all the above employment of nonsense syllables, no use whatsoever was made of a change in the form of words to indicate the relationship of one word to the other. (Questions of plurality concern numbers involved—not the roles played.) The order of the words was more than sufficient to show that it was a *W* who *X*'d a *Y* to a *Z*.

The "sure, why not?" of a certain number of readers will stand as epitaph to a faulty tradition which has haunted Western

Europe for the last 2,000 years: the tradition of Classical Grammar.[1] Its fault lay in the smugness and self-righteousness of its speakers with regard to other tongues. Some idea of this linguistic self-adulation may be conveyed when we notice that throughout their entire histories, neither Greek nor Latin ever bothered to note down the details of a single other language—this, in spite of the Greeks' reputation for lively curiosity and alertness. *Barbarian* was once a Greek word which meant merely someone who spoke another tongue than Greek; originally the word meant *a stutterer*. Sinclair Lewis's George F. Babbitt could have done no better.

This snobbery in matters of language would have done no lasting harm if it had died with the classical world, but it did not. Great was Rome, and glorious was Greece. The memory of those dead nations, the shadows of their great men, awed the scholars of succeeding centuries who could see themselves as somehow huddling in the ruins of vanished greatness. Respect for a culture grew into idolatry of a language in which the culture had been expressed. (And Greek *had* been beautiful, Latin was *still* of importance in the Church and universities, let us be fair. In the two halves of what had been the Empire, they provided something like international languages.)

Thus the notion grew that, insofar as a language resembled the classical tongues, it was rational, deserving of some attention —though the implication always was: What a pity it isn't Latin.

Time passed, and new, upstart languages (including the Romance tongues—simplified descendants of Latin) sprang up as the vehicles of young and vital societies. Unfortunately, their ways of expressing meaning were often a far cry from the linguistic habits of the Greeks and Romans. It was their fate to fall into the hands of Scholars Who Knew Their Latin. (After the fall of Byzantium in the 15th century, the number would include Scholars Who Knew Their Greek, too.)

---

[1] "Classical" because it was a cult which held the perfection of logic and language to be inherent in the categories of Greek and Latin—the chief tongues of the Western World of classic times.

And of course these Scholars wrote grammars of the new-comer tongues—when they bothered to write them at all—as if they were the incorrect babblings of a proletariat with neither the good sense nor the taste to use the categories of thought of Socrates or Caesar. It has been precisely this sort of scholar who, until recent times, wrote the grammars which troubled each new class of luckless schoolboys. Even today, a little of that Scholastic spirit lingers on.[2] Let us take a look at two of the pillars of righteousness which supported Grammarians-with-a-capital-G for so long in their faith . . . Declension and Conjugation.

Declension (a Latin term meaning literally "a turning away from") refers to the changes made in nouns, pronouns, and adjectives to indicate the logical and/or grammatical relation-ships between them. The name arose from a particular image which classical grammarians had of this system of changes. Ac-cording to this picture, the nominative form—used as the subject of a sentence, such as *man* in *the man is coming*—was considered as being vertical. Other forms, which in English would be ex-pressed by phrases such as *of the man, to the man, from the man,* and so forth, were visualized as turning away from the pure uprightness of the nominative. (One still finds in rather old-fashioned grammars of Latin, Greek, Sanskrit, and the like, the term "oblique" used in connection with such forms.) Thus a tabulation of changes was truly a "declension." Carrying the anal-ogy one step further, each particular form was called (in Latin) a *casus,* a *falling* away from the perpendicular. From this *casus* comes the English grammatical term *case.*

From this image spring those nominative, possessive, objec-tive (and sometimes dative) cases which may still plague the memories of readers. In English, this case system survives only in the -'s and -s' of our possessive case in nouns (*the voter's*

[2] As an example: ". . . authority of general usage, or even of the usage of great writers, is not absolute in language. There is a mis-use of words which can be justified by no authority, however great, and by no usage however general." White, R. G., *Words and Their Uses,* Boston: Houghton Mifflin Co., rev. ed., 1899, p. 14.

friend, the cousins' houses), and in the *I/mine/me, he/his/him, they/theirs/them* (and analogous forms) among pronouns.

But Greek, Latin, and other tongues have preserved this system of changes in form in its full glory. Latin, as perhaps the language of this type best known to Western Europeans and Americans, will serve as a good example.

The literary language of Caesar and Cicero, of Tacitus and Tertullian had five such cases: *nominative, genitive, dative, accusative,* and *ablative.* Each, in theory, served to indicate a specific function of the particular word declined. According to the ideal scheme which first-year Latin students have often encountered, these cases were arranged as follows (using English equivalents):

Nominative:	*man,* as in *the man* sees the dog
Genitive:	*man,* as in *the man's* house
Dative:	*man,* as in he gave it *to the man*
Accusative:	*man,* as in the dog sees *the man*
Ablative:	*man,* as in the ball rolled *away from the man*

There were, in addition, two other cases: the *vocative* ("calling") and *locative* ("locational"). These, however, existed only in a small number of nouns. A separate vocative case was found only in masculine nouns ending in *-us: Marce* ("O Marcus!") from the nominative *Marcus.* The locative was even scarcer, a mere handful of place-names accounting for its existence: *Romae* ("at Rome") from a nominative *Roma* ("Rome"). The vocative may be remembered from prayers in Latin beginning with *Domine* ("O Lord") from *Dominus;* and the *et tu Brute!* cried out to Brutus by the dying Caesar.

Even a quick glance at such a tabulation must give the reader a hint of troubles to come. Though such a system of cases is claimed to represent relationships between one noun and another, it is readily apparent that there are far too few forms. There are, after all, many more possibilities in life than *of, to, away from,* and the status of actor and acted-upon. There can be *next to a man, inside a man, through a man, in spite of a man, past a man, beneath a man,* and so on till convulsions set in. Life is far too complex to be caught and pinned down nicely by a paltry five (or even seven) cases. If the Romans had been limited to this poverty-stricken number of expressions, they would never have succeeded in conquering Rome, much less the Mediterranean world and additional acreage. Even the Romans recognized this.

As long as the language remained Latin, their remedy lay in the judicious use of both word-order and prepositions—but neither in excess. There is evidence that the average Roman-in-the-street arranged his words in a rather standardized fashion, and even the toga'd aristocrat probably did this in speech, though not while writing. In theory, it mattered little whether one said *Petrum Paulus vidit, Paulus vidit Petrum,* or any other possible combination of the three words; the *-us* of *Paulus* indicated that Paul was the actor, the *-um* of *Petrum* that Peter underwent the action. *Paul sees Peter* was the meaning of the statement no matter what the arrangement—changes would merely lay psychological stress on the importance of Peter, Paul, or the act of seeing. But such verbal high jinks were in all likelihood too much for the average plebian; in various parts of the Empire he settled for one pattern or another to express his meaning. And of course when he did, the nominative, dative, and accusative endings became unnecessary. This helped to produce the Romance languages; but then of course it was no longer a matter of the language being Latin. French, Spanish, Italian, and their cousins had made their debut.

In addition to a systematized order of words, came the use of prepositions. The very purest of Latin might be: *carnefici dabo* (I shall give to the executioner) with *carnefici* in the proper dative; but Plautus could write *ad* (to) *carnificem dabo,* in which *carnificem* was the accusative; the preceding *ad* made the meaning quite clear.

This process continued at such a pace that in the Romance languages of the West, there is no trace left of separate noun cases at all. Aside from the distinction between singulars and plurals, the typical noun in a Romance tongue stands one and unchangeable. Even the possessive case is missing as a direct form. *Livre*, for example, is the French for *book, livres* the plural. Neither can be changed in typically Latin fashion. *Le livre frappe l'homme* can only mean *the book hits the man,* just as *l'homme frappe le livre* can have no other significance than *the man hits the book. Paul voit Pierre,* and *Pierre voit Paul* both in word-order, and in meaning, are identical with the English *Paul sees Peter,* and *Peter sees Paul.* The nouns can no more be interchanged in French than they can in English.

Even the -'s of English, a holdover from a case-rich Anglo-Saxon, is absent in these stripped-down grandchildren of Latin. In contrast to our *Peter's book,* French can say only *le livre de Pierre;* Spanish *el libro de Pedro;* kindred tongues use similar phrases—all of them literally equivalent to *the book of Peter.*

As in English, however, even these streamlined "modern Latins" have preserved a measure of distinction in case among their pronouns: analogous to the *who/whom* of English, French has its *l'homme* qui *me voit* (the man *who* sees me), and *l'homme* que *je vois* (the man *whom* I see).

The classical tongues carried the affair of declension one step further than was perhaps necessary, even granting the logicality of the basic case-system: they forced their adjectives to keep step with the related noun, all the way through the maze of declensions. Thus, a good girl who was doing something was obediently nominative—*puella;* and not merely the girl, but her goodness also stressed her activeness—*bona puella.* The house of the good girl belonged to her admirable quality as well as to herself—*domus bonae puellae.* And if you happened to see a good girl, you saw a *bonam puellam.* One would think that even the dullest Roman of them all might have eventually decided that, given the endings which were attached to the noun, the goodness of the particular girl was fairly obvious. (The Romance tongues have preserved a distant trace of this cadence of adjective-and-noun in the agreement or concordance of these two parts of speech with regard to number. Thus, in French, one interesting book—*un livre interessant,* but several "interestings" books—*plusieurs livres interessants.* Even English has two fossilized remnants in the plurals of *this* and *that: this* man, *these* men; *that* house, *those* houses.)

There has been a good deal of misplaced admiration for concord as it existed in the classical tongues—many *ooh*'s and *ah*'s over the "logical fashion" in which relationships were indicated and associated words kept together by this goose-stepping of noun with adjective. In point of fact, such concord is but a poor makeshift in comparison with the thorough system used in many of the Bantu languages of Africa, in which there may be as many as 20 separate classes, each with its own concord-marks. "That big lion who roared is still alive" would in such languages be translated as: "Animal-that animal-big animal-lion animal-who animal-roared animal-is-still-alive." The word that we have translated as "animal" before each of the other words, however, would not be the separate word for "animal," any more than our *-'s* could be used by itself as the equivalent of "of."

Whatever the ultimate reasons for such thoroughgoing classification and agreement of parts of speech—and they are hopelessly lost in the far-distant past—it cannot be placed at the doorstep of some special rationality possessed by the ancient Romans or Greeks. It is a habit of language, largely superfluous, and that is all.

*　　　*

Conjugation may be considered as merely a special term to describe the declension of verbs. The word is a relic of Rome's agricultural foundations, for the first con-jugation (*con,* together + *jugare,* to yoke) took place when a couple of beasts were tied together to drag some crude wooden plough over the spring fields.

There is no particular reason why there should be one term applied to nouns, pronouns and adjectives, while another is used of verbs; it is merely convention. But the convention is a long established one which would be too much trouble to break.[3]

Just as the classical languages used separate forms of noun, pronoun, and adjective to express relationships indicated in many current-day languages by word-order and helper words; just so, Greek and Latin depended on changing forms of a single verb to specify ideas which we make clear with a sequence.

With all their differences, however, classical and modern verbs have at least four basic notions in common:

(1) the idea of *person*   (i.e. *who* is performing the action?)
(2) the idea of *number* (i.e. *how many* are performing the action?)
(3) the idea of *time*   (i.e. *when* is the action being performed?)
(4) the idea of *mood*   (i.e. *what* is the attitude regarding performance?)[4]

It should be stated at once that modern languages have not moved nearly so far from the classic pattern in the case of verbs as they have with nouns. Though the case-system is largely a fossilized myth carried over from the days of Rome, such is not true of person, time, or number, in most European tongues to-day. These categories are distinctly alive and kicking.

It is safe to say that the Romance languages, so ruthless with their nouns, have simplified their verbs but little since the days of their Latin ancestor. Even the Teutonic tongues—German in particular—have some distance to go before they strip their verbal apparatus down to a bareness of structure comparable with the modern noun. (We shall see this in chapter 14, dealing with the Teutonic languages, and which traces the course of our own

---

[3] *Conjugation* might be the better term of the two to use for all purposes, since it does express the idea of a bringing-together of related objects; whereas declension owes its existence to a rather unusual notion of perpendicularity. However, it is probably too late to change things now.

[4] Needless to say, there are other notions expressible in verbs—see the comments on aspect in the preceding chapter—but these four categories constitute a common denominator between the classical and the modern languages. Furthermore, statements concerning these four categories are unavoidable when using either type of verb—i.e. these categories are primary.

language. The Scandinavian languages and English have made considerable progress, nonetheless.)

There are still differences in approach, however—especially with regard to *mood*. This, the fourth category listed above, is perhaps the vaguest to present-day ways of thought.

In English, it is almost a dead issue. The live example still preserved of what the classical world would have felt as mood is the imperative. There is a world of difference—even to us— between the noncommittal statement: "You close (are closing) the door," and the command "(You) close the door!"

Thus, the imperative still lingers with us, if only as a state of mind. It was fully as much a reality to the Greek or Roman, but as might be expected, he used different forms of his verbs to indicate the difference between statement and command. This difference in form is preserved even in many modern tongues, as well.

The true "mood" thought of by present-day speakers when they think of the category at all is the subjunctive, which lends a color of doubt, wonder, hope, or wistfulness to a statement. The creature is well-nigh extinct in English—deader than *whom* in all probability. "Were he only here!" "If he leaves the house I shall be disappointed," and "If his word be trustworthy" are usages found today only on the tongues of purists, pedants, and—foreigners.

For this subjunctive still lives on in languages other than English. The Romance languages and the Teutonic (with the notable exception of English) have preserved, in varying degrees, a distinct set of subjunctive forms which are still used. However, if the speakers of these various tongues were asked what the subjunctive *meant,* they would be hard put to give a straightforward answer. For by now, the subjunctive is often nothing but a mechanical linguistic reflex: the Frenchman will employ it after his word for *although* ("quoique"); the German will use it in reporting, indirectly, the words of another; each language which preserves this mode increasingly employs it in stylized ways which merely fulfill the demands of good usage.

However, there still remain—in Italian in particular—a number of situations in which the use of the subjunctive is discretionary. The speaker (or writer) will have a choice between it and the mood of normal assertion—the *indicative*. It is only in such situations of choice that the subjunctive retains something of its old color, its old touch of the other-than-matter-of-fact.

One can feel a tinge of regret at the passing of this category—for it *is* passing. Though none of the other languages of Europe have gone so far as English in its abolition, the subjunctive is not holding its own. Colloquial French, German, and others of the breed are losing this "mood of the hesitant." In 500 years, it may be gone even from Italian, the most faithful of Latin's Romance children.

*   *

Amo, amas, amat, amamus, amatis, amant. Anyone who has ever taken a week of Latin will recognize this as the conjugation of *amare* ("to love") in the present tense, indicative mood, all three persons, singular and plural numbers. Its English equivalent is *I love; you love (thou lovest); he, she* or *it loves; we love; you love; they love.* We have already touched lightly on the question of moods (suffice it that Latin had alternative forms for the subjunctive); let us, therefore, examine briefly the remaining three categories of meaning basic to both classic and modern verbs: *person, number,* and *time* (tense).

Person and number are, at first glance, rather simple concepts. Person embraces the tri-partite idea of speaker, audience (person spoken to) and subject (person spoken of); these three being labeled first, second and third persons, respectively. Number is simply the grammatical distinction between a single subject and more than one.

As subjects of verbs, the English first-person pronouns are *I* (singular) and *we* (plural); second-person pronouns, *you* or archaic *thou* (singular) and *you* or archaic *ye* (plural); *he, she, it* (singular) and *they* (plural).

Yet English no longer uses—save in biblical or pseudo-archaic style—the *thou lovest* (or *he, she, it loveth*) forms. In the present tense, our only remaining mark of person, and that only in the singular, is the *-s* of the third person: e.g., *he loves*. First and second persons singular, and all three persons in the plural, bear no distinguishing marks whatsoever. By a linguistic convention, *love* when used alone is understood as a command (that is, as the imperative mood).

This absence of endings accounts for the obligatory subject-pronouns which we place before every verb we use, with the trivial exception of such a statement as *I love, cherish and adore her.* Compare *I love and cherish* with *I love and you cherish.* Verbs in unbroken series, or with a connecting "and," can carry the thread of the subject's identity clearly; the contrast of a different subject requires an explicit pronoun.

Languages such as Latin or Greek however, possess a full complement of endings which simultaneously indicate both person and number. In the conjugation of *amare* given above, *-o* is an unmistakeable indicator of the first person singular ("I"); *-ant* an equally unambiguous sign of the third-person plural ("they"). All other persons in both numbers are assigned similarly definitive labels. Thus, in simple statements, there is no need for use of pronouns to indicate the actor. (Separate pronouns do exist, though, and are used for emphasis, as in *ego amo* —*I* (not some other person) *love.*

The mere fact that a language possesses a full set of personal endings is no guarantee, however, that the subject-pronouns will be avoided. It is true that Italian, Spanish and Polish have as complete a collection of endings as Latin, and similarly avoid subject pronouns; but there are odd departures from this general rule of "if-endings-then-no-pronouns."

Russian, a close linguistic relative of Polish, has a full set of personal endings, yet the use of the subject-pronouns is extremely common; the Russian equivalent of *amo, amas,* etc. is: *ya lyublyu; ty lyubish'; on, ona, ono lyubit; my lyubim; vy lyubitye; onyi lyubyat.* In theory, there is no reason why *ya, ty, on,* and the rest could not be dropped. Yet they are probably more often used than not—even though endings make them logically unnecessary.

Welsh, too, has endings for its verbs, yet adds subject-pronouns (*after* the verb). Some languages, apparently, are happy with a little extra luxury.

We have dealt with person and with number together, because they are usually combined in a given ending or pronoun. The Latin *-ant,* for example, cannot be broken down into a third-person part, plus a plural part; *-ant* is a single indivisible unit conveying the notion of third-person-plurality and that is that. Similarly, the English *they* combines the same two notions of person and number into one unsplittable word.

There are, however, occasional examples of usage where the concepts of number and person are divided. In English, *you* indicates second-person-ness only; singularity or plurality are not implicit in the word.

In contrast, the German *sie* may—on occasion—ignore the question of person, often meaning either *you* or *they.*[5]

It is in matters of tense, that the modern verb lies perhaps closest to the old classical model. Like the notions of person and number, the idea of time is still paramount in the verbal equipment of European tongues. But whereas the mechanism of person and number has often radically changed over the millennia (see above), but still preserved the concept; time is still expressed by much the same devices as it was by the Caesars—or even the legendary kings of the Indus valley. Though there are a number of present-day tongues of the West which have replaced changes in form (*flexion*) by use of pronouns to indicate the *who* and *how many,* no Western language has yet given up flexion entirely to speak of *when.*

It is true that the Germanic tongues have perhaps gone furthest in this direction, reducing the verbal system to a pair

[5] When meaning *you,* it is spelled with a capital S.

of simple tenses—present and past—together with a number of highly flexible compound formations. Thus the English *I have, I had, I will have, I would have,* etc., corresponds in meaning to the French *j'ai, j'eus, j'aurai, j'aurais,* etc. The French here exhibits four simple (single, unitary) forms, two of which are translated into English by compounds formed with "will" and its past tense, "would." As might be expected, Latin goes even further in representing time distinctions by a single word—with person, number and mood thrown in, of course—such as *habuimus—we have had, habuissetis—(that) you-plural had had* (subj.), and so forth.

But even though English, German, Dutch, and kindred tongues have stripped their verbal apparatus of some of its gewgaws, nonetheless the flexional tenses are still intrenched in even the most modern of languages. It is the rare European verb indeed which makes no distinctions in its form between the possible "when's" of human activity. English does have a limited set of such verbs, on the model of *I set the table* (yesterday), *I set the table* (now), and *I set the table* (tomorrow); but even in English such verbs are the exception—and English has gone furthest along this road of verbal simplification.

* *

We have dealt with four notions expressed in common by all European tongues, past and present: person, number, time, and mood. Grammarians in the audience, or those who remember their highschool English, may object at this point at the failure to mention *voice*.

Voice can be considered as the device by which a language may indicate the direction of action. In the active voice—normally the most common, and in some tongues the only one—the subject acts and the object receives the action. Thus, *Peter hits Paul* is active in voice, Paul receiving Peter's action—presumably his fist. *Paul is hit by Peter,* on the other hand, is passive. But though *Paul* is now grammatically the subject in this re-phrasing of the original sentence, he is still the one who acquires the black eye, bloody nose, or whatever.

At this point, a number of sharp-eyed readers will probably begin to feel decidedly uneasy. This passive voice, now . . . How can the subject receive the action? Is not the subject, *by definition,* the actor, person, or thing which takes the initiative?

Normally this is how we think of it, and for most purposes—since the active voice is far more common than the passive—there are few difficulties. It is, however, when we deal with the passive that we see how arbitrary the idea of *grammatical* subject and object really is. In all honesty, subjects or objects of grammar can be defined only within the "traffic-regulations" of a particular language. Thus, in English, the subject is the person, object, or whatever which comes directly before a particular form of a verb: *I saw, you touched, we loved, Paul is,* all contain a noun or pronoun which is a subject by reason of its position in the phrase.

We can see the truth of this in two such sentences as:

Peter   hits / is hitting   Paul

Paul   is hit / is being hit   by Peter

If this passive-voice acted-upon subject troubles the reader, let it be noticed that even in the active voice there are a number of instances in which the grammatical subject is in reality not the actor. In *Peter sees Paul,* Peter is far from performing a deed marked by activity; his eyes merely take in—quite passively—the light-rays reflected from Paul's anatomy. Once the retina at the back of his eye has been stimulated, furthermore, Peter has no choice as to whether the nerve impulses evoked will travel to the visual center of the brain. They will, whether or not he wishes it. (It is true that there is activity involved in the opening of the eyelids, and the converging and focussing of the eyes. *Peter opens his eyes,* or *Peter focussed on Paul* would combine both grammatical and logical subject. But the mere idea of *seeing* is physically a passive notion. Even with eyelids propped open by toothpicks, Peter would still see Paul.)

In reality, the "subject-ness" or "object-ness" within any given statement is a product of the particular language in which that statement is made. It is a matter of grammar, or rather of particular grammars. Many languages have the active-passive option, and can interchange the two grammatical categories while still preserving the description of what actually happens (see the example given above). Many other languages, however, lack the passive. When it is a matter of Paul having a bloody nose and Peter sore knuckles, the only statement which can be made is one equivalent to our simple *Peter hits Paul.* In such languages, we have only the actor-subject and acted-upon-object. A smaller number of tongues prefer a passive, however; in them, what we would consider the grammatical subject is the recipient of the action. Paul will always be hit by Peter in such tongues; Peter will never hit Paul.

Most of these passive-dominated languages are obscure and little-known save to professional students of language. There is one type of statement, nevertheless, in which even fairly well-known tongues use a passive-like construction where English employs the active: a statement regarding possession. Thus, Russian or Latin is in the habit of saying *there is a house by me* or *a house is by me,* where we would say *I have a house.* Compare the archaic English *methinks* or *methinks it,* with the modern *I think.* In the first, the person in whom the thought is flashing is the grammatical object; in the second statement, he is the subject. Even today we can say either *I think,* or *the thought occurs to me that* . . .

*   *

We have dealt with the question of voice last of all because it is perhaps the most dispensable of verbal distinctions. There is a

logical difference between whether *I hit you* or *he hits you*
(person); *I love her* presumably means a different thing to the
girl concerned than *I loved her* (tense); *he is eating* implies
a smaller grocery bill than *they are eating* (number). Even the
distinction (ignored increasingly) between *if he was here* and
if he were here shows some difference in the certainty of the
supposition, or at least a hesitancy in the speaker's attitude.

The variation in voice, however, serves only two purposes,
neither of which reflects reality. And both of these functions
may be expressed by alternatives which do not involve a passive
construction. The passive can emphasize the importance of
someone (or something) other than the normal grammatical
subject—and it can side-step the mention of a specific actor.
Peter is hit by Paul brings the identity of the victim into greater
prominence than the equivalent active-voice statement; while
Peter is hit establishes the fact of some injury to the hapless
fellow, but leaves the cause safely anonymous.

But both of these goals—emphasis and indeterminancy of
actor—can be just as well achieved by other means, and in many
tongues are. "Peter is hit by Paul" may bring Peter to our especial
notice and sympathy or astonishment; but vocal stress and the
script device of italics serve equally well: "Paul hits *Peter*."[6]
Anonymity or ignorance of the actor or causative agent may be
expressed by means other than the passive, as well. Thus, where
English would say *The rifle is fired,* French would assert that
One fires the rifle, since the implication is that someone pulled
the trigger. Similarly our *He is talked about* would be in
Hebrew *They talk about him,* with a vagueness-implying absence of the pronoun (the verb-ending being sufficient to indicate third-person plurality). In a similar vein, a German will
often—a Frenchman even oftener—say *The door opens itself,*
to express what we would mean by *The door is opened.*[7]

[6] And in languages with well-developed case-systems, "Peter" can be placed
first with no ambiguity. *Petrum ferit Paulus* still leaves Peter the object of
the hitting, yet mentions him first.
[7] A careful distinction must be made here, because of the imprecision of English. We often use a passive to indicate not merely real action performed,

These last two chapters have probably drawn the reader's attention to the less-than-ideal fashion in which languages reflect the inconceivable complexity of Reality. A little thought on his part will soon show that this is scarcely a cause for surprise—or dismay. From the beginning, Man found himself in a thing-and-event-becrowded universe more intricate than he could have guessed. Small wonder that the human instrument of Language has failed to achieve perfection in mirroring the glory and the frightfulness of the world around—and within—him.

"The world is so full of a number of things, I'm sure we should all be as happy as kings." But as James Thurber pointed out in this, our 20th century—we all know just how happy kings are.

("The door is *opened*"), but also to mark the *results* of such an action which itself took place in the past ("The door is *open*"). Only in a few instances, as this one, does our language take explicit notice of the distinction, and then via the adjective (*opened/open*). German and Danish, however, can distinguish the two by a change in the helper-verb used: German "Die Tür wird geöffnet" (the door is *opened*) and "Die Tür *ist* geöffnet" (the door is *open*). Our "the door is shut" is, like the majority of such instances in English, ambiguous. It could mean either (1) that the door is in the process of being shut, or (2) that the door rests in a shut condition (as a result of prior action). (1) is a true passive, referring to present time; (2) is a pseudo- or statal passive, whose reference is to the past. We may distinguish the two meanings where necessary, by an English re-wording: (1) the door *is being* shut; (2) the door *has been* shut.

𝒫 5

… And how they snub us

AND in contrast to these, there is the simple, moving, and perfect beginning of Bunyan's *Pilgrim's Progress:* "As I walked through the wilderness of this world, I lighted on a certain place where was a Den, and I laid me down in that place to sleep: and, as I slept, I dreamed a dream." The language sounds quaint to us today, but it was an artist's approximation to the true speech of his time, the 17th century.

Yet the contrast between James and Bunyan cannot be reduced to a simple matter of literary style growing more complex with the passage of time; Hemingway is as influenced by the directness of current speech-rhythm as the inspired tinker was by the language of his day. And Sir Thomas Browne in his *Hydrotaphia* out Henry'd James, though he wrote a hundred years before Bunyan.

These two traditions of language have been with us for centuries. Each has done its part in speaking of fact, or calling up mood. All the same, we feel something bookish in one, while the other we think of as more "spoken" (though all use of words springs from talk in the beginning).

The preceding paragraph is how a Bunyan writing in our century might have put the matter. Henry James, dealing with the last two sentences, might have given us something like this:

It must, nonetheless, be admitted, if one is to be strictly honest (and this, an honesty to one's self—not to that nebulous, inward, and chastely abstract dedication at the shrine of "the writer's craft"), that the homelier of the two traditions—the abruptly forthright—*is,* after all, conceived of as being perhaps a trifle, leagues, in fact, closer to the pieties and innocences of syntax *a la parole* (as if *any* language were not—ultimately—spoken!).

*   *

We may ask the origin of such divergent strains of language. Is such a contrast between the simple and the complex merely an oddity of English linguistic history, or do all other languages share it as well? The answer seems to be this: Any language which possesses a written language probably does have two styles—the "high" and the "low"—but the reasons for their development will often vary immensely from one part of the world to another. In China and Japan, for instance, bookish style was largely the product of a particular system of writing (see chapter 13); in Russia, the survival of a liturgical language.

But throughout Europe the cause was something else, and here again the root of the trouble can be traced back to the Classical World, though in this case it was the style that men loved which lived after them. To a large extent, it was the tradition of Latin syntax which made a Thomas Browne or Henry James possible.

As we have already seen, the word-order of Latin and Greek was capable of wide variation, since noun-and-verb endings would generally indicate the relationships which existed within any given statement. In theory, this meant that any Roman or Hellenic citizen could express himself with close to absolute freedom so far as the order of words used was concerned.

In actual fact, your average Roman Marcus or Grecian Markos in-the-street had a rather fixed and stereotyped set of sentences for everyday use, different only in detail, but not in rigidity, from the limited variety of types used today. However, this rather simply-ordered speech of day-to-day life was only rarely reflected in the language of oration or written composition.

The reason for this divergence is not hard to find. Latin and Greek could arrange the words within a sentence with a—to us— amazing freedom. The creators of poetry could—and did—take advantage of the liberty their tongues offered.[1] They used a system of arranged syllables which came to be recognized as appropriate to "high matter," since it possessed a measure of form and regularity which satisfied the human desire for pattern and structure.

Just as any language, at any level of style, is the imposing of pattern on a bewildering universe, just so, the conventions of poetry were a patterning of language itself. It is quite possible that this ordering of particular elements arose as a mnemonic— memorizing—device; it is notoriously easier to commit any collection of ideas to memory if one can detect in it any regularity. For example, "Thirty days hath September," etc., uses the two

[1] Prose developed later, as a literary form, but followed a similar path.

devices of stress and rhyme to hammer home the confusing truths of the calendar.

But when we speak of the "high matters" to which patterned language (originally poetry only) was thought appropriate, we should not overestimate their height. Hesiod's *Works and Days* was a Hellenic version of The Old Farmer's Almanac. *On The Nature of Things*, by Lucretius, dealt with what today we would consider astronomy, physics, and evolution. In neither case is the content something which we would think of as "poetic." Even the *Iliad* and *Odyssey* were doubtless considered as half-novel, half-history (though not historical novels in our sense) as they were chanted by some minstrel in the smoky halls of feudal 9th century B.C. barons in Maecenaean Greece.

This tradition of artfully designed utterance, differing widely in construction (and often in vocabulary) from the types used in everyday speech, became embued with notions of intrinsic beauty. These notions were largely justified, since the arrangements used took advantage of the particular opportunities offered by the language in question.

The unfortunate thing was that though the intricacies and conventions of a Pindar or Catullus might fit the genius of Greek or Latin to perfection, they could not successfully be imported lock, stock, and barrel into the "new Latins" (the Romance tongues) which developed after the fall of Rome. Still less could they blithely be grafted onto the widely different Teutonic languages of the North, of which English is one. They could not be, but because of the tremendous reputation of the Classical World, they were.

Sir Thomas Browne, Francis Bacon, John Donne, Milton—these masters of various brands of high style were schooled in the two tongues of the Classical World. In many respects, the English they wrote was a translation. Constructions, idioms, and literary conventions galore were hammered firmly into the language by reason of these men's undoubted genius. Their graft took, but it was foreign fruit on an English tree, all the same. And though such complete literary identification with Greece and Rome withered with the centuries, nonetheless the intricacies of Classical prose survived in the doctrine that "to write deep is to write full and ample."

It was into the dying world of such a tradition that Henry James was born. Doubtless such a deeply and intricately subtle man in his own right would have produced prose of subtlety in any case; but a good argument could be made for the theory that at least half of Jamesian syntax represents the shade of Cato or Tacitus, uncomfortably wandering through the brick-fronted houses of Washington Square.

* *

We have spoken of the "low" style as being somehow closer to the origins of language, somehow nearer to *spoken* language. Yet, what *is* spoken language? How does it differ from the intricately woven conventions of the high language of classical times, of Sir Thomas Browne, of Henry James, and of others beyond counting?

* *

There is the matter of vocabulary. The two styles often use different words for the same thing or concept. "Concatenation," "interstices," "elevated," are words which are restricted to "elevated discourse"—if used at all. The very phrase "elevated discourse" itself is a perfect example of words which would be used in actual speech only by a theologian, philosopher, or critic (who sometimes combines the more disagreeable characteristics of the first two into one).

However, the vocabulary of high language is not merely a matter of long words. "Eventide" is a rather short word, as is "steed"; yet both are to be found only in a rather outmoded type of poetry, or in that "poetic" prose which is the last refuge of certain historical novelists. In point of fact, much of this high—

but short—diction was at one time decidedly lower-class rural dialect, made fashionable by a certain school of nature poets in early 19th century England. A reading-through of the rustic parts in many Shakespearean plays will show that such terms as "e'en," "quotha," and the like were formerly thought of as hallmarks of the uneducated boor who trotted onstage with a silly gawk on his face and a farmer's pitchfork in hand.

We have taken our examples from English since they are most familiar. But it should be noticed that throughout Europe such a pigeonholing of vocabulary is well-nigh universal. No German in his right mind will speak of a *horse* as a "Rosz" unless he is trying to write another *William Tell;* "Pferd" is the everyday word for the critter. (How many recognize in this last word a simplified pronunciation of "creature"?) Similarly, a French playwright, under the demands of a 12-syllabled poetic line which must rhyme with its follower and the exigencies of noble speech, will use the word "funeste" rather than the everyday "triste" (sad) or "fatal." And before the days of Socialist Realism, many a Russian poet (or high-styled novelist) would mount his "kon' " rather than climb onto his "loshad'." Whichever he did, though, he always ended up by sitting on a horse.

There seems to be something about this animal which tugs at the mind, understandable enough when we think of its importance in the long millennia before cars, tractors, or tanks. Curiously, the original word for the beast has disappeared in many languages. In Old English (Anglo-Saxon) the basic word for the creature was "eoh," while "hross" (allied to the German *Rosz*) referred to one particular type. The most famous case of horsey heritage is the word "caballus," however. This word is not to be found in the works of classic Roman literature, where the term "equus" was the only one thought proper by authors; "caballus" was *vulgar* (common, everyday) Latin. (It may have had some of the overtones of our word "nag.") Yet what heights were reached by such a word of humble origins. It was truly a Horatio Alger hero among words, for from it came *caballero,* *chevalier, chivalry* and a host of other terms in a handful of tongues, each bearing connotations of the brave, the valiant, the noble. Unrelated in genealogy, and by a similar process of social climbing, the German word "Ritter" rose from the simple idea of a "rider" to the high-born concept of "knight." And, for that matter, our "knight" once meant nothing more than "servant." But this falls in the province of Semantics, covered in the chapter after next.

*   *

So there is usually a difference in vocabulary between the high and low styles. Usually, but not always. If we examine the Beerbohm parody and the Jamesian original at the head of this chapter, we will notice that "big words" are by no means a majority. "Predecessors," "dynastic," "resolved," "want," (in the sense of lack), and "tacitly" can probably be considered elevated, but such words are only a small fraction of the total in each quotation. There is something more which makes the style an elevated one.

And that "something more" is their syntax, the general principles by which the sentences are assembled.

Though it would be hard to guess from the literary works of days past, men probably spoke as simply as they do today. "So I walk up to him and I tell him 'Say look here, Mac . . . ,'" "Yeah, that's the street. That's the place where it happened." "Sure, that's the guy. I gave him a bust inna mouth, you betcha!"

Something like this must be heard every day in all parts of the world. And (with differences in vocabulary and language) much the same sort of thing has probably been characteristic of everyday speech since the beginning of Language. The particular tongue or idiom will change with the centuries and the territory, but the urgent realities of human life have doubtless made themselves audible in much the same words—and sentences—world and time over. Anger and contention will be themselves no matter where or when.

And so will love: "Honeybun, I never saw a girl as pretty as you. You're the greatest." "Hey, lookit that girl there! That's a cute one!" And after Nature has taken its course: "Marcus (or Karl, or Ivan, or Avram, or Hsien), keep an eye on the baby for a minute. I don't want him to hurt himself."

Grief, too, finds its words without self-consciousness in such uncomplicated sentences as: "If it only hadn't happened! Why did it have to happen to *me?*" "It shouldn't have happened, she was so beautiful." And of course, perhaps the most famous cry of grief and mourning in Western Literature, David's cry of agony at the loss of his eldest: "O my son Absalom, my son, my son Absalom: would God I had died for thee, O Absalom, my son, my son!"

Then too, there are the countless utterances of everyday existence, unmarked by any earth-shaking emotion, yet inescapable if Man is to live: "A cruller and a coffee, black!" "I really didn't notice that 'No Parking' sign, officer." "What's good on TV tonight?" "I guess I'll clean out the cellar on Saturday." "He said he'd take the papers he forgot back to the office."

What can we say of such a diversity of statements? Is there much—or anything, for that matter—which they can possibly have in common? Even living in syntax, as they do?

One thing, at least, we notice as a common denominator throughout all the examples above: a simplicity of form. The typical statement of fact, intention, or opinion will most often consist of a subject, verb, object, and period. And the average question or exclamation is just as rigidly pared down to a small number of elements arranged in a decidedly standardized order.

In everyday speech there are few of those parentheses within parentheses which mark the profound thinker contemplating the world from the security of his study—and often from behind the barricade of a safely independent income. It may be an exaggeration, but there is a fair amount of truth to the thesis that style has become simpler as "modest competences" have grown scarcer.

One characteristic of the spoken language is *parataxis;* it might in fact be regarded as *the* characteristic. Though of a rather imposing cast, the word refers neither to cabs dropped from planes by parachute, nor to some insidious disease just discovered (and presumably caused by some pleasure of the human animal). The Greek words from which the term has been formed mean only *a placing-beside*, and that is—for once—what the word means today.

This placing-beside, however is restricted to linguistic discussion. The Latin equivalent, *juxtaposition*, has a somewhat wider range of applications (though probably not much greater use), but parataxis is a bit of exotic fauna to be found only in the company of philologists, classical scholars, and professional students of rhetoric.

I sat down, he got up. He owed me some money, the room got chillier. Easy come, easy go. In the most limited sense, these three sentences are purely paratactic. There is a definite logical relationship between the major elements of each sentence, but it is indicated only by placing them side-by-side. Often the *order* of placement is important as well; *he hit her, she cried* would make different sense if its two components were reversed; and the world might be pleasanter if it were true that *easy go, easy come.* Nevertheless, many a paratactic statement is true independently of the order of its parts: *the room got chillier, he owed me money* is as true as the original version, since the coolness between the *he* and the *me* is the result of something which began before the particular moment in the particular room.

Although parataxis in the strictest sense of the word refers to the device of placement pure and simple, the term has been broadened to include a closely related device, the technique of grammatical *coordination*. This may best be summed up as the use of certain joining words (coordinating conjunctions) which give flexibility to the statement. *And, also, but, or, (n)either . . . (n)or*, and the like are typical examples of such conjunctions.

"Coordination," means literally "an ordering with." When we

speak of coordination of physical activity, in the back of our minds we call up the idea of harmonious ordering of one type of movement with another. Grammatically, however, the emphasis in the word is on the "co-" (with) portion. For opposed to coordination is another syntactical device: "subordination"— "an ordering *beneath*."

A good example of a sentence which uses coordination to associate more than one idea would be: *I sat down and he got up*. If we compare this with the earlier example of parataxis given (*I sat down, he got up*), we can see how closely the two methods are allied. The second sentence, the one using "and," is a little smoother to our comparatively sophisticated ears; but in all probability, the first man to make use of such a word was thought distinctly avant-garde. (Just as *I sat down, he got up* may be equated with *I sat down and he got up*, so *I sat down, he didn't get up=I sat down but he didn't get up, I didn't sit down, he didn't get up=Neither I sat down nor he got up*, and so on for the other coordinating conjunctions.)

Sentences in which coordination is the only device used to attach one statement to another are known as *compound* from the Latin *con* (with) + *ponere* (to place). In these, the meaning of the whole can be considered as the sum of the meanings of the separate parts. Each of the constituent sub-statements can be regarded as equal in importance to each of the others. Furthermore, it is merely a convention of style and punctuation which makes a single sentence of the statement at all: there is nothing intrinsically irrational about—*I went out of the house. And he came in*. But generations of schoolmasters have fulminated against it successfully, and there is little hope for an immediate change in policy. It should be pointed out, though, that many a recognized writer has treated this particular convention (as well as others) with a full measure of contempt. Our eyes have grown used to a certain pattern of periods and capital letters on the page and any radical departure from the pattern makes quick recognition difficult; however, the orthographic convention which makes of every compound sentence a single entity has no necessary relationship to the logic of statements. (The reader will notice that I could have used a period instead of a semi-colon within the sentence preceding, and then capitalized the "H" in "however." The result: two sentences where there had been one.)

So much for coordination. Now this matter of subordination . . . It came onto the linguistic scene latest of all. There are in fact a number of languages which have never evolved it, or at least have never completed its development. Such languages as Welsh and Hebrew, for example.

A typical—and simple—example in which subordination can be seen is *While I was reading, my wife made dinner* or—irrefutable logic!—*After dinner was finished, I washed the dishes.* In these sentences there is a solidly independent core (. . . *my wife made dinner, . . . I washed the dishes*) which can stand alone as a statement pure and simple. Attached to these cores (usually known as independent clauses) are elements which can not lead a life of their own (dependent clauses). *While I was reading . . . ,* and *After supper was finished . . .* certainly say something about the situation described, but they do not normally have enough structure[2] to constitute independent statements of themselves. In answer to such questions as *When did your wife make dinner?* or *When did you wash the dishes?* they can honestly be considered complete—but only because they draw on the previous context of the questions asked. (In such instances, these independent dependent-clauses are known as "elliptical sentences"—though there is nothing whatsoever oval about them.)

The attachment of such qualifying (and parasitic) statements to an independent core is known as *subordination.* It is "an ordering beneath" in the sense that one element of such a sen-

[2] This applies to all the languages of Europe and most of those elsewhere. There are some tongues, however, which would accept these as legitimate sentences.

tence can do without the other (and still remain whole), but the other remains dependent on the first. In such a situation, the idea of rank is an obvious one. Just as the colonel is considered the superior of the private (and can order him about as proof of it)—just so the independent clause is considered superior (grammatically) to the dependent, which is truly subordinate to its more free-wheeling partner.

The matter of independence is not quite so simple as we have pictured it, however. One can dissect *While I was reading, my wife made dinner* into two sections, and stand the independent clause on its own two feet as a complete sentence—but this cannot be done in all languages.

German is an example of a tongue in which the procedure of isolating the dependent from the independent element is decidedly more complex. Let us take as an example that statement about my wife, dinner-making, me, and reading—and translate it into German. The result is *Während ich las, bereitete meine Frau das Abendessen,* (literally: While I read, prepared my wife the evening meal). But isolation of the independent clause—in German—requires a bit of reconstruction; the German equivalent of *My wife made supper* is not . . . *bereitete meine Frau das Abendessen,* but rather *Meine Frau bereitete das Abendessen,* with the same word order as in English. Thus, in German (and Dutch as well) the dissection of a subordinating sentence[3] into its components requires a recasting of word-order

Historically, however, it might be more proper to say that it is the assembling of subordinate elements around the *simple* sentence which requires a re-ordering of parts; since it is the subordinating sentence which is a late-comer on the grammatical scene.

We have mentioned that there are certain languages which do not seem to have evolved this device of subordination. Two of the better-known tongues still at this stage of syntax are

---

[3] The grammatical term for such a sentence is *complex,* as contrasted with the compound type formed through coordination. The basic, independent cores we have spoken of—clauses in compound or complex sentences—are known as *simple* sentences when standing in self-sufficient isolation.

Hebrew and Welsh.[4] In such languages, one type of subordinate clause in particular—the relative clause—actually does not exist. Quasi-subordination in such sentences as *I knew that he had come* however, can be achieved, as we shall see.

In one respect, though, these languages (and Russian as well) are a little more realistic than the familiar tongues of the West. In indirect quotation, they make use of the original statement's true (original) tense. We must say *He says that he* is *happy* or *He said that he* was *happy*, in which the subordinate verb must reflect the tense vagaries of *says* or *said*—even though the man's words were "I *am* happy." Russian, Hebrew and Welsh will keep closer to the tense of his original declaration: *He says* (or *said*) *he is happy*. Similarly, if his words were: "I was happy," these languages will state: *He says* (or *said*) *he was happy*.

The convention may strike us as odd, but at least it avoids the bugaboo of the "sequence of tenses" remembered ruefully by everyone who has taken Latin. And even the sequence of tense can fail us: *He said that he had been happy* could refer to two possible utterances: "I have been happy," or "I had been happy." The two fuse in our usage. We must resort to quotation-marks.

It is in the use of relative clauses, however, that a number of languages depart strongly from our familiar custom—and not merely in the use of tenses to indicate the time of an action. A relative clause can best be regarded as a particular type of subordinate clause in which reference is made, within the subordinate element, to a person or thing presented in the independent clause. *This is the house in which he lives* is a good example of a sentence in which such a clause is hidden; it becomes more apparent when the statement is reworded to read *This is the house that he lives in*. The *that* in *that he lives in*

---

[4] Needless to say, the absence of this device in these two languages has nothing to do with the intelligence or level of culture of their speakers. The Russians as we shall see, are burdened with a cumbersome case-system, yet their recent achievements in applied science—to say nothing of their political acumen—are of an indisputable order of intelligence. Similarly, Welsh song and poetry are almost clichés of excellence, and the Hebrews shaped the magnificence of the Old Testament while heeding no subordination in the strictest sense.

refers to the house mentioned in the independent statement *This
is the house*. Similarly, *I know the lady to whom you were speaking* links *to whom* in the subordinate clause to *the lady* of the
independent clause.

Many languages do not possess such relative clauses. The
relative pronouns *who, whom,* and *that* (or their equivalents in
the languages of Western Europe) have no true counterparts
in Hebrew, Welsh, or a host of lesser-known tongues scattered
across the globe. The Hebrew translation of *You see the house
that I live in* is *You see the house that I live in it. This is the
man to whom I was speaking* becomes *This is the man that I was
speaking to him.* In each case, the Hebrew uses a single form,
sheh (or the longer form which is interchangeable with it:
asher) for which more familiar tongues would employ *that,
who, whom, to whom, about whom, which, over which,* etc.

Welsh does almost the same thing, but often does not even
use a special word (such as *sheh*) to indicate the relationship.
Thus, *Dyma'r plismon y mae ei fab yn feddyg* is Welsh for *This
is the policeman whose son is a physician;* but word-for-word the
sentence reads *Here is the policeman whose son is a physician.*
It is only a matter of speech-rhythm, or the use of a period and
a capital *Y* which distinguishes this utterance from: *Dyma'r
plismon. Y mae ei fab yn feddyg. Here is the policeman. His son
is a physician.*

In such languages, the word which grammars often call the
relative pronoun is nothing of the sort; it is merely a particle
standing between two clauses. The Hebrew *sheh,* the Welsh *y,*
can almost be considered mere "punctuation" which leaves unchanged the essentially independent nature of the clauses joined
together. Just as much can be said in these languages as in ours;
writers in these languages are capable of fully as much subtlety
—often through the use of tenses, constructions, or idioms unknown to the West—as a Henry James or a Sir Thomas Browne.

But close to the surface in such tongues there is always the
simple sentence, though often joined to its fellow to form compounds. Of true subordination in its most recent sense—"rel-

ativization"—there is little or none. Though we may feel such a deficiency keenly, nonetheless there can be much beauty, clarity —and power—in such languages. If nothing else remained to prove it—there would still be that book called Genesis.

✐ 6

A word is a word is a word—sometimes

Ehkiwinamohtatiwach.   *Fox.*

Inialudam.   *Chinook.*

Audiuntur.   *Latin.*

Qu'est-ce qu'il y a?   *French* (written).

Kesskeeya?   *French* (spoken).

What do you mean?   *English* (written).

Wachameen?   *English* (spoken).

"In the beginning was the Word," said St. John, and in the context of Hellenistic civilization, where *Logos* was familiar, that sentence established an immediate understanding; but to us who think of "word" as a particulate shape of speech, or as a cluster of inky shapes on paper divided from each other by a stretch of white, the term carries very little emotional charge, if we bother to think of it at all.

And yet the idea of "word" is a tricky one indeed. The profoundest of linguistic scientists, when pressed to give a definition, have sought shelter in generalities and circumlocutions, such as: "The smallest significant unit of speech and language" (Ullman), "the smallest speech-unit capable of functioning as a com-

76

plete utterance" (Palmer), or the like. Bloomfield defines a word as a "minimum free form," (a unit which can have meaning when used alone) yet Jespersen—one of the profoundest students of language—is still in a quandary as to the nature of a word after four pages of closely-reasoned discussion of the matter.

At first glance, most of us would probably accept those definitions which depend upon meaning—for does not a word have fundamental importance only insofar as it *signifies*? Seen in such a light, significance and completeness of utterance play the predominant role. But if meaning be the criterion—what then makes *triangle* a single word, and *three-sided figure formed by lines* a five-word phrase?[1] What makes *Bacchus* a word, though no one would consider the string of letters (or spoken sounds) *the Greek god of wine* any such thing?

Perhaps then, Franz Boas' definition might be taken as the closest approximation to the truth: ". . . a phonetic group which, owing to its permanence of form, clearness of significance, and phonetic independence, is readily separated from the whole sentence." According to this, *triangle* and *Bacchus* can safely keep their "word-hood" in the face of the phrases which we gave as their logical equivalents. *The, Greek, God, of, wine*: none of these taken singly expresses the meaning summed up in that one collection of sounds—*Bacchus*. *Bacchus* can summon up a meaning from the vasty deep, whereas no one element of the many-worded paraphrase can—by itself. The same is true of *triangle*.

But as Jespersen points out, there are many "words" which are not free. Just as a noun or pronoun must follow *both* and *and* just so the French *je* (I), *tu* (thou), *il* (he), and *ils* (they) must be followed by some form of the verb. *Je parle* ("I speak") is permitted, but in answer to the question *Qui parle?* ("who speaks?") the answer must be *Moi* ("I"). *Je* cannot stand alone, nor can the other forms mentioned.

Just so, with *with*. Although *avec* (French for *with*) does have a certain liberty of position, this is far from the case with a number of other languages. In many of the Slavic languages

[1] We shall ignore the question whether "three-sided" is one word or two.

(Russian is a good example) there are a handful of prepositions which consist of a single consonant only. Russian for *with* is "S" (written "C"); *toward* is "K" (written in our same fashion); and *in* is "V" (written as "B").[2]

These single letters (single sounds, for that matter) can be used only before a following noun or pronoun. In Russian, *s offitserom* ("with an officer") is a permissible form, but an isolated "s" in answer to the question: "Did you go *with* the officer, or *after* him?" is not allowed. Permissible answers would be "Da, shol s offitserom," or "Nyet, nye shol s offitserom." And since "s" can be used before pronouns, one might substitute "*s neem,*" in English, "with him," instead of using the word for "officer." But the Russian *s, k, v,* can not be used independently as in the English: "Are you with him or against him?" "With."

Where then can one draw the line? Certain students of linguistics have gone so far as to state that forms such as the French *je* or the Russian *s* are not, in fact, words at all. Just as no one would consider the *-o* of the Latin *amo* (remember chapter 4?) or the *'s* of *John's hat* as being words, (though the *-o* expresses "I" in "I love," and the *'s* is merely another way of saying "of"—compare "the hat of John" . . .); so there are linguists who would insist that *je, tu, il,* and the like are merely prefixed beginnings to verbs in the same manner as *-o, -as, -at,* and so forth are endings.

According to the linguists of this radical school of thought, the single-consonant prepositions of Russian (and related languages) are simply prefixed (placed before) forms, analogous to those endings of languages such as Latin or Greek we have discussed before. In this case, one would have to consider such a word as changing at both its beginning and end. Thus, from the nominative "offitser," would be derived the form "s-offitser-om."

In all honesty, one must admit that here the division between

---

[2] There are certain expanded forms which make pronunciation of these words easier before certain other words. "Soh" for "s" before words beginning with two consonants, such as "mne" (*me*), is one of these. But these variants do not militate against the course of the following discussion.

word and ending is tenuous indeed. "Offitser" is one form of the utterance which a Russian-speaker would apply to an "officer"; "soffitserom" would be another. Is there any good reason for breaking "soffitserom"—as it is actually pronounced in speech—into two words, "s" and "offitserom"? There is, but only for one reason. "Offitserom" can occur alone (with certain verbs, or when the -om ending means "by means of," rather than "in the company of"). Otherwise, the "s" might be considered as a beginning-flexion.

Something like this ambiguity is often encountered in the Celtic languages, once spoken over a wide extent of what is now known as Europe. One characteristic which they share in common is "initial mutation" (changes at the beginning). Thus, the Welsh word for "child" is *plentyn*. "My child" is, however, *fy mhlentyn*, "thy child," *dy blentyn*, and "her child," *ei phentyn*. A good question might be raised at this point: what *is* the word for "child"? Granted that *plentyn* is the form used when no other word precedes (and when all but a handful of words *do* come before), why think of *plentyn* as *the* word? Is not the actual form *lentyn?* with prefixed *p, mhl, b,* and *ph?*

The only trouble with this notion is that *lentyn* never occurs alone as an utterance in Welsh speech. Never.

There seems to be, in such cases, almost a matter of majority rule. If *offitserom* were a form which occurred alone, or it came most frequently in speech, or if—say—*mhlentyn* were; then perhaps these would be considered the forms which were *the* word. If so, then the alternates (*offitser, plentyn,* and the others) would be considered as various derived forms of the central word. Such, however, is human psychology that the form given to the principal focus of our attention—the person to whom initiative is attributed: the grammatical subject—is considered, at least in standard grammars, as basic.

Even here, however, it is oftentimes difficult to tell exactly what a word is. There can be a flowing, an interpenetration, which many a time makes glib distinctions difficult. In numerous situations words are warped, changed, altered when there is nothing so clear-cut as the question of logical priority. The Irish *Oileanach* (islander) becomes *tOileanach* after the definite article: *an tOileanach* (the islander). The Welsh *cadair* (chair) becomes *y gadair*. Which is the real word in each pair?

The nice and easy schoolmarm will here be mistress of a simple certainty, saying: "The noun following the definite article changes in such-and-so a fashion." All well and good. But what then of the Hebrew, where often the *article* changes? *Yeled* is the word for *boy; hayeled* the word[3] for *the boy. Khalutz* is the word for *pioneer;* but it is *hekalutz* (not *hakhalutz*) which has the Hebrew *the.* Considering the sneaky way in which that "h" adds now one, now the other, vowel—how can we speak of *a* word for "the"?

Just in case you wish to brush this off as an ancient Hebrew idiosyncrasy with regard to a single word—*the*—let it be pointed out that even so everyday a linguistic element as the pattern for *and* undergoes similar metamorphoses: "and the boy" is *vehayeled,* but "and who" is *oomah* and "and Jerusalem" *vi-Yerooshalayeem.* Like the Hebrew "the" (*ha-*), "and" is integrated into the following linguistic event. Is it a word? And if it is a word, what word is it: *ve-, oo-,* or *vi-?*

*   *

Often this question of "What is a word?" can be reduced to a matter of spelling conventions. *Like* is—in Hebrew—a "k" written solid (compare *ha-* and *ve-*) before whatever word comes next: *k'Mosheh*—"like Moses." But there is no real reason why this *k-,* with its blurry indeterminate vowel like the "a" in "sofa"— should not be written separately; i.e., *k' Mosheh.* It can not be the mere indistinctness of the vowel associated with *k-,* for it is

[3] In Hebrew the definite article is considered—and spelled—as a solidly-fixed addition to the noun following. In this case, too, what is one word? What is two?

the same vowel as that which occurs in our English *the*, which is considered a word in its own right.[4]

'Twas (or earlier, *'T was*) and its present-tense twin *'Tis* (*'T is*) were once everyday contractions. In all likelihood they were considered as almost single words, at least by those many who use language without thinking about the instrument they handle. The varied spellings of the present- and past-tense forms give some hint of the diverse view held concerning the unity—or lack of it—within the utterance: *'t is* and *'t was* are definitely recollections of the original *it is* and *it was;* and *'t is* and *'t was* still show, by the white space between components, a remembrance of a day when each form was a twosome. Such forms as *'Tis* or *'Twas,* however, reflect the short memory of Man, for orthographically these words are a unity, and it is only a short step to such rarer transcriptions as *Tis* and *Twas*—at which point juncture is in all respects complete.[5]

This process, as we have just seen, can be largely a matter of scriptorial whim. But such whim—reflecting speech habits—can do more than merely collapse two sets of syllables into one. In the case of *'Tis* and *'Twas,* at least, the speaker was marginally aware of the original meaning of the parts, and aware of their former separation. But the process can go much further, to such a point that all awareness of the original words is lost in the new word. For such a change to take place, however, there must be radical changes in the sounds, accentuation, or spelling involved —or any combination of the three.

The Frenchman's *voici,* as in *voici la parapluie de ma grand'-mère* (*here is,* or *behold, the umbrella of my grandmother*); or *voilà,* in *voilà la capitulation de M. Laval* (*there is Mr. Laval's sell-out*); provide good examples of words which were born of pairs of words: *voici* is historically an abbreviation of *vois ici*

[4] Consider, however, the poetic usage of 150 years ago, during the age of Pope, Dryden, and their contemporaries; "th' enammeled touch of art" is an example of a blending which was commonplace during that era.

[5] Bernard Shaw, as might be expected, was somewhat ahead of his time in this matter; he insisted on such forms as *cant, shant, shouldnt, wouldnt,* and so forth. They are to be seen in any faithful edition of his writings.

(*see here*), as *voilà* is of *vois là* (*see there*). The pronunciation of these two collapsed formations is not too different from the pronunciation of their component parts—mostly a difference in speech-rhythm. But there is every evidence that the average Frenchman is no longer conscious of the original pair of words which went into these convenient expressions. For *voilà*, in popular speech, has largely replaced *voici*, even in situations in which there can be no idea of distance from the speaker: "Give me the letter, please," is answered, "*Voilà*, monsieur" (*here* it is, sir). *Voici* is now largely used in conversation only to differentiate one object from another: *voici votre place et voilà la mienne*—"here is your place and there is mine."

This is a comparatively simple example—though even here we see how quickly the idea of separate words can slip from the consciousness. Carried to the ultimate, two words can so join that no one but a professional student of linguistic history would ever guess that there had ever been more than the one word in the first place. Our everyday *lord* is a perfect example. Who in his right mind would ever dream that *lord* actually carries within it the notions of bread and its guardianship? Yet this is the case. Originally one spoke of the *hlaf-weard*, "the guardian of the bread."[6] Such is the invariable laziness of the human animal that in the course of time such contracted pronunciations as *hlafeard, hla'ward, hla'ord, laord* (or at least forms very much like this) soon came into popular use. And from the particular phrase which spoke of him who held custodianship over the staff of life came—with forgetfulness of the *hlaf*—one word: a word descriptive of power and dominion generally. Natural enough that this new term should come to be used (when capitalized) as the title of the Creator of all created things; but behind this word of awe and authority stands the humble and vital ear of grain, all the same.

[6] *Hlaf* has come down to us in the form *loaf*, but its first meaning was that of bread in general; only later did it acquire the sense of "a piece of" the general substance. (See the chapter following for a discussion of semantics, the science of meanings.) *Weard*—guard(ian) or keeper—comes from the same root as our present-day "warden," or the "ward" in "Watch and Ward Society."

A good deal humbler (not to say profane) example can be found in the sad decline and fall of the word *hussy*. Such is the force of change and alteration that no one today would care to make the acquaintance of such a creature, save in historical novels. (This may be a naïve assumption of the author's, but let it pass for the sake of argument.) Who would normally suspect that *hussy* was once a term of respectability? but so it was. Tracing the word backwards up the stream of time, one can discern such traditional forms as *hussy, hussif, huswif* . . . and we end with the old English form of our familiar *housewife*. (Apparently the Anglo-Saxons had their domestic troubles, too.)

As with *hlafweard*, another radical change of meaning came about thanks to a profound change in pronunciation. Granted that there is a connection between Divinity and the staff of life, let us hope that the transition from "mistress of the hearth" to "wanton" is not an obvious one. For such a process of change to take place, speakers must probably be unaware of the once-extant group of words (and their meanings) which have coalesced into the one word in question.

*　　*

The reluctant reader may by this time grant that the distinction between one word and a number of words—and hence, the very definition of a word itself—can be a blurred one. Nonetheless, he may still insist that this sort of ambiguity is an exception, one of those interesting curiosities of linguistic history which only goes to prove the rule. ("Prove" originally meant "to test the correctness of," "to probe"; however, the meanings of words change, as we shall see in the next chapter.)

German is a notorious example. Mark Twain has probably given the best-natured accounts of difficulty with the language, but there are doubtless many who still bear psychological scars from their encounter with the language of Luther, Goethe, Heine, and Bismarck. The difficulty of the grammar has often been exaggerated,[7] but even to the student to whom languages come naturally, there has probably come a moment—the moment—when he first was fazed by a German Word.

Untergrundbahnhofseingang, for example. This can faze. It is true that about 95% of the difficulty lies in the stubbornness of the human eye, which grows too accustomed to the familiar. *Untergrund bahnhofs eingang* might still look a trifle uncouth to the English or American eye, but it would at least be something with which the good citizen could cope: *Underground roadcourt's ingoing*. It is not too much to ask of the prospective Germanophile that he accept this as *subway entrance*. (It will be a good deal easier for the Englishman, who is Anglo-Saxonoid enough to call his public-transit institution "the underground"— no half-Latin *subway* for him.)

But it is not merely that the German *writes* as a single word what would be three to our way of thinking. He *treats* the whole thing as if it really were one word, and probably even thinks of it as a single entity. Thus "of the subway entrance" in German is *des Untergrundbahnhofseinganges*, and "subway entrances" are *Untergrundbahnhofseingänge*. The *-es* of the possessive singular, and the *ä* and attached *-e* of the plural, are incorporated into the *-gang*; though in theory one might add some mark of plurality at least to the *-grund-* coil of this German serpent.

However, before we grow too superior in our patronizing of the luckless *Fritzchen*, let us admit that speakers of English often do much the same—but are not honest enough to admit it. It is too easy to say that *we* would never be guilty of such offenses against typography (to say nothing of eyesight); for in fact we handle many a dragon-like word in the same fashion, though conventions of printing may blind us to it.

Every time that we speak of *the head of the firm, the man of the household, a friend of the family,* we are guilty—if guilty is the word—of just the same sort of word inflation. How many of us would say *it is the job of the man of the household,* or *the wife of a friend of the family?* In normal conversation (and

[7] Yes, it is possible to do this.

writing) the expression would be: *it is the man of the household's job*, and *a friend of the family's wife*. In each case we attach the mark of possession, the *-'s*, to the last word in the phrase, precisely as the German does with his *Untergrundbahnhofseingang*, or even *Antivereinigtenstaatenconstitutionsverbesserungspirituosenwarenhändler*.

In older days, when combined phrases were thought of as a grouping of honestly independent words, writers of English were true to the logic of theoretical grammar. One did not write *the King of England's crown* but *the King's crown of England*; for the crown was the King's, not England's. (This was before there were any pettifogging arguments about constitutional monarchy.) But as time went on, and *the King of England* grew to be felt as a unitary utterance (for after all, was it not reference to a single person?), so it came to be treated as a single word. Just as *man* had *man's* as its possessive form, just so, *King of England* had *King of England's*.

Users of the English tongue have not quite exercised the thoroughgoing logic of the German, however; and some original soul is bound to ask why we have never summoned up enough courage to write *afriendofthefamily*, or at least *a friend-of-the-family*.

It is because—in spite of our half-conceding that such phrases are more than a simple collection of isolated words—we have never taken that final step which would carry us over the brink. In the one context of possession, we do treat *a friend of the family* or *the King of England* (being good democrats about it) as a single word, even though we spell the components separately. But we have gone no further linguistically. We may have *a head of the household*, but not many *head-of-the-households*. In matters of plurality, we still form the phrase as though there were a collection of words—and for this purpose, there are.

If the objection be made that we *must* make the plural in this fashion so as to distinguish between one head of one household and one head of two or more households (*a la* the Old Testament or Muhammad), it should be pointed out that German gets around this difficulty very simply—even though it is rigorously consistent about attaching the plural sign at the end. *Untergrundbahnhofseingang* is a single entrance; *Untergrundbahnhofseingänge* are a number of entrances; and an *Eingang zu x Untergrundbahnhöfe* refers to one entrance to x subways. In fact, everyday English does treat such word-phrases with the same honesty as do German, Dutch, Swedish, Danish, and Norwegian (to name but a handful of tongues). We speak of one *mother-in-law* and *a mother-in-law's temper*. And so far the popular and the correct forms are in agreement. It is in the form *mothers-in-law* (plural) that correct grammar shows a distressing lack of understanding in matters of honest English. First of all, *mothers-in-law* (and analogous formations such as *courts-martial*, etc.) are simply not said. This will not daunt your purist; according to him, so much the worse for common—as against educated— usage. But once given *mothers-in-law*, what is the possessive plural? *Mothers'-in-law? Our mothers'-in-law hats* is not even possible—much less good—English.

But English is *our* language, and since this particular inconsistency belongs to us, there is a strong temptation to concede it with a disarming "so what?" Perhaps we *are* inconsistent and unable to decide exactly what a single word is. So? If we are not strictly logical (such an argument would run) it is because there is no way—short of back-breaking words—to treat the problem logically. Certain utterances (concepts, rather) are more than a word, but less than a simple cluster of words.

The defense sounds logical, but is it true? Unfortunately, no.

There is a choice other than the long, long logic of German, or the inconsistent half-way house of English. Among languages best-known to us, it is the choice made in French, Spanish, and Italian. (It is a choice made also by Chinese and by Pidgin English, for that matter; but these smack of the exotic. The closer to home, the more sharply will the contrast in approach to words strike us.)

To take perhaps the most familiar example, French is famous (or notorious, if you dislike that sort of thing) for its numerous constructions with *de* (*of*) and *à* (*to, at, for*). By means of these two prepositions, French forms a host of what are—at least orthographically—phrases, to express what English often and German more often express as a single word.

There is a kind of hierarchy by which German is most, English next, and French least, likely to assemble a collection of ideas into that thing which each language treats as a single word. Thus the German will enjoy himself in a *Vergnügungspark;* the American will have his fun in an *amusement park;* while the Frenchman will take his rational pleasures in a *parc des attractions.*

This grading is not an absolute thing: the Parisian *boulevardier* speaks of the document which lets him pass through customs technicalities at a foreign port as a *passe-port* (and treats the utterance as a single word). Even the German may speak of what we call a *bruised fruit* (in French a *fruite frottée*) as a *Frucht mit Druckstelle*—literally a "fruit with squeezespots." There are, after all, exceptions to almost all rules.

Nevertheless, there is a definite tendency: the German will be most prone to a lumping of concepts into one solid block of print (which he will then treat as a word). The Frenchman will tend to dissect the same concepts into their individual parts. The speaker of English? As before, he will not quite be able to make up his mind. The utterance under consideration may be one word, it may be many, but then again . . .

If there is ever invented an electronic brain which can give itself its own commands (rather than having them programmed for it by a human being), the Germans may well invent the word "Selbstprogrammierender" (self-programmer), or at least "Rechnungsmaschine mit Selbstberichtigung" or even "Selbstberichtrechnungsmaschine." The French, if they were to follow the historical trend of their language, would probably know it as a "machine à computer programée par elle-même," or possibly as a "machine sans direction humaine."[8] For an English term, perhaps "auto-programmer" or "self-programmer," or perhaps "computing machine without extraneous programming," might be possible. English has the sort of flexibility—or lack of formal plan—which enables it to encompass these two extremes of potentiality; but in all likelihood we would find some middle ground—a phrase such as "self-programming computer" which would lie midway between the Germanicism of "Selbstberichtrechnungsmaschine" or the Gallicism of "machine à computer programée par elle-même."

We began with the question of what a word is, and we have seen that even such familiar languages as French and German (which are ultimately kindred) can disagree as to the degree of "wordhood" in a particular context. Obviously, when three languages, all related, can regard a given aspect of reality as one, two, three, . . . or even more, words—there can be no such simple an equation as: *x words for x objects*. Granted that a given piece of electronic hardware may be regarded as (1) a totality or (2) a sum of half a million parts; still, given that it is regarded as a totality, it is a matter of linguistic idiosyncrasy whether it will be a "Selbstberichtrechnungsmaschine," a "self-programming computer," or a "machine à computer programmée par elle-même."

Nor can the matter be so easily decided by the number of divisions made in writing; if words were to be defined only by the location of white space on a page, those tongues without systems of writing—and there are many—would have no such thing as a word constituting a linguistic unit. Furthermore, such a definition would oftentimes smack of the most hair-splitting sort of triviality: it is one thing to say that the French consider *machine*

---

[8] In point of fact, the Germans will quite probably call the hypothetical gadget a *Komputor*. Almost as certainly, the French will know this Frankenstein-monster as a "computeur auto-programmé." The reason for this is that most languages of Western Europe are taking their cue—and words—from English, which has assumed dominance in the field of technology. The same sort of thing happened *to* English once upon a time: Anglo-Saxon *here weard* (army leader) gave way to the Norman French *general*.

à écrire as a three-word phrase, while English users regard *type-writer*—a group of sounds referring to the same sort of phenomenon—as a single word; it is another matter indeed to claim that the English *cannot* is a different linguistic event from the American *can not*. Some distinction must exist between words—though to date there is still some quibbling over details of the distinction—but mere orthography can be no more than the last refuge of the unimaginative.

Though professional students of language may disagree as to the precise wording of their definitions, we are ultimately driven back to the idea encompassed by so many of their attempts: *"a word is the smallest unit of language which can meaningfully stand alone."*

Spelling conventions may often reflect the true state of affairs, but they may often conceal it as well. In *we are all here,* the division between *all* and *here* does reflect a real (to English speakers) division of concept: *all* does have a certain measure of meaningful independence. Such analogous sentences as *we are all drunk, we are all hungry, we are all in love with Julia* can be formed, in which *all* plays an identical function, independent of the word or words which follow.

But again, from an English-speaking point of view, there is a true distinction between *all ready* and *already;*[9] *already* is so much a different thing from the simple sum of its parts that it can no more be considered as two words than can *lord* (although once *hlaf weard*).

Spelling may often conceal the "phraseness" of what we normally regard as a word, however. Grammarians admit—logically —different spellings for *all ready* and *already* as a reflection of the separateness and unity in the respective utterances. But foolish conservatism prevents them from being just as logical about *all right* and *alright*—to choose just one example.

To formalists, *We were all right* is the only permitted spelling of an answer to two different questions: (1) *How many of you*

---

[9] As in *we are all ready to go* (no one is unprepared), contrasted with *we are already prepared to go* (you don't have to wait for anyone).

answered the question correctly? and (2) *Were any of you sick?*
Yet it is a linguistically correct instinct which prompts most
people—in the face of schoolmasters—to consider . . . *all right*
as the correct response to (1), and . . . *alright* as the answer to
(2). *All right* is to *alright* as is *all ready* to *already,* and it will be
only a matter of time until the books catch up with the truth of
the matter. For *alright* is *not* a combination of two words (except historically); it is a synonym for "healthy," "happy," "well-
off," "acceptable," and the like; and in another sense it may be a
mark of affirmation equivalent to "if you wish," "O.K."

In short, "all right" as "all correct" is alright; "alright" as
"healthy" or "yes" is also[10] alright. But "all right" meaning
"O.K.," or "alright" for "all correct" is all wrong—or would it be
alwrong?

This is the real reason why *like* is not truly a word in Hebrew
in phrases such as *he is like Peter;* the Hebrew *k-* cannot stand
alone. The Hebrew *like,* just as the Hebrew *the,* exists only in
the context of some following word. They can no more stand
alone than the English possessive *-'s.* One could never say in
Hebrew *whom is he like?* but only something equivalent to *like-
whom* (one word) *is he?—k'mi hu?*

If the reader is still with us, he may be inclined to say: "That's
all very well, but regardless of the exceptions and ambiguities, a
word is still basically a fundamental thing. The Germans may
ram them together; the French may split them into little pieces;
we may not be sure about what makes for one word or more than
one; Israelis may take words such as *like* and *the,* and treat them
as if they were parts of other words. Nevertheless, they all distinguish one word from another. *Nobody* treats a whole statement, a whole sentence, as if it were a unified lump, densely all
compact!"

Unfortunately, some peoples do. A number of them have a decided preference for bringing together what we would consider
separate words into a single form—the Turks, for one. In Osmanli

[10] Another example of what were once two words which are now considered—
and spelled—as one. Alright?

(standard Turkish), it is perfectly possible to say—if one feels energetic enough—*oturmayalim,* "let us not stay seated." Anyone with ambition will regard this as praiseworthy, and anyone with some grammar will regard this as an English sentence. In Osmanli it is also a single word.

The number of technical linguistic terms presented to the reader so far has been kept deliberately small; though an acquaintance with the standard terminology of grade-school grammar has been assumed. The author has tried to keep the number of *zero-grade mutations, paramorphemes,* and *contact vernaculars* to a minimum. Here, however, we must step into some rather chilly water, and admit that certain Amerind tongues are more or less *polysynthetic* (as are Eskimo and a number of other languages to greater or lesser degree).

Polysynthetic. The term does not imply that the languages involved are spottily artificial, but only that they are extensively put together. And the natural question will be: What do they put together? One might pardonably expect that the answer would be: *words.* It is not so. In polysynthetic tongues, the assembly-line deals with—*elements.*

In the preceding chapter we spoke of the Latin habit of using numerous endings to express what we, in English, would indicate by separate words; thus, Latin *audiuntor = be-they-heard-in-the-future.*

From the standpoint of our language, this is a rather remarkable bit of compression; to a lesser extent, *sumpseram* ("I had taken") also seems a respectable feat. In each case, Latin has taken a basic root (*aud-, sūm-*) and attached to it a number of units which particularized the basic idea inherent in the root. Yet the attachments mean nothing in themselves, and there is no such logical rule as "one unit, one meaning." (Both -*o* and -*m,* for example, can convey the idea of "I" when attached to verb-roots; yet "I" as an independent word is "ego.") Much the same sort of process occurs in the handling of nouns (see the discussion of case-systems in chapter 4). Languages such as Latin, in which roots fuse with essentially arbitrary elements are often known as *amalgamating* languages: that is, their predominant characteristic is one of melting together (Greek *malakos*—"soft").

In contrast, another type of speech—typified perhaps by Hungarian—has been called *agglutinating*. In an agglutinating language, as in the amalgamating, various elements are added to a root; but in agglutinating tongues these elements have a clearly specified meaning—which often can exist when the element is used by itself. Thus a Hungarian's word for "man" is *ember;* his word for "in," *benn. In (a) man* becomes—by scrupulous logic—*emberben.* The sign of plurality (equivalent to our *-s*) is *-ek,* and—placed as it is between root and other elements—*in men* is expressed by *emberekben.*

Analytic languages may be described as languages which split apart. Compared to Latin, English is such a language; consider *parabamus* and *we were preparing.* Using the earlier-mentioned criterion of independence to define a word, we may say that English splits into a number of independent particles that which Latin can express only through a monolithic utterance which must stand or fall as a whole.[11]

Using these newly-acquired technical terms, one might set up a scale in which German (with regard to nouns) is more amalgamating than French: *Gemüsegeschäft* as compared to *marchand de légumes.* In such a scheme, English might take a middle place with its *vegetable store.* But though amalgamating in the matter of nouns, German would be analytic (as would English) in the matter of verbs: *ich werde gehen* and *I shall go* as compared to the French *j'irai.*

It is when we come to polysynthetic languages that these other distinctions seem to become unimportant, so strange does polysynthesis seem to non-Amerind Americans—and to Europeans too, for that matter. As with amalgamation, agglutination, and analysis, polysynthesis too is only a comparative affair—though

[11] These terms: *agglutinating, amalgamating, analytic* and *polysynthetic* are relative. Compared to Chinese, English itself must be regarded as at least partially amalgamating; the English contrast between *hope* and *hoped* is a more amalgamating device than the Chinese *hope* and *hope finish* (the latter indicating "pastness").

Osmanli is basically agglutinating, we gave a polysynthetic example at the top of page 91. But even in its diluted form it strikes us as a strange mode of speech.

Briefly, polysynthetic languages go one step beyond even amalgamating tongues. Whereas an amalgamating language treats many concepts as formal parts of some other word (e.g., the *-o* [I] in Latin *amo—I love;* the English *-s* [of] in *brother's—of* the, or a *brother;* the Russian *-om* [*by means of*] in *p'erom—by means of a pen*), a polysynthetic tongue regards *most* concepts as attached elements. The process can go so far that some languages of the polysynthetic type have no nouns or verbs which we would recognize. Their equivalents are merely elements which must occur in intimate blending with other units.

We may get some idea of this by devising a hypothetical example based on our own language. Let us imagine that there were no word for "boat" in English, but only the syllable *-bo-* which could no more exist independently than can our possessive *-'s*. One could speak of *thebo,* or *abo* (*the* or *a, boat,* respectively), or make the statement "Iseeabo" (*I see a boat*); but *boat* as a word—that is, a form capable of standing alone—would not exist.

Carrying the example one stage further with *Iseeabo,* we notice that the verb *see* no longer exists as a word either. It is not merely that *Isee* constitutes a single, unified utterance, for the Latin *amo* is also a single entity, i.e., an amalgamating form. If *Isee* could stand isolated, then one might say that our hypothetical language was merely amalgamating in its verbs. But *Isee* can not stand alone; it must (by our new rules) always be a case of *Iseesomething, youseesomething, heseessomething,* etc. Since "-see-" is no more independent than "-bo-", one may truly speak of polysynthesis as the dominant theme in our "new English."

The example given was hypothetical, and doubtless seemed far-fetched. Yet there are languages (many of them Amerind, as mentioned earlier) in which just this sort of approach is taken to the problem of uttering a statement. Some go even further, and make what we would consider adjectives or adverbs just as integral a part of the flow of unified sound as their not-word nouns and verbs.

It would be unfair to say that this is simply quibbling and to insist that the words really are there, but buried in the web of sound (or letters). It would be somewhat closer to the mark to say that the building blocks of a polysynthetic sentence-word are *roots,* analogous to the *am-* of the Latin *amare* ("to love"), or the *zhenshchin-* of the Russian *zhenshchina* ("woman"). Roots of this type can never exist in a statement as themselves, but only as "incarnations" which give rise to words when attached to endings (thus, *amas,* "thou lovest," and *zhenshchiny,* "of a woman"). But both Latin and Russian are synthetic languages, and they carry this procedure of root + ending only so far. A polysynthetic language lumps a vastly larger number of elements into the affix category—the category of elements which cannot stand alone.

We have already said that agglutination, amalgamation, and analysis could best be regarded as comparative qualities: hence there is in most cases little information conveyed by the term "analytic" alone. A tongue such as French may be more analytic in its nouns than even English—which has moved far in that direction since its days as Anglo-Saxon—yet decidedly more amalgamating (addicted to inflections) with respect to verbs. (There are certain tongues which have gone amazingly far in one direction or another, however. Thus Chinese with analysis, Sanskrit with amalgamation, Nenets [a Finnish-related tongue of the Soviet Union] with agglutination. For an extreme example of polysynthesis, read on.)

But the relative nature of analysis, amalgamation, and the like goes further than merely the comparison of their use from one language to another. It is ultimately possible to regard these four categories of word-use as variations in degree, rather than as completely unrelated, opposing concepts. We have already seen how a number of separate words (an originally analytic construction) can collapse into a single utterance treated as a single word: *vois là: voilà, hlaf weard: lord,* etc.

Such collapsings can do more than merely give rise to one word where two existed, however. In a very real sense, this process of blending can produce new endings—either devoid of meaning when used alone (amalgamation), or still carrying clearly specified associations (agglutination).

A good example of the first type of change can be seen in the development of a new future tense in the Romance descendents of Latin: the average Roman-in-the-street did not use the future tense found in grammars of Classical Latin—the type studied in our highschools; he avoided such forms as *favebo* (I shall favor), and made use of an analytical construction with "have," saying: *favere habeo* (literally: *I have to favor*).[12] In the course of time, the various forms of "have" which followed the main verb were blurred in pronunciation, much as the "not" in our contractions *can't, won't, didn't,* and eventually came to be felt (and spelled) as endings to the principal verb.

Thus Italian, Spanish, and French now have new amalgamating forms: *je parlerai, yo hablaré, io parlerò,* all meaning "I shall speak," and all—historically—degenerate forms of "I to-speak have." Yet none but a linguistic historian among the native users of these tongues is conscious of the "I have" forms *ai* (Fr.), *he* (Sp.), and *ho* (It.) as the remnants of former words.

Such forms as the *-a* in the French *fera* (*he will make*)—and other Romance equivalents—is a single, highly un-free form in itself. Portuguese, that Latin dialect closely akin to Spanish, occupies a middle position in this respect. For *you will see me,* Portuguese says *ver-me-as* in contrast to the Spanish *me verás.* Since Romance languages place their object pronouns before the inflected form in positive statements, the fact that Spanish places *me* in front of *verás* indicates that *verás*—to a Spaniard—is one undivided entity, i.e., a word. The Portuguese habit of inserting *me* before *-as* would seem to show that *-as* has kept alive some of its force as a verb in its own right: "thou hast." Nevertheless, in cases where both languages can put the object after the verb (that is, when the object is a noun), both tongues regard the

[12] Compare the futurish flavour of *I have* (*got*) *to go, he has* (*got*) *to help,* etc.

future form as a unity. The Spanish *verás la fuente,* and the Portuguese *veras a fonte* are equally three-worded in saying *you will see the fountain.*

If we keep alive a realization of how words can fuse together —how formerly independent elements can blend into a singleness in which the parts can no longer stand alone—we shall not find it so difficult to realize that one man's word is another man's prison. Just as it would strike us as a violence to common sense to use -'s independently (rather than *of*), just so there are a number of tongues in which a "word" is much less than it is to us.

If a member of the Kwakiutl tribe living on the Pacific coast were to give someone else a fair share of blows with some instrument as yet unmentioned—and the Kwakiutl are as jealous of social standing as we are—an interested bystander might describe the situation to a friend in the following form: *mixeideks.* This could best be translated as *he hits him with it.* Believe it or not, an approximate translation of -*k*- is roughly "him"; -*s*—"with it." These two elements can only occur in the context of what would be to us a complete sentence. They do not stand alone.

Going beyond the simple matter of pronouns, one can take an even more impressive example from one of the dialects of Eskimo. The English phrase "he begins to see" can be expressed only by the word *takulerpok.* This is truly a single word. It is true that *taku-* means *see;* but only in the same way that -'s means "of." *Taku-* has just as little independent existence as our possessive ending. -*ler-*, too, is only the creature of its context; though it denotes "beginning," it demands something before it, and something (analogous to our pronoun) after it. *He sees,* or *he begins* would require distinctly different constructions.

In the Oneida dialect of Iroquois the single utterance *watgajijanegale* expresses that which we might say by "the flower pops open." The *wa-* is a mark of the present tense, -*t*- indicates that the action is all of one piece and to be regarded as a whole, the -*g*- may be translated as "it," while -*jija*- and -*negale* are the elements which signify "flower" and "open suddenly," respectively.

The idea that such concepts as tense, aspect, and person (*wa-*, *-t-*, and *-g-*) should be parts rather than independent words may not strike the reader as too peculiar—but almost any speaker of a European language will be somewhat startled to learn that the elements which denote "flower" and "open (suddenly)" are just as secondary and dependent. Neither *-jija-* nor *-negale* can exist alone any more than our possessive *'s* or plural *s*. But the fault, dear reader, lies not in the words, but in ourselves.

We have spoken of the "thing-dominated" nature of Western languages. These familiar tongues are also concerned with actions, but largely as they can be "thingified"—sharply delineated in terms rigidly analogous to those in which we think of objects. To the extent to which things-and-even-actions strike us as basic to the universe, to that extent perhaps we think them deserving of "wordhood." And within limits, we are possibly right. For there are few languages—if any—which systematically reduce "things" or "actions" to mere flexions, while consistently elevating "abstractions" such as futurity, negation, possibility, and so forth to independent status.

But there *are* languages which are somewhat more equalitarian than those which we study in highschool. There are tongues which deal with the total situation—or at least with more of it than modes of speech which regard nouns (and perhaps verbs and adjectives) as somehow primary to the universe at large. The Pawnee who said *tahikstuen* ("I make an arrow") was something more of a democrat—linguistically—than we. The word *riks* ("arrow") can exist independently, but he buries it in his declaration (in the form *-hiks-*) and it becomes a mere phonetic element in the totality of his involvement. Even more democratic is the Oneidan Indian who stalked around New York state's Lake Otsego, and who saw nouns (such as *-jija-*, "flower") and verbs (*-negale,* "popping open") as only part of reality. "When" and "how" were just as important, and all were parts of one word.

Of course, this question of Amerind "democracy" or European "thingness" can be carried only so far—and not too far, at that. Chingatchgook, last of the Mohicans, spoke as he had learned to speak, from his ancestors. So did Natty Bumppo. They were both—within the limitations of their provincial creator—good men. The decency—or evil—of such men is largely a product of much that went to shape them, but it would be foolish to think that an entire philosophy of existence was manufactured deliberately by the founding fathers of their particular tongues. However, language was one of the things which *did* form them.

Whatever the cause, there have been a thousand-and-one ways of looking at the world, and as many ways of speaking of it. And when men began to speak of how they spoke, when they learned to write of how men wrote, they found themselves driven to acknowledge the splendor and power of language.

One would think that the heart of language—the word—would be an easy thing to discover, but perhaps it is always the kernel of experience which is most hidden and obscure. The Preacher spoke of the heart of Man, and called it "deceitful above anything." It is likely he was right. Words, we know too well, can be deceitful, and it would only be just if they were secret as well. And like all well-kept secrets, they have always been hidden in the most obvious of places.

Tricky to catch, the word has always been a gay deceiver, even though it lies—in both senses of the word—on the lips of all men who have ever lived.

7

What I *really* meant

was . . .

I prevented the dawning of the morning
—*Psalms* cxix:147

I anticipated the dawn

And here the smug* and silver Trent shall run . . .
—Shakespeare, *1 Henry IV*, iii:1

WHETHER or not it is easy to tell exactly what a word is, we are generally rather certain as to what it *means*—if, of course, the language happens to be our own. At any rate, so far Man has managed to make himself understood by his fellows reasonably well. However, as Mrs. 'Arris the eminent scholar has pointed out, "There is always room for improvement."

Misunderstanding occurs often enough so that it has even evolved an entire branch of humor as its own—the pun. Yet carried far enough, confusion can lead to the worst of tragedy. There is evidence that the war with Japan may have been continued unnecessarily when the official news agency of the Japanese government mistranslated a term in replying to the surrender ultimatum given by the Allies at Potsdam. The reply of the Emperor's regime contained the word *mokusatsu* which the Domei agency turned into the English "ignore." More properly, *mokusatsu* carries the meaning of "reserving an answer until a

* smug = fair

decision is reached." If, in fact, this mistake did confirm America's resolve to drop the atomic bomb, the error may well have been the most costly linguistic blunder in human history.

Misunderstandings or mis-borrowings might conveniently be classified under four headings:

1. Mistranslations from one tongue to another
2. Differences in the meaning of a word—within one language—from one part of the world to another
3. Changes in the meaning of a word over a period of time
4. Multiple meanings attached to a given cluster of sounds or written symbols (i.e., puns both serious and humorous).

The hypothesized blunder of some nameless Japanese cited above is perhaps the most horrible example one can give of a type (1) misunderstanding, yet it is possible to find scores of similar translations which are happily less bloodcurdling. Many, in fact, have their humorous side.

There is the classic schoolboy story example of the budding young French-scholar who insisted that Parisians were—reputation to the contrary—the most impolite people in the world. In justification of his stand, he pointed out that the French were always *demanding* one thing or another; they were never content to simply *ask* for a thing.

It is easy to smile at this when one reflects that the French "demander" is simply the verb "to ask" (*exiger* expressing what we would translate as *demand*); but similar howlers and worse have been committed time out of mind—and not by schoolboys.

Perhaps the most commonly-encountered mistranslations are those by which many a nation describes various foreigners. It has been known for a term that began as an insult to achieve the status of a name. (Unfortunately, this example of fossilized bad manners is not rare. The various Slavic words for the Germans (Russian *n'em'ets*, Polish *niemiec*, etc.) all stem from a root meaning "mute, dumb, unable to speak." Compare the Greek term for all foreigners: *barbaroi*, "the stammerers." In pre-Tsarist days, the Russians called one tribe native to Siberia *Samoyedes*

—literally, "self-eaters," "cannibals"; under the Soviet policy of theoretical broadmindedness, the official term is *Nenets*, the Nenets' own word for themselves. As one might guess, *Nenets* means simply *people*. Such misconstruals of meaning are natural enough in the first days of rough-and-ready interpreting. One can find examples of this in the terms "Dutchman," "Polack," and "Yid," which are only the terms used in German, Polish, and Yiddish (a medieval German dialect written in the Hebrew alphabet) for: "(a) German," "Pole," "Jew." And of course, the generally derogatory connotations attached to such words—secondary, in the beginning—frequently became primary terms of abuse. Yet often enough, a people's name for itself means simply: *people*. In origin, such terms as *Bantu, Dutch*(man), and the Latinized Teutonic name for a tribe of ancient Germany—the *Alemanni*—are simply utterances which assert the unique humanity of the speakers. *Bantu* is a word meaning "the Men," "the People"; the same significance originally attached to *Dutch* (German *deutsch* from a word originally meaning "People").[1] As for the Alemanni: one can say only that the self-confidence of this ancient tribe must have been immense for them to call themselves "all the men." Such egotism was, however, a natural bit of ethnocentricity in a world of limited geography; the Germans were not the only folk to indulge in it. Traced back to ultimate roots, the great majority of terms—if not all—used by such peoples for themselves might be found to mean something on the order of "the Men," "the People," "the Speakers," "the Dwellers," and so forth.

The great bulk of other mistranslations can be ascribed either to simple ignorance on the part of the translator of the original language—as when a French rendering of Fenimore Cooper's *The Spy* gave the Wharton residence named *The Locusts* (from its locust trees) as *Les Sauterelles* (the grasshoppers!)—or

[1] In an earlier day we speakers of English employed this term properly, i.e., in speaking of those who call themselves *deutsch*—"the Germans." *Pennsylvania Dutch* is a holdover from this earlier usage. At about that time we were still calling the modern-day Dutch that which they call themselves: "Netherlanders," or more commonly "Hollanders."

to the fact that very few languages "map the same territory" precisely.

This second sort of difficulty is natural enough, if we take the time to realize that no two people see the world in exactly the same way. This is all the truer if languages develop during times of geographical isolation. Good examples of the way in which languages fail to agree in "drawing a map" of the reality around them have been given in earlier chapters. We saw that what one tongue regards as obvious common-sense logic another may regard as balderdash (or at least as relatively insignificant). But differences of outlook are not limited to formal grammatical categories or pigeonholes for logical concepts; even so simple a thing as what the meaning of a word is can be a matter of dispute.

The Yakuts (another tribe indigenous to Soviet territory) have no separate terms for *blue* or *green:* one utterance, one word, serves to translate what to us would be expressed by either of two different terms. However, it would be foolish to jump to the conclusion that this tribe suffers from collective color-blindness. They see as well as the rest of us, but their language does not draw the same set of verbal distinctions as ours does between two certain segments of the elctromagnetic spectrum—two segments labelled by distinct terms in most Western tongues. Every language must play false to reality in one fashion or another, and color is a good example. The number of possible modes of vibration within the visible limits of the electromagnetic spectrum climbs into the millions. What language can boast that it has unique words for even a fraction of the total number?

Lest we be tempted to shrug off the Yakuts as nothing more than a herd of obscurely-situated and flea-bitten savages who know no better, let it be remembered that even such highly-respected folk as the ancient Greeks once had no one word for the hair color which we know as "yellow" or "blond"; they described the children of what were probably Germanic peoples as "polioi": *gray-haired, with-hair-like-that-of-old-men.*

Even such a highly-technological people as the present-day Germans will lump together a number of what seem to us separate concepts under a single linguistic rooftop. *Zug* has proved a notorious stumbling-block to many a potential Germanophile, ranging in meaning as it does from "railroad train," to "suit of clothes." Yet, when forced to, even Germans can tailor an acceptable dinner jacket, and can certainly build a serviceable locomotive. Their ability in matters mechanical is a cliché among the other peoples of Europe, and their efficiency is well-known to most of the General Staffs of Armydom.

This overlapping of meanings from one language to another could prove the subject of an entire book, and not all of them can be blamed on such difficulties as selection of a word to express the Yakut *greenblue* or German *Zug*. Often it is languages nearer home which get the most delightful manhandling. Was it not a famous French critic who once rendered Macbeth's "Out, out, brief candle!" as "Get out of here, candle!"?[2] And even Victor Hugo himself was not above translating "peajacket" as a "paletot à la purée de pois" (a coat in pea soup style).

One rather interesting type of misunderstanding occurs in the borrowing of foreign terms: the fallacy of *erroneous extension*. Often the borrower has some idea of what the word means, but fails to gauge the full limits of its meaning. Oftentimes, the change in significance springs not from ignorance, but from a desire to give an exotic flavor to some aspect of an otherwise well-known bit of reality.

As an example of this latter tendency, the French will refer to "un cherry," but by this they do not mean the fruit; rather, the term denotes the liqueur we call *cherry brandy*. An example of our borrowing in the opposite direction can be seen in the very word "liqueur"; the term when first borrowed by us meant any liquid whatsoever, but is now restricted to a particular type of ardent spirits.

However, such deliberate touches of the exotic are the province of a relatively small number of *cognoscenti*—who show that they are "in the know" by avoiding the word *connoisseurs*. By and large, errors of extension are the result of either ignorance

[2] *Sortez, chandelle.*

or sheer desperation. The first Russian peasant did not add the word *dog* to his vocabulary because he lacked a native term; Russian has two words, *pyos* and *sabak,* which can stand for Man's Best Friend. But hearing his master refer to the new bulldog as "dog," Ivan Serfovich, knowing no English, understood the foreign word to refer to the particular breed, and from that moment *dog* = *bulldog* for him.

It was roughly a similar state of affairs which gave us terms for a variety of meats of all kinds. Like most languages, English originally used the same word to speak of both the flesh-food-on-the-table and the animal it came from; this is still the case with such words as *lamb,* and most varieties of fowl (*chicken, duck, goose,* etc.). But the larger creatures which end up on our dining tables, have a vocabulary of edibles that is from the French.

For a long time following the Norman Conquest, England (like the Russian of the 18th and 19th century) had a peasantry which spoke one language, and a nobility which spoke another. The ox, lowing gently over the fields was a *buef* to the Norman, an *oxa* to the Saxon. A French invader saw a *veel* tottering along beside its mother, the cow, where the Saxon cowherd saw a *cealf.* And both invader and invaded wore in chilly weather clothes made of wool sheared from the *molton* (Norman), otherwise known as a *sceap* (Saxon).

In time, the two languages spoken by the nation died away, to be replaced by a vastly altered Anglo-Saxon much of whose vocabulary was French. In that new tongue (which even we today would recognize as English) there were now sharp distinctions between *beef* and *ox, veal* and *calf, mutton* and *sheep, pork* and *swine* (or *pig*). However, in France today—which was not exposed to a large-scale contact with a foreign tongue—the words *boeuf, veau, mouton,* and *porc,* like the old Saxon terms, refer indifferently to animal or entree.

These changes in the extension of a word have been examples in which the range of applicability was restricted: *un cherry, cealf* and *veel, dog,* all lost a good deal of their total significance when taken into another tongue; but of course it is far from inevitable that the change will always be in the direction of narrowing.[3] There are numerous instances in which an imported term has *expanded* its domain.

Such was the case with the Russian term, *pareekhmakher* (now meaning "a hairdresser"). This term was borrowed from the 18th century German *Perrückmacher*—"a maker of perruques,"[4] but with the decline and fall of knee britches, buckle shoes, and the aristocratic heads beneath those perruques, the word generalized itself to encompass all those whose business it was to keep the human pelt in style. Since *perruque* (or the variants *Perrück, pareekh*) was not an indigenous Russian term, the meaning of the two components in the word was not perceived, and there was little incongruity felt in broadening the meaning of the term. Strangely enough, the Germans dropped *Perrückmacher* from their vocabulary at about the same time that it became truly acclimatized on Slavic soil. Their present day term for a hairdresser is *Friseur*—another French import.

English, too, has often broadened the scope of terms taken in from a foreign source. A prime example is the term *virtue*—which in one sense or another has been a cause of enough dispute to last even a language's lifetime. Taken from the French *vertu*, the word stems ultimately from the Latin *virtus* and originally meant nothing more than "those properties characteristic of a man," or more specifically, "strength, courage." In English, the term appropriated to itself connotations of moral worth and religious excellence which would have surprised the ancient Romans beyond measure. (Among those with a knowledge of Latin, however, the word kept many of its old associations of maleness; hence the King James Bible's "Who can find a virtuous woman?" Who can, indeed, if one be faithful to the origin of the

---

[3] Nor do changes of extension take place only in the course of inter-language borrowing. As we shall see throughout the remainder of this chapter, this type of change is one of the important means by which a language's word stock can —and does—change in and of itself, with no help from abroad.

[4] A French word for a certain kind of wig. The word "wig" itself is another example of expanded extension, through the transitional form "periwig." Unlike the original "perruque," our word "wig" refers to any variety of artificial cranial pelosity.

word?) In the light of the double-standard it is somewhat ironic that "virtue" when applied to a woman has undergone a subsequent re-specialization to mean "chastity"—especially since that meaning was developed when most men would have found such conduct rather decidedly unmanly.

When dealing with problems of translation, however, one could close on no better a note than the effort of some nameless immortal who once attempted an English version of the Biblical "The spirit is willing but the flesh is weak." His achievement was perhaps a trifle *too* faithful to everyday idiom: "The liquor is agreeable, but the meat is bad."

*   *

It is when we move to consider misunderstandings *within* a language that surprises make their appearance. We can expect anything of strangers, after all, but to be confused by speakers of one's own language seems base treachery. Yet it happens.

Best known of such confusions is perhaps the pandemonium which stems from *geographical* variation. Bernard Shaw observed that the English and the Americans were two peoples divided by a common language, and as short a time ago as 1940 there was much truth to the remark. The fact that an Englishman might huddle before his *wireless* through which *programmes* came if the *valves* were functioning, doubtless baffled Americans who enjoyed *programs* on the *radio* as long as the *tubes* held out. (H. L. Mencken devoted much space to a listing of such differences in his *American Language* in an effort to substantiate his claim that the two dialects had achieved the status of separate languages.) Increasingly improved communication has, however, brought the two varieties of speech closer together—especially English to American, to a number of Britons' dismay.

Such differences are not peculiar to English, of course. Any language spoken over extended territory will show variation from one part of the country to another. The Parisian will refer to

"80" as *quatre-vingts;* yet many Belgians whose native tongue is
also French would designate the same number as *octante.* As for
German—an apocryphal story says that two men from opposite
sides of the same valley need an interpreter. This is an exaggeration, yet a German who spoke only Swiss dialect such as in
's isch schad für sini bsundre Gab (Standard German: *Es ist
Schade für seine besondere Gabe*) or one who spoke only Low
German with its *Anna stun vaer Stratendaer* (Standard German: *Anna stand vor der Strassentür*), would certainly have
problems in communicating with those who spoke only the
official High German taught in schools.

It is these inevitable differences creeping into geographically
separated segments of a single tongue that can give rise—in
course of time—to what are recognized as separate languages.
The distinction between two dialects of one language and two
related languages is often a matter of politics. The languages of a
Liverpool slum-dweller and a homebody Yorkshireman differ
as much as Danish and Norwegian, yet both are considered
forms of English since both speakers are—we trust—loyal subjects
of Her Majesty the Queen. If the Iberian peninsula had remained politically united, there would probably be no separate
Portuguese language, but only a strongly-marked regional dialect. In fact, there is today such a dialect—Gallegan—spoken
within the boundaries of Spain; it is considered a Spanish dialect,
though indistinguishable from much of what is considered
Portuguese.

We have already spoken of the Romance languages, referring
to them as "new Latins." In their case we are fortunate, in that
there is sufficient documentation to enable us to trace the process
by which one language gradually shifted in various directions,
ending as a handful of mutually-unintelligible dialects—languages, in fact. Though there is nothing like Latin's wealth of
written material extant for Germanic and Slavic tongues, the evidence is still overwhelming (see chapter 9) that once there was
a Germanic and *a* Slavic, each of which subsequently dissolved
into such languages as German, Swedish, Icelandic and English

on the one hand, and Russian, Polish, Czech, and Bulgarian on the other. As we shall see later, there is even strong reason to believe that these parent tongues, together with pre-Latin, pre-Celtic, and others, were only dialects of a still earlier language: Indo-European.

Geographical variation is fairly familiar to speakers of every language, especially in these days of efficient communication (which are paradoxically helping to negate it). *Temporal* changes, however—the alterations which occur over a period of time—are generally less well-known. There are very few of us who live long enough to remember how our great-great-grandfather spoke, and not many people busy themselves researching dusty manuscripts of another century.

Although this type of change (together with geographical variation) is a basic element in the development of new tongues, languages grow so slowly that no one generation of men is normally aware of the magnitude of the alterations implied. And just as the unsophisticated tribes of the earth called themselves "the Men," believing that their kind was the only kind, it is also an unconscious assumption of most of us that words are pretty much fixed—they haven't changed and won't change too much. They have, and will, but the slowness of the change is insidious. The world does not turn upside-down overnight—nor do words. Yet given enough time, anything can happen.

This kind of topsy-turveydom is precisely characteristic of our word "nice." It began as the late Latin adjective *nescius,* "ignorant" (from the negative particle *ne* + the *scius* from which comes our "science," literally a "knowing"). In its French descendant, *nescius* became *nice,* orginally a two-syllable word rhyming with "see-say," later reduced to one which rhymed with "niece." The word came into English about the year 1290 with the meaning *foolish, ignorant,* as in "They said he was a fool . . . and that they never saw so nice a man." Later, the word carried the sense of *rare, odd, strange:* "Diverse manner of nice beasts and whale-fishes." From this, the word can be seen to gather to itself the idea of *delicacy, coyness,* and later, *shyness.*

It is from this idea of refinement and/or squeamishness that the word moves toward a related connotation—that of "highly precise"—still implicit in the stereotyped expression, "a nice distinction,"[5] i.e., a carefully accurate distinction. In 1666 it was still possible, for instance, to speak of "a nice pair of gold-scales" in the sense of high accuracy in measurement.

But just as "dainty" has acquired the connotations of *fastidiousness* from the earlier idea of *deliciousness,* so, in an opposite direction, "nice" has moved from *fastidious* to *pleasant.* After all, any object whose purpose was practical was most probably "nice" (in our sense of the word) if it was "nice" (in the older meaning, i.e., an accurate functioner).

But it is possible that the shift from "precise" to "pleasant" came about through a slightly different process: approving of an object because it was carefully made, rather than because of the pleasure which its efficiency gave the buyer. Such a sentence as "Some of these pastries would appear to be very nice" would, after all, seem to apply more to the skill in the baking than to any particular function of the cup-cakes in question. In either case, the primary meaning which "nice" bears today can be seen as an understandable extension of the immediately preceding one.

And, of course, words do not stand still; "nice" is still changing. Even at its best it implied only a mild degree of pleasantness, but it is rapidly becoming an example of vapidity *in excelsis,* a mark of vague approval to be used when one does not wish to bother looking for a stronger or more precise term. Often it is nothing more than a device which satisfies some obscure desire in the user for speech-rhythm; "That's a nice lousy situation you got yourself into, Buster" strikes some ears as more euphonious than the bare and unadorned "That's a lousy situation . . ." etc., etc. Often the phrase "That sure is a—" is used instead. In either case, the extra word(s) can best be regarded as a sort of vocal punctuation.

[5] More often today, "a fine distinction." And even now, "fine" is beginning to lose its meaning of "precision."

Each of the transitions in the meaning of "nice" is fairly plausible; none shock us with amazement. But this is only because each is presented in rough sequence, in the approximate order in which it occurred. It is only natural that each change should appear fairy reasonable, for otherwise it would never have taken place; men do not decide one morning to give that which they knew as "black" the new name "white." But black can shade to gray through all the intervening hues—especially if the change requires 15 generations or more.

Much the same sort of thing happened to that presently somewhat contemptuous word: "silly." Once upon a time it was a word of high praise, as those readers who know some German may have guessed already. For our "silly" is ultimately the same as German's present-day *selig*. And *ein seliger Mann* has nothing of the silly about him; he is a man who suffers in his own way, a man marked off from others by his capacity for agonies and joys. He is the blessed man. And once "the silly man" was *holy* too, in the speech of the English.

There are those who would say that the spirit of the practical conquered the speakers of English a little earlier than the rest; but that is a sort of cheap-and-sleazy mysticism which writers about language fall into all too frequently. (Linguistics has occasionally been caught mooning over the supposed Anglo-Saxon instinct for self-government, "natural" Slavic profundity, the African's "inborn sense of rhythm," and the like.)

Whatever the cause, "silly" moved through something like the following series of stages: *blessed, unworldly*—uninterested in the bustle and scurry of this world below; *naïve*—erring through ignorance of the practicalities of everyday life; and finally, *ignorance,* impure but simple.

There is really no reason for the speakers of English to single themselves out for special shame, however. If the present sad estate of "silly" says something about our way of life, much the same has happened in other languages.

Our "cretin" (one marked by dwarfism and mental deficiency

due to a lack of iodine in the diet) is, for example, nothing but an anglicization of the French *crétin;* originally the word for "christian." The present day French term for one of the Faithful is *chrétien*—a later coinage, modeled more closely on the ancestral Latin *christianus.*

Even among the Russians—whose devoutness was almost as fabled before the Soviet era as the Negro's supposed ability to dance—the early word for *christian* became in time merely the word for *peasant,* and by extension, *hick.* A newer variant was evolved to cover the idea of religious affiliation in and of itself, but even so there is a close obvious relationship between *krest-'yáneen* and *khresteeanéen.*

We have already discussed the changes in extension which take place among words borrowed from a foreign tongue; *nice, silly, cretin,* and *krest'yaneen* are evidence that the same sort of process can occur *within* a language. A word may become specialized over the course of time, or it may grow more general. Given favorable conditions, it may undergo one type of change and then the other. Of the four words listed at the beginning of this paragraph, *krest'yaneen* is probably closest to a simple case of specialization. Of the totality of christians within the country, one variety (the peasantry) was singled out for description by the term—the notion that virtuousness is more typical of the countryside somehow seems to be pandemic.

The changes that occurred in the other three words cited above are rather more complex. In them one sees specialization, true, but there is association of ideas as well. Perhaps such changes can best be visualized if we think of a word as being something like a circle. At the center one finds the basic core of meaning borne by the word, while along the circumference lies an entire set of associated ideas.

The central idea attached to *silly* was originally "blessed"; but even then there must have been a peripheral feeling—in the businessman's mind, at least—that such devotion to an impractical ideal smacked faintly of the foolish. It is possible that this half-unconscious feeling was brought to the forefront by such factors as the growth of hard money and a merchandizing economy; then too, the French *sainct* ("holy") had ousted *halig* as the title given to saints, leaving *holy* with less work on its hands.

Whatever the causes, and they can only be guessed at with varying degrees of certainty today, *silly* grew more and more to mean "unworldly," originally one of the circumferential ideas associated with it. Eventually the word's center of gravity must have shifted—slowly—and this formerly marginal idea became the focus of meaning, the center of the circle.

It is as if this circle had gradually melted into something resembling an ellipse; for a while there were two foci, during which time the notions of blessedness and other-worldliness were equally present to the speaker. But gradually the ellipse contracted to a circle again, this time around another point as its center. What had once been the primary idea of *silly* now lay at some distance from the center, and as time passed it moved further and further from the direct consciousness of any who used the word. With each new change in the central meaning of *silly*, the idea of sanctity fell ever more into the background. Eventually—as we know today—the idea of blessedness passed beyond the circumference of the circle entirely. At that point, "blessed" was no longer a meaning, secondary or tertiary, of the word in question.

Much the same sort of thing has doubtless happened to each word as it underwent—and undergoes—the inevitable change of a living language. "A living language . . ." We have used the metaphor of a circle to describe the process by which words change, but a circle is a lifeless, geometrical abstraction. There is something in the behavior of Language which carries with it an inescapable impression of vitality. It often strikes us as having a life of its own. It is a false impression of course, since Speech is almost as much of an abstraction as Geometry; but if it is a lie, it is a lie like truth. For since Language is born of men's needs and nature's it shares the flexibility and transience of the living creatures who make it. As their lives and outlooks change, so do the words which reflect the flickering inconstancy of human situations.

*   *

But the human situation is not only inconstant, it is also ambiguous. It is not merely that things and words change, but that a thing or word in itself may be an entire multitude.

The Aristotelian may claim the primacy of the Law of Identity: *A* is *A,* and it is true that a thing is itself—but what *is* the thing? As a later philosopher said (perhaps exaggerating, but not much): "The logical content of any real thing is inexhaustible." A tree is certainly a tree, but depending on the observer and circumstance, it is a prospect of shelter from rain, a bit of shade on a hot day, an assemblage of cellulose-surrounded cells of the classes *Gymnospermae* or *Angiospermae,* a specified amount of newspaper pulp, *x* per cent of a Cape Cod cottage, a low-cost housing project for birds, or a poignantly sharp silhouette on the skyline at sunset.

Just so, words—either the visual or audible representatives—can exhibit a similar manysidedness, best seen in what might be called *the pure pun,* together with its half-siblings: *eye-* and *ear-puns.* The pure pun is a given constellation of sounds, with one standardized set of written symbols to represent it, which bears a multiplicity of meanings. The bow of a ship and the bow of a courtier fall into this class, as can be seen in the rather poor joke to the effect that "A ship is the gentleman's means of transport, since with it bows always come foremost."

The *eye-pun,* as might be guessed, consists of a number of different sound clusters (with separate meanings) all represented by the same sequence of written symbols. An illustration of this can be seen in the reason given for describing the battle of Agincourt—at which the archers of Henry V defeated the knights of France—as the most polite encounter in warfare, since "French nobility was met with bow after bow." Here, *bow* is taken to rhyme with *slow*. Spoken, the pun means nothing unless one remembers the spelling involved. The closely allied device of eye-rhyme was formerly quite popular in poetry, but has largely dropped from use; to rhyme *wind* with *behind* or *through* and *bough* was permissible in Coleridge's time, but today it merely strikes us that the poet has a tin ear, or that the device is being used to jar deliberately.

The *ear-pun*, which can be immediately appreciated even in the swift flow of conversation, has proven far more durable. As we might expect, this type of half-ambiguity (as with the eye-pun) gathers additional savor in those languages whose orthography is notoriously capricious—such as English. In more sanely written languages, there is not the troublesome gap between sound and symbol which plagues the 2nd-Former or 1st-Grader: *too, two, to,* are particular horrors of the English-speaking, as are *four, fore, for; two more, tumor; know, no; straight, strait,* and a host of even more hideous examples. However, be of good cheer —English is not the only offender. As we shall see in the next chapter, there are other languages whose scripts are fully as idiotic as ours—or almost so, at any rate. And though far from being the worst offender, because of certain features of structure as well as spelling, French can perhaps lay as good a claim as any tongue to the possession of *homophones:*—words sounded alike though spelled in different fashions: *sang, sans, cent, sent* (*blood, without, hundred, feels*) is as good a case of identically sounded confusion as one is likely to discover anywhere in the Western World. Since so many of its words can have the same pronunciation, though different in spelling, French even more than English has a poetry of ear-rhymes. In fact, there is one particular couplet—in itself, a pun without parallel anywhere else in Europe—in which each syllable of one line rhymes with each of the next:

Val, amant de la Reine, alla, grand tour magnanime,
Vallament de l'arène à la grande Tour-Magne à Nîmes.

(Val, the Queen's lover, went—great magnanimous feat—
Valiantly from the arena to the big Great-Tower in Nîmes.)

Spoken rapidly, these two consecutive lines sound identical. The closest approximation we can cite is one of the few triple puns we have:

When the Texas triplets were asked why they had renamed the ranch they had inherited from their father, giving it the new title *Focus*, they answered, "Because it is where the three sons (sun's) raise (rays) meat (meet)."

A poor thing indeed in comparison with the Gallic. Given fifteen seconds, any Frenchman of normal intelligence could probably come up with something as good or better; he may, without realizing it, do precisely that during the course of an average day's conversation.

We have spoken of pure puns, eye-puns, and ear-puns, when a more traditional discussion would have spoken of *homophones* and *homographs*. In part, this has been because we have tried to avoid the technical jargon of linguistics insofar as possible. There was, however, another reason as well. The reader may call it a quirk of misplaced piety, if he wish, but by considering such ambiguities as "puns," we have tried to resurrect a little of the wide acceptance such a device once had.

The Pun has fallen on evil days indeed; it has been called "the lowest form of humor"; a 17th century writer claimed, half-seriously, that the punster "would not scruple to pick a pocket"; even the gentle Charles Lamb dismissed it as "a pistol let off at the ear, not a feather to tickle the intellect." Though the reader has probably heard these things before, nowadays, of course, "the lowest form of humor" is not really that low after all. The pun is a legitimate instrument of humor—appearing in the best of humorous poetry *a la* Ogden Nash—and no one supposes that it is really a mark of stupidity or defective moral character. Yet, even today, after a partial resurrection, the pun is still *humor* and nothing more. Only rarely is it serious, and to most of us, this is natural.

William Empson knew better. In his *Seven Types of Ambiguity* (1930) he discussed the many-faceted contexts in which language—for his purposes, literary language—can express or imply a "diversity of creatures" in a single utterance. Perhaps only two of Empson's seven types would strike the innocent reader as pun in the normal sense of the word, but by an imaginative extension of the word such a form as the *allegory* can be regarded as one long, dedicated, and intricately woven pun. Though one is no longer necessarily dealing with simple words which mean more than one thing—note the names in used allegories, however—the entire allegory itself is a use of language to describe different levels of reality in one and the same discourse. Thus, in the *Pilgrim's Progress,* Christian is not only the typical Christian confronted by the snares of this world; he is also a man named *Christian* who—for the purposes of the narrative—passes through certain concrete adventures. Vanity Fair is not only a symbol for the fripperies and deceitful springes of the worldly life; it is, as well, an honest-to-goodness (or dishonest-to-badness) Fair. As Bunyan describes it, the Fair is a rather vividly portrayed assemblage of booths and stalls close by the town of Vanity, in which are sold such tangibles as jewels and gold—as well as such strictly allegorical commodities as pride and idleness.

*   *

We began this chapter with a brief discussion of causes of misunderstanding, and have moved to some observations on the nature of Pun as Allegory, which in a more general form is the question of Language as Art. The distance travelled would seem to be a long one, but the trip is shorter than one might think. Remember, Plato banned poets from his Ideal State—for in his stern vision of perfect knowledge and ideal virtue, the Poet was the Liar, the Deceiver.

Indeed, the poet—or any serious user of language, for that matter—is making use of dangerous tools which slip easily from the grasp to do injury. We have seen how easily language can betray meaning when placed in a foreign setting; how even within a single tongue the sense of words can shift with a change in time, a place, or the context of statement. And when we think of what a Goebbels, a Savanarola, or a Huey Long was capable of doing to stir men's passions, we may have a little more sympathy with poor Plato faced with the problems of political architecture.

There is one school of thought—General Semantics—which lays extremely strong stress on the trouble-making potentiality of language. There are many who say that these Semanticists place too much emphasis on language as the root of all evil, but considering the fervor with which men have died for a word—or at least the idea that is supposed to lie behind the word—there is doubtless more than a germ of truth to the assertion that men are often the slaves, not the masters, of language.

Ultimately, the problem of misunderstanding reduces itself to the question *What is the meaning of "meaning"?* If there is any harder word to define adequately, the author has never come across it. "Word" presented difficulties, as can be remembered; but at least a word, whatever it is, is an event or activity *in* language. Meaning, in contrast, is thought to be something *above, conveyed by,* it.

As we shall see in the very last section of this book, this entire problem of Meaning is one which is the subject of some highly-sophisticated (and mathematical) debate. Boas' definition of a word was taken as perhaps closest to acceptable, but in the final analysis one of its terms begged the question: " . . . clearness of significance . . ."

It may well be that "meaning" is one of those "primitive terms" which escapes definition precisely because it is so important, so basic. Even in mathematics, which prides itself on being the most logical and definitive of human activities, there are certain concepts which must be accepted for the sake of any progress whatsoever—"axioms." Perhaps "meaning" is such an axiom, but as more is learned about the nature of thought, the less this seems likely. Men do not give up so easily.

Whatever meaning should finally prove to be, there is at least one thing which binds together man-in-the-street, poet, and propagandist: the need to be understood. The desire for a pair of shoes, the passion which demands a pinpointing of the Truth, the urge to convince—all of these are equally human. And all of these can so easily be thwarted by the vagaries of Language.

"He's not bad—he's just misunderstood": this is often taken to be the caricature of the progressive attitude toward crime and evil. And yet in one way or another, from pun to poem, from haggle to "horatory," we all are misunderstood—or misunderstand. We do the best we can, and, as with fine literature, we often turn ambiguity to advantage. Like democracy, Language "may not be good, but it is still the best we have." We are only human, and Language is only man made; yet Language does pretty well.

But men have battled or grown angry over the spelling of a single word. What we call democracy another people may regard as a curse. The very purpose of language—the communication of meaning—may often be mocked even with the best of intentions, and it may be that William Butler Yeats' epitaph was truer than he thought, if we only add two pairs of quotation marks:

> Cast a cold eye
> On "love,"
> On "death,"
> Horseman ride by.

8

Sounds and scripts

We have, till now, dealt with Language and languages as if they were so many abstract patterns divorced from concrete human activity: a humanizing institution; a mirror in which are reflected the hundred-and-one preconceptions held about the universe; a constellation of hard-to-identify things called "words," and so forth. What we have *not* done is to view this patterning of perceptions as a here-and-now job of work. The vignettes scattered here and there through the text may have lent some vividness to our discussion of Speech, but we have yet to consider the actual process of speaking—or the writing which has occasionally come afterward. The physical expressions of linguistic behavior have rested largely in the background.

For there *is* labor involved, of course. Language originated as a sequence of sound modulations produced by the flow of air from the lungs—a flow of air modulated in its passage to the outer world by such organs as the vocal cords, the uvula, the palates (hard and soft), the tongue, the teeth and lips, and even the nose. Since the earliest days of Language there has probably been only a small degree of change in the apparatus which produces and shapes this articulate breeze; and we are burdened with much the same sort of work in conversation as were our cave-man forebears.[1]

The number of phonetically distinct utterances which the human vocal apparatus is capable of producing is—though far from infinite—extremely large. When one considers the possible permutations and combinations of such factors as *length of utterance, position in the mouth at which a sound may be focused, degree of tenseness of the vocal cords,* and the like, one can readily see the reason why it takes baby as long as it does to learn to speak. The job is a hard one, even leaving the psychological problems of word-meaning to one side.

Even so basic a matter as the accurate imitation of a given sound so that it is accepted as correct by members of the child's speech-community is a fantastically difficult accomplishment. When we consider the tiny distance in positioning of the tongue which separates the s of "sign" from the *sh* of "shine," (try it yourself, and see), we can get some idea of the physical acrobatics involved in the process of learning our own language's pronunciation. Compared with it, the problem of learning to walk on the precarious stilts of two legs, or even the matter of tightrope dancing, become relatively simple questions of routine muscular coordination.

We have somewhat glibly mentioned the difficulties involved in the production of acceptable, articulate sound, and paid

[1] There are also processes of infinite complexity involved in the reception of speech and its interpretation by the brain: patterns of density and rarefication register upon the eardrum and are passed along eventually to a series of minute hairs within the inner ear. Somehow, a varying electrical impulse is then brought into being which travels along the auditory nerve and makes its way to a specified portion of the brain (a speech center) where it is—again, somehow—understood. Unfortunately, we know a good deal more about the crudities of speech production than we do of its interpretation within the human animal. Luckily for the purposes of linguistic—rather than neurological—investigation, the genesis and nature of utterance is more immediately important than the subtleties of its reception and ultimate destination. The basis of Language as a series of events in the nervous system is nonetheless of the greatest theoretical importance, and may have vital implications for humanity in the near future. See chapter 15.

proper respect to the impressiveness of the feat—but what *are* the sounds? If Linguistics can claim to be a science—and it does make the claim—how are these various creatures of the human voice classified? What is their natural history?

There are a number of systems of pigeonholing the audible offspring of human vocalization, but by and large they differ in the ways in which they transcribe the utterances themselves, the ways in which they leave some record behind of the transient quiver of air which is Speaking. (Of this more later.)

What most systems agree upon is a *classification by physical characteristics*. Just as modern biological taxonomy (the science of pigeonholing a given species of plant or animal life in relation to other creatures) establishes its categories by means of reference to structure and to the types from which the present forms sprang; in a similar manner, phonetics (the science of uttered sounds) classifies its subjects according to physical characteristics and birthplace.

This system of classification produces some rather odd results at times: the sound [p] and the sound [f] turn out to be first cousins. (Another first cousin, on the other side of the articulate family-tree turns out to be the often-ignored [h], a runt of the litter.)[2]

Repeating these sounds will give the reader a good idea of the relationships among the members of this trio: the acrobatics performed to produce [p] are highly similar to those used in the pronunciation of [f]; the principal difference is that whereas [p] involves a closure of the lips, [f] is the result of our resting the upper teeth lightly on the lower lip only. A natural consequence of this is that [f] may be continued indefinitely in pronunciation: "f-f-f-f-f-f," while [p] closes itself off automatically, as it were. [h], in turn, is a sort of "super-[f]," in that it departs even further from the lip-closure of [p] than does [f]; there is not even the

[2] The square brackets: [ ] are used to indicate the actual *sounds* indicated by the letters inclosed within, rather than the letter's name or the letter as a visual symbol. More of this later, in the discussion of alphabets.

tooth-to-lip contact of the latter sound, but only the passing of exhaled breath through the slightly-opened mouth.[3]

This inability to continue the pronunciation of a given sound is characteristic of an entire group of consonants: [p, b, t, d, k, g], and for this reason they are often known in linguistics as *stops*. Such sounds as [f], in contrast, are known as *spirants* (from a Latin word meaning "breathe") and may be continued in utterance as long as one's breath holds out.

So far, we have divided the sounds produced in human speech into two categories; but this does not carry us very far. We can —and will—make further distinctions.

One such sub-division already *has* been made: that involving the role of the lips in articulation. We have called [p] a *labial* consonant because it is articulated by the lips alone, while [f] has been described as *dento-labial* in that it is produced by the teeth and lips acting together in concert. *Dental* consonants are those, such as [t], which result solely from contact of the tongue with the teeth.[4] Amplifying this classification-by-origin, we may add the *gutturals* such as the [g] in "go," which stem from the back of the throat, and the *palatals* exemplified by the [k] in "kill," in which pronunciation the tongue is raised somewhat toward the roof of the mouth.

We now have two interlocking systems of classification—one in terms of continuance, the other in terms of place of origin—by which consonants may be classified. There is, however, still

---

[3] The close relationship of these three sounds can be seen in the extent to which any one of them may shift to become one of the other two. Thus, the Latin word "ferrum" (iron) changed its articulation over the centuries in most of the Iberian peninsula, so that the modern Spanish word is today "hierro." The Latin "pater" and the English "father" also have a common origin in a long-lost word of ancient Indo-European which presumably began with a [p]. Our Germanic ancestors were the innovators here, changing from the *labial* (lip) pronunciation of [p] to the *dento-labial* (tooth-to-lip) articulation which forms [f].

[4] As you will see in attempting to pronounce it, [t]—in English—is not truly dental, since the tongue is brought into contact with the gum ridge immediately behind the upper teeth. Such modified dental consonants are known technically as *alveolars*. The [t] of French, German, etc. is, however, a true dental.

some possibility of error remaining. How may we distinguish, for example, between the [p] of "pull" and the [b] of "bull"? Both are stops, and both are labials. Any taxonomy which failed to specify these to us different-seeming sounds would be sadly lacking in thoroughness.

Another, an additional standard is needed to assist the two already established: the standard of *voice*.[5] If we pronounce [p] and [b] alternately, all the while touching our Adam's apple (larynx), we find that there is one characteristic which does distinguish the two closely-related sounds. With [b] one detects a marked trembling of the larynx; with [p] there is no such vibration. This is because the only distinction between [b] and [p] is that the first involves active use of the vocal cords, while the second is produced by omitting them from sound production. In philological jargon, [b] is *voiced,* [p] *voiceless*.

With these three sets of criteria, it is possible to roughly characterize most of the consonants found in the languages of Europe in somewhat the following fashion:

	Dental		Labial		Palatal		Guttural	
	Stops	Spirants	Stops	Spirants	Stops	Spirants	Stops	Spirants
Voiced	[d]	[đ]	[b]	[v]	[g']	[ĵ]	[g]	[γ]
Voiceless	[t]	[θ]	[p]	[f]	[c]	[ç]	[k]	[χ]

(*Note:* Since few languages are perfectly logical about spelling conventions, and the conventions themselves shift from one language to another, the International Phonetic Association (IPA) has devised a notation which makes use of a standard set of symbols having approximately fixed values. Some of the characters employed are familiar to us both in shape and value, others are borrowings from tongues and scripts other than English. Thus, [đ] has the value of *th* in "this"; [θ] = *th* in "three"; [γ] = the Dutch *g* in "gegangen"; [χ] is the "throaty c*h*" of German "Nacht," and [ç] the palatal counterpart in "nicht." [k] is used

---

[5] This is the "voice" of phonetics, not to be confused with the active and passive voices of grammar (see chapter 4, p. 56).

to represent the guttural first sound of the English "camera," while [c] may stand for the palatal variant found initially in "kill." Both [ɟ] and [g·] are rare as standard sounds in the tongues of Europe, though they may occur in dialect or as personal peculiarities.

The tabular presentation just given represents adequately most of the consonants of familiar languages, but a moment's reflection will show that it is by no means complete.

There are the *nasals,* for one thing: such sounds as [m], [n]. The palatized variant of [n] found in the Spanish "cañon" and the final sound of "sing," are also common examples. These are usually given a separate nasal classification since they are marked by a continual passage of air through the nose during pronunciation. (In the IPA alphabet, [ɲ] is used to represent the "ñ" of "cañon," and [ŋ] stands for the "ng" so often encountered in English.)

It is not absolutely necessary to consider these nasal consonants as a category peculiar to themselves. One could easily integrate them into the table above by making the quality of nasality of equal standing with stops and spirants.

The only remaining simple consonants of great importance yet to be accounted for are the *sibilants,* the hissing consonants. As might be guessed, [s] is one of them—the snake's hiss *par excellence.* Its voiced equivalent is [z]. Closely allied to these are the *turbulants,* produced by a turning-up of the tip of the tongue while otherwise continuing as for the sibilants. The results are (1) the voiceless sound represented in English spelling by "sh," in French by "ch" as in "champagne"; and (2) the voiced counterpart which is encountered in English only in the middle of words such as "pleasure," but which is fairly common in all positions in French: "gentil," "ajouter," "dommage"; IPA [ʃ] and [ʒ].

We have now accounted for the consonants most commonly found in the languages of the West—or have we? The sharp-eyed reader may voice an extremely loud note of protest at this point. Righteously rigid, or loquaciously longing, he may have noticed the absence of [r] and [l]. Nevertheless, it is still true—

we have accounted for most of the *consonants* usually encountered in the Western World.

[r] and [l] were omitted because they are not, all appearances to the contrary, purely consonantal. Together with the "y" of "yet" [j], and the "w" of "wet" [w], [r] and [l] fall into a hybrid category of their own. They are only *"semi*-consonants" (or equally correct, and more usual, "semi-vowels").

Most people will recognize the relationship between the "y" of "young," and the "ee" sound in "evil." Pronounced extremely slowly, "young" can be seen to decompose into something resembling "ee-oung." In like manner, [w] bears a rather obvious relation to the "oo" of "tool."

But [r] and [l] have never, to the average Westerner, been smirched with this sort of ambiguity. This is largely the fault of our orthographies, however, which have been molded largely on the expected and time-honored patterns of Latin, in which [r] and [l] do not, in fact, function as vowels. Yet what are we to make of such a word—and a distinctly pronounceable word, at that—as the Czechoslovak "vlk" (wolf)? Or that city known to the Yugoslavs as "Trzbsk"? (We are more familiar with it under the Italian form "Trieste.")

Such combinations might be written off by those with delusions of Western superiority as the aberrations of mere Slavs who know no better; but unfortunately for us, English is also full of those words in which [r] and [l] do serve as full-fledged vowels. Perhaps the most common instance of this lies in the multitude of words which are spelled so as to end with *-er*. That "e" which stands before the final letter is merely a sop to our prejudices, for a moment's honesty will show that it is not pronounced—not even as the blurred vowel found in such a word as "purr." By all rights, forms such as "robber," "eager," "wonder," and the like, should be re-spelled as "robbr," "eagr," "wondr," etc. There are almost as many sorts of words in our language in which [l] serves as a vowel, as well. The most frequently met-with words of this type are those in which the following sequence of letters is seen: any consonant + [l] +e. Thus, "bottle," "whistle," and similar forms are two-syllabled words in which the second syllable is unmistakably [l].

The true "vowelishness" of these two consonants can be clearly seen in examples drawn from (1) the Southern English of England, and (2) modern French. When the Englishman drops his "r," as in "wawtuh" (water) or "silvah" (silver), it is in reality a matter of changing the vowel rather than dropping a consonant. The vocalic[6] [r] has opened and moved toward the front of the mouth in its articulation so that it approaches the blurred sound which ends such words as "sofa," "idea," etc.

A similar process of vocalization has produced those words in modern French which terminate orthographically in -au, and many of those ending in -eau. Thus, "vau" (valley) and "marteau" (hammer) were at an earlier stage of the language "val" and "martel."[7] These words were pronounced approximately as they would be in English today. Gradually, the [l] came to be pronounced as a "oo," however; something of the sort may be seen in our hasty pronunciation of such a word as "trail" as though it were spelled "trai-uh," or even "trai-oo." At such an intermediate stage, the words "val" and "martel" must have sounded something like "va-oo" and "marteh-oo," respectively; the first of the pair rhyming in rapid speech with our "vow." Further sound changes brought the two into their present state in which they rhyme: "voh," and "martoh."

Though [l] and [r] are the consonants which most often play the role of vowels in European languages, any voiced element can play a vocalic part in speech under the appropriate circumstances. Thus, in rapid conversation, "could" often loses its normal vowel (which rhymes with the "oo" of "good"), and the [d]

[6] "Vowelish." The corresponding adjective for consonants is more regular: consonantal.

[7] English borrowed a number of such words before the shift occurred, which accounts for the fact that many of our forms are reminiscent of the Old French, rather than the speech of Paris today: Eng. novelty, O. Fr. nouvelte, Fr. nouveauté; Eng. assault, O. Fr. assalt, Fr. assaut. The French, even today, have kept many of these antique forms as names of persons or places. Charles Martel, the medieval hero, still known by that name in French texts, rather than as "Charles (le) Marteau" (Charles [the] Hammer).

assumes a vowel-like function. Phonetically, such a pronunciation might be transcribed as [cd], and dialect spelling, in fact, often uses the form "c'd." [l] and [r] excepted, perhaps the most commonly encountered consonant-vowel in our own language is [n], which we meet with each time that a word ends in an unaccented "-en." Phonetically, "straighten," "toughen," "oaken," and so forth, terminate in [tn̩], [fn̩], [kn̩], or more generally, follow the formula: consonant + [n̩].

From these halfway-houses it is only a short step to the vowels (and combinations of vowels) themselves. Unfortunately for us —the speakers, readers, writers, and hearers of English—it is rather difficult to focus precisely on what the vowels *are*. "A, E, I, O, and U" is the conventional answer; but though these are the *names* we attach to five letters of our alphabet, not one of them represents the primary sound of the vowel referred to.

"A" for example, rhyming with "sleigh," is not a vowel at all, but a *diphthong*—a combination of two vowels pronounced in one syllable; it consists of a vowel (allied to the vowel of "same") followed rapidly by the "y-glide" found at the end of such words as "boy," "clay," etc. The name of "E" itself is misleading, since to most of us to whom English is native, that name represents the "long double-e" (actually the "i" found in "machine").

The International Phonetic Alphabet approaches the problem of vowels via the Continental System, which though perhaps unfamiliar to those with no other tongue but English, has the virtue of simplicity.[8] According to this system, five vowels common to many languages are represented by the following phonetic symbols:

> [ɑ] as in "father"
> [e] as in "they" (without the final "y-glide")
> [i] as in "machine"
> [o] as in "go"   (without the final hint of a "u")
> [u] as in "rule"

[8] To those with some knowledge of Italian, Spanish, or German, the "Continental" values for the vowels are simply the long or short pronunciations of *a, e, i, o,* and *u.*

As we can see, these vowel sounds occur in English, though our spelling conventions often conceal their presence; [ɑ] is evident in general American "Tom"; [e] will be found in "sway"; [i] is the vowel of "please"; [o] is hidden in "though"; and [u] masquerades in fancy dress in such words as "fool," "prove," "Reuben," and the like.

Some languages manage with these vowels alone, and diphthongs built up from them. Italian is one such, Hawaiian another. In fact this set of vowels is often spoken of as "Continental," because it accounts for most of the vocalic elements in a large number of tongues spoken over the whole of Europe.

There are other communities of speech, however, whose phonetic equipment is far more complex. English itself is a language peculiarly rich in its vowels.[9] The Continental System may have the virtues of simplicity, but it has failed to account for many of the most familiar sounds of American (and British) everyday speech. Additional symbols must be introduced to do even elementary justice to the sounds of our native tongue.

Each of the vowel sounds (the Continental as well as the specifically English) may be either long or short; however neither of these terms must be taken in the sense in which we normally use them. In the commonplace usage of many an English grammar, we find the following set of opposing values:

"long" vowels	*"short" vowels*
"a" in "mane"	"a" in "man"
"e" in "reed"	"e" in "red"
"i" in "mind"	"i" in "mid"
"o" in "tone"	"o" in "tot"
"u" in "ruby"	"u" in "rub"

From what we have already said of vowels, however, it is easy to see that these "long" and "short" forms refer in actuality to entirely different vocalic entities.

Yet there *is* a sense in which we can speak of long and short

[9] As we shall see in chapter 14 of this book, this abundance of vowels accounts in part for the difficulties of English spelling.

vowels. Insofar as one and the same vowel sound is extended over a greater or lesser segment of time, such a distinction makes good sense. The [i] of "peep" is "longer" than the same vowel in the derived form "peeper." In the IPA alphabet such a genuine difference in vowel length is indicated by the use of a colon [:] after the long form. Thus, "peeper" would be transcribed as [pipr̩] (or [pipə] if recording the speech of a southern Englishman), while "peep" would be written (for either American or English) as [pi:p].

"A,E,I,O,U" is the normal order in which all of the languages of Europe set forth their basic vowels, but this is a mere accident —attributable to the rather arbitrary sequence in which the letters of the Latin alphabet have been arranged. Just as we have been able to devise a number of criteria by which one can classify the consonants—stop, spirant, labial, voiced, and so forth—just so, we may categorize the vowels by their points of origin, as well as other factors.

For Western European purposes we can assume that all vowels are voiced, and to that extent resemble such consonants as [b], [d], [g].[10] Since this characteristic is *assumed,* it may be ignored in making further distinctions; the principal characteristics which are used to differentiate one vowel from another in everyday Western usage are (1) *point* of articulation; (2) *level* of articulation; and (3) degree of (lip) *rounding.*

It takes no great powers of observation to notice that [i] is produced much further forward than is [a]; we can feel the difference almost immediately. [ʌ] comes somewhere between. [i] therefore, is classed as a *front,* [ʌ] as a *central,* and [a], as a *back* vowel. ([ʌ] = "u" in "but.")

If one wishes to subdivide the continuum of resonant utter-

[10] There *are* such things as voiceless vowels—we use forms very much like them when whispering—and they occur as integral parts of a number of Amerind tongues. But for all practical purposes in the non-Amerind world one may regard vowels as by definition voiced quantities. One definition of a vowel which partially distinguishes it from what we normally regard as consonants is: "A voiced utterance which owes its character solely to the resonating shape of the oral-nasal passages."

ances according to the height of the tongue—close to the roof of the mouth (palate), somewhere midway in the oral cavity, or depressed toward the lower jaw—a convenient classification is: *high, mid,* and *low.* This particular tri-partition may be somewhat more difficult for the average English-speaker to observe than that of front, central, and back since mid-vowels—though extant in our language—play a rather secondary role in English. Through accident one might pronounce "the" in the slightly unfamiliar fashion [ðœ], rather than in the more acceptable form [ðə]. There would be little chance of misunderstanding, however, since [œ] exists in our tongue only as an accidental variant of the to-English-normal [ə]. Though this new set of distinctions may be a bit difficult for the English-hearing ear to grow accustomed to, let it, nevertheless be granted that the following categories can be established:

$$[i, u] = \text{high}$$
$$[e, ə, ʌ, o] = \text{mid}$$
$$[ɪ, ɛ, æ, ɑ, ɔ] = \text{low}$$

Still a third mode of description can be employed, in which the degree of lip-pursing is specified. According to such a scheme, one may speak of *rounded* or *unrounded* vowels, and the same basic eleven resonants (vowels) may be classified in this fashion:

$$[u, o, ɔ] = \text{rounded (with pursed lips)}$$
$$[i, ɪ, e, ɛ, æ, ə, ʌ, ɑ] = \text{unrounded (with unpursed lips)}$$

By combining these three types of classification, we may characterize any of these vowels by a descriptive triad of adjectives; [i], for example, may be specified as *front, high, unrounded,* while [ɔ] is almost precisely its opposite: *back, low,* and *unrounded.* Such a trinomial system is often found in elementary textbooks. By means of it, we are able to set up a tabular presentation of vowels similar to the table of consonants given on page 123.

All the ingenuity devoted to this system of names, however, has become sadly obsolete. Modern technology has passed the vagueness of such descriptions by, save as a set of convenient approximations to be used when diagrams present difficulty to the typographer. With the invention of the X-ray which can represent cross sections of the nose, mouth, and throat; the fluoroscope which presents the same picture in actual motion; and the spectrograph and oscilloscope which diagram visual profiles of the sounds themselves, even the IPA alphabet shows itself to be no more than a sadly imperfect scheme of notation.

The following diagram, for instance, is an approximate cross sectional view of Man's vocal apparatus; the IPA characters inscribed within are set at the points of origin of the sounds represented.

POINTS OF ORIGIN OR ARTICULATION

OF VARIOUS SOUNDS

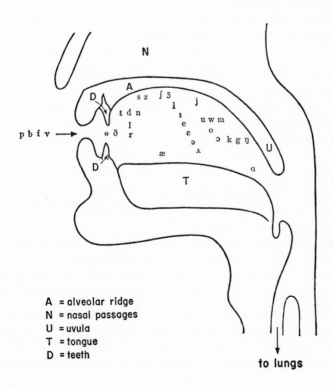

A = alveolar ridge
N = nasal passages
U = uvula
T = tongue
D = teeth

to lungs

The sounds represented here are those of Standard English. It would be possible to re-draw this diagram so as to present the complement of phonetic elements peculiar to any language spoken by the tribes of Man, and in few—if any—of them would the precise locations of any set of sounds be identical with their placement in our tongue.

In interpreting this diagram it should be understood that: (1) such sounds as [t, d, s] have been located within the picture at the points at which the tongue is placed; (2) the vowels have been positioned at their point of resonant focus; and (3) for pronunciation of the nasals (and the nasal vowels which occur, for example, in French or Portuguese), it is necessary that the uvula-U be open as it is in the sketch itself, so that the breath stream from the lungs can fork into the mouth and nasal passages (N) simultaneously.

In light of this diagram, it is possible to set up a rational arrangement of the consonants, beginning with the labials at the entrance to the mouth, and moving back via dentals and palatals till we reach the gutturals which originate in the neighborhood of the uvula itself.

A closer look will also reveal the underlying logic of vowel classification, for the entire trinomial nomenclature proves to be only a crude verbal attempt to picture relationships which spring naturally from human oral anatomy. Of special interest is the triangular pattern in which the vowels are arranged. In one form or another this "vowel-triangle" is a feature of many textbooks, though it is often presented in isolation, divorced from the fleshy context which determines it.

Such diagrams as the above—or those oscilloscope/spectrograph images which represent phonetic elements as vibrational frequency plotted against the length of time required for an utterance—are *structural*. Physical characteristics of origin or frequency are graphically represented. Such structural representations have proved of primary importance to the phonetician, whose province is humanly produced sound, not necessarily considered in its capacity as a bearer of meaning. From this purely phonetic point of view, these images or recordings have implications only partially concerned with human linguistic activity: speech therapy, physiology, and anatomy have obvious relevance here. Then too, an understanding of speech-mechanism can set the limits of human vocal behavior. (It would seem highly unlikely, for example, that any human community will ever use as an element of speech the vocable produced by the placing of the uvula at the alveolar ridge of the lower teeth: anatomical considerations alone would almost certainly forbid it.)

The story of the IPA alphabet is rather more complex. Nonstructural, this *functional* system of notation consists of conventionalized shapes each of which was intended to have a specific phonetic value. This was the original goal, and to a limited extent attempts are still made to use it in this manner.

The development of the various scientific devices mentioned above, however, soon showed that the IPA alphabet had become phonetically obsolescent shortly after its birth. As an arbitrarily arranged system of written forms it was inferior to actual pictures of vowel or consonant formation; and the shape of the symbols could tell nothing *per se* of the auditory realities (sounds) represented. Even though through continued invention of additional symbols one might—in theory—represent all possible individual human utterances, such a system would rapidly grow too unwieldy for use. Phonetically, so it proved, the IPA alphabet was at best a makeshift—useful, but only within limits. Fluoroscopy, frequency graphs, and—most convenient of all—the phonograph record were far more faithful to the manifold aspects of spoken reality.

"Spoken reality." There lay the crux of the matter. The spectrograph might show varying patterns of light and dark which represented the individual sounds of a language, but the same device soon showed that there was more there than met the ear.

We can most easily appreciate this when it comes to the matter of foreign accents. Even those who know no French can imitate many of the characteristic pieces of linguistic behavior which mark the Parisian attempting the language of William Shakespeare or Casey Stengel. Yet if forced to explain the differences between "accented" and "unaccented" English, we are often hard put to tell exactly what the distinguishing marks are.

Take [t], for example. There is something about the Frenchman's pronunciation of that simple sound which sets it off sharply from ours, yet how many of us can tell what, precisely, it is? Unless we are gifted with an extraordinarily sharp ear, it is only by a process of trial-and-error that we finally pinpoint the distinction: whereas our [t] is formed by placing the tip of the tongue at the base of the gum ridge (alveolus) behind the upper teeth, the French shape theirs by placing the tongue at the base of the teeth themselves.

The change in positioning of the tongue is miniscule, yet is more than enough to mark the one sound as native, the other as unmistakeably alien. However, even though the Gallic [t] is not ours, we still perceive it as at least a variation on the familiar theme. The question is—why? There is nothing natural about our perception of similarity, for in fact French [t] is as different from American [t] as American [t] and [d] are from each other.

The solution to this problem—as well as the story of how the IPA script received a new lease on life—can be summed up in the one word: *phoneme*. Briefly put, we may say that our English-hearing ear catches the Parisian's [t] as in some manner akin to ours from the fact that both varieties are, *in English*, mere variants (*allophones*) of one and the same phoneme.

There is more than the tooth vs. gum ridge distinction which marks off the French from the Anglo-American [t]. The French [t] also lacks *aspiration*, an outward puff of breath, which is natural to us in such words as "tell," "trance," "torrid," and so forth. Yet in spite of this double difference, the Frenchman's [t] is still only an exotic (to us) variation of an old, familiar sound. This is because even though the aspirate, alveolar [t] is normal to us, we can use the other form without changing any English word into another. Often in our lifetimes we may have used the dental and/or unaspirate (French) [t] but have never run the risk of being misunderstood. Our accidental slip was not enough to cause us to say something that sounded like some other word.

[d], on the other hand, is in English a phoneme separate from even the French dental; there are a host of English words which do differ only in the voiced vs. voiceless distinction: *tin*/*d*in, *citer*/*cider*, *lit*/*lid*. These three pairs of words show that, initially, medially, or terminally, there are distinct words differentiated only by the voiced or voiceless alveolar, alternating within a single, specified position in the pair. Since [t] and [d] can—and do—occur as distinguishing sounds in one and the same location among otherwise identical groups of sounds, they are said to lack *complementary* (mutually exclusive) *distribution*.

Lack of complementary distribution is vital to their separateness in English. Conversely, since the two varieties of [t] mentioned earlier can occur in the same otherwise identical word without generating a difference in meaning, they are considered mere variants of the same phonemic unity.

Usually the variation within the limits of a given phoneme is not a question of a slip of the tongue, however, but the consistent change which springs from the adjoining sounds (phonetic environment). The initial [t] of such words as "tap," "telephone," for instance, is marked by an outward puff of air; *initial* [t] in English is aspirate. But [t] following an [s], as in "stain," "sterling," "stone," lacks this outbreathing, i.e., is unaspirate. In such a case there is truly an instance of complementary distribution since initial [t] never—save by accident—lacks the puff of breath, and conversely the [t] in the [st] combination never possesses it. Unlike the chance "Frenchy" (dental) [t] of accidental pronunciation, these two allophones of the single phoneme [t], are encountered regularly and as a matter of course; they are *positional variants, consistent* allophones in English.

It must be pointed out that the range of allophones which one language lumps together in one phoneme, another language may divide quite sharply. There are a number of tongues, for example, which distinguish no words whatsoever by the simple alternation of voiced and voiceless sounds, i.e., they lack such almost-identical twins as the English *tin*/*d*in, *tap*/*tab*, and so forth. If this be the case, then our [t] and [d] fall together into another, single phoneme in the hypothetical tongues concerned.

Conversely, these languages may utilize the aspirate-unaspirate distinction, which occurs in English only as positional variation, as a means of distinguishing otherwise-identical sound groups. In such a case there will exist words such as *tap* and *t'ap* in which the only difference is the vital (to the native-speaker) distinction between aspirate [t] and the unaspirate utterance [t']; these two will be as truly separate phonemically as our [t] and [d].

Such is the psychology of hearing that the speakers of these languages will hear the (to us) unnoticeable presence or absence of aspiration as we do the characteristic of voice; the distinction *means* something in their tongues. By contrast, the speakers of these languages will seem oblivious to the t/d, p/b, s/z, k/g, pairs which stand out to speakers of English in loud, clear tones. For voice—to us so important in distinguishing meanings—will be to such folk a positional variant at most.

It must be emphasized at this point that these differences in perception have nothing to do with physical acuity of hearing. There is nothing in the anatomy of a Hindustani-speaker's ear, for example, which makes it more physiologically sensitive to as-piration than the Anglo-Saxon's; nor does the Anthapascan Amerind suffer from a peculiarly selective deafness with regard to voice. It is merely that all human beings are particularly ob-servant of those distinctions which have importance to them. Thus a horse breeder can tell how many Clydesdales, Tennessee Walkers, Welsh Pit Ponies, and Thoroughbreds there were in a given field after a cursory glance; his botanist friend will carry only a vague memory of "horses." Yet when walking through a forest, the botanist will have his turn, speaking knowledgably of Boletus and Polyporus, Amanita and Psalliota; his ranching com-panion may write off their field trip with, "We saw an awful lot of mushrooms!"

So far we have defined a phoneme as a group of allophones in complementary distribution with one another; but as we shall see, complementary distribution alone is not enough. If it were, then in English it would be impossible to choose between the unaspirate varieties of [p] and [t] for selection as the proper allophone to aspirate [t].[11]

The particular example given here permits a half-instinctive, yet justifiable, solution; namely that we exclude unaspirate [p] from inclusion in the [t] family because of its labial character, in contrast to the alveolar nature of the twin varieties of [t].

This particular dilemma, however, is a relatively easy one to resolve. Unfortunately, there are more obscurely distinguished groups of sounds, and the ultimate question must come down to this: Granted that a number of phonetic elements may be in identical complementary distribution with some one given sound (X)—is there some set of criteria by which we may single out one of them as somehow closer and therefore *the* co-allophone of (X)?

A tentative, yet plausible, answer to this problem has been proposed by the Prague School of linguists, which has attempted in some sense to silhouette "the essence of phonemicity." According to Prague theory we admit that many sounds share some or all of a number of characteristics (tension or slackness of vocal cords, voice or lack of it, etc.); but certain of these may be isolated for any given language as hallmarks of any one phoneme— and hence, of its allophonic variations. These hallmarks, plus the crucial element of complementarism would constitute the criteria for definition of a phoneme in any particular tongue. Thus, in Standard English, the essence of [t]-ness might be considered as some limited fraction of all humanly possible physical —i.e., phonetic—traits, and within this limited boundary exist a

[11] The justification of this seeming paradox is somewhat technical, but may be summed up as follows: [p] after [s] behaves as does [t]; i.e., only in that position does it lose its aspiration. Therefore, unaspirate [p] never will occur in the same phonetic environment as does aspirate [t]. That is, the two are in complementary distribution. Thus, if complementarism be taken as the sole criterion of a phoneme, we are left with no way of choosing between unaspirated [p] vs. unaspirated [t]; either might be regarded as the legitimate co-allophone. (It would be illegal to admit both unaspirated forms to brotherhood with aspirate [t], since then they would share the same phonetic environment—the immediate post [s] position—and could not, by definition, be allophonic variants.) If this seems overly abstruse, the reader may take it safely on faith. The chain of deductive logic *is* correct.

number of particular constellations of muscular setting (allophones), determined by phonetic environment.

In this manner we may—for demonstration purposes only—"fence in" the Standard Anglo-American phoneme [t] by the characteristic of alveolarity (a phonetic trait); all possible sounds which might be generated from alveolarization would then be allophones of the phoneme [t], *provided that they were complemental in distribution.* (This insistence on complementarism serves to exclude the voiced alveolar [d], which in Anglo-American *does* make for differences in meaning within a given phonetic environment: e.g., *t*ent/*d*ent.)

We qualified the example of the [t] phoneme with the phrase, "for demonstration purposes only," out of a sense of justifiable prudence. It is extremely difficult—time consuming, at least—to specify all of the permissible allophones of a given element, and from them to reason backward inductively to the lowest common denominator which isolates the phonetic determining portion of the phoneme itself. However, just as it is possible to reduce all possible poker-hands to a combination of four suits and thirteen numbers, so certain linguistic theoreticians (Roman Jakobson, for instance) are piecing out the primary physiologic acts to which the huge gamut of human speech elements can be reduced.

Even granting the usefulness—correctness if you wish—of the Prague formulation, it must be pointed out that it is still not a completely satisfactory definition of the phoneme—especially when comparing two languages.[12] With minor reservations, the Prague definition of a phoneme (phonetic character + complementary distribution) may be accepted for the sound system of a particular language, but when applied to observances *between* tongues, there may be difficulties. The notion of complementary distribution is unambiguous enough, but what is "phonetic similarity?"

---

[12] Even within a given language it leaves the problem of homophones unresolved: English *knit* and *nit,* French *la reine* and *l'arene,* for example, are not only phonemically, but phonetically, identical.

To Europeans in general—not merely speakers of English—
it may seem natural enough that unaspirate [p] be excluded
from the [t] phoneme on grounds of insufficient phonetic likeness, but would all peoples see the matter in this light?

Again the Welsh, to choose but one group, offer some tentative insights. Their habit of initial mutation (see chapter 6),
has produced positional variants which are not allophones included within some one phoneme; for example the d/n alternation in such expressions as "y dant" (the tooth) and "fy nant"
(my tooth). Though this shift from *d* to *n* is determined solely
by the presence of a preceding "fy,"[13] the two sounds are not
positional allophones of one and the same phoneme since there
exist pairs of words distinguished only by [d] vs. [n]; e.g., "dawn"
(talent) and "nawn" (noon).

There exists in Welsh another, analogous, transformation.
This one is from [t] to [d] when following the word "dy" (thy);
thus "y tad" (the father), but "dy dad" (thy father). Again, the
variation is not allophonic, since there are pairs of words—"de"
(southland) and "te" (tea)—whose sole difference lies in the
voiced/voiceless distinction. If there were no such pairs, however, there is little doubt but that the two variants would be
considered as allophones; the phonetic similarity (dentality)
strikes us as primary, the question of voice as merely an em-
bellishment.

But what then would we do with the d/n shift, which differs
only in the preceding phonetic context ("fy" instead of "dy")?
It, too, influences words beginning with [d]; it, too, follows as a
regular consequence of a foregoing possessive pronoun. If there
were no pairs of words distinguished only by [d] and [n], could
we speak of these two sounds as allophonic variants of a single
phoneme? One is a dental, the other a nasal. If the Prague definition of "phoneme" is, in fact, valid, then whatever "phonetic
similarity" exists in such a case must be a very, very subtle
thing.

[13] Compare this with the shift from aspirate to unaspirate [t] after a preceding
[s] as mentioned earlier, in such pairs as "top" and "stop."

The mere fact that such questions can arise is testimony to the vigor and aliveness of modern linguistic science. The science is marked today by new horizons in such diverse fields as mathematics, computer theory, and neuro-physiology; such vitality argues well for its future, a brief discussion of which is found in the Epilogue.

*   *

We spoke of how the concept of the phoneme has provided a new use for the IPA alphabet, even in the face of modern transcription devices which are infinitely more accurate in setting forth the actualities of human speech. The revitalization of the script has come about through a simple transformation: IPA letters have largely dropped the pretense of being a *phonetic* alphabet, and have become *phonemic* in character.

The task of representing the hundreds of possible phonetic utterances formed by human speech organs tends to be left to machinery which can most efficiently carry out the task; the differences between aspirate and unaspirate [p], dental and alveolar [t], have by and large been assigned to the province of the spectrograph and oscilloscope. In the broad (phonemic) transcription increasingly employed by users of the IPA script, one assigns a single character to a single phoneme since phonemes are the meaningful sound distinctions found within any given tongue.

Thus, in using the IPA alphabet to set forth the sounds of French, one uses [t] to represent the phoneme which is an unaspirate-dental. No matter that there may be occasions on which this [t] acquires a measure of alveolarity, aspiration, or even voice; such changes, if they occur, are only positional. In the broad transcription they will all be written as [t]. If, on the other hand, the alphabet is used to transcribe a language having—say— aspirate and unaspirate [t] occur as meaningful differences in one and the same environment (Hindustani is one such tongue), then the IPA script will use two different characters, because two different phonemes will exist.

It would be untrue to say that the IPA alphabet is consistently used in a phonemic manner; this is decidedly not the case. Part of the still-extant ambiguity may be traced to its earlier history, when there were still hopes that phonetic transcription could be achieved in a practical fashion via a limited battery of symbols.

Such a phonetic use of the alphabet is exemplified in the "narrow transcription" of such words as the English "calm" and "king" by [kɑ:lm] and [ciŋ], respectively. The [k] and [c] symbols are used to differentiate the initial stop of each word, since the first is a guttural, the second a palatal. Similarly, the [ɑ] used in transcribing "calm" has the colon [:] which customarily marks long vowels (see p. 129, this chapter).

This is a phonetic use of the IPA script, and is useful in the absence of better methods to indicate the actual sounds constituting the two words transcribed. It is completely superfluous, however, in terms of English's own internal logic; for neither the guttural/palatal stop distinction, nor vowel length, are meaningful (i.e., phonemic) categories in English. Using the IPA script *phonemically,* both words could be set down far more simply as [kalm] and [kiŋ]. (If, however, the alphabet were being employed to transcribe Arabic, then the [k] and [c] symbols *would* have to be employed, for the language of Islam is highly aware of vital distinctions made by means of the alternation of these two phonetic entities.) In like manner, the colon-of-length would be vitally necessary in languages which use vowel duration as a device for distinguishing meaning between two otherwise-identical words. Classical Latin is a familiar example of a tongue in which vowel length is a phonemic category: *puellā* and *puellă* have decidedly different significations, expressed only by their respective long and short *a*'s.

When used consciously in a quasi-phonetic fashion, the IPA alphabet serves a perfectly legitimate stopgap function: spectrograph tracings are somewhat exotic fare for the man-in-the-street, and their accuracy is such that it is often difficult to separate the essential from the accidental (the same person, repeating the same word, will usually give noticeably distinct tracings to the expert's eye). What *would* be disturbing would be an apparent indifference to, or ignorance of, the distinction between phonetic and phonemic elements.

The use of "narrow transcription" in a schoolboy's dictionary, for example, would be a sadly misdirected effort at accuracy— unless the book were being used to teach pronunciation to a foreign-born student, whose ear might be struck by accidental variations which the native-speaker's ear ignores. The only purpose that the use of colons-of-length—to cite one example only— would serve in a dictionary for Americans, would be to assert the need for a standardized American accent. Otherwise, differences in vowel length constitute a normal and non-phonemic source of individual and regional variation.

*   *

Since this book is largely oriented around the concept of Language-as-Speech, no attempt will be made to give a detailed story of the scores of scripts which have been devised at one time or another to commit the Word to paper (or parchment or clay or banyan leaves). Nevertheless, any account of Language would be incomplete without *some* mention of writings of the present and past. Discussion of this matter is particularly appropriate following our treatment of phonemes, for as we shall see, the everyday alphabetic scripts scattered across the globe today are essentially the product of phonemic analysis. From the Devanagari letters of Sanskrit to the bold sans-serifs of a restaurant menu in Idaho: all the alphabets of the world seem to have sprung from a common source in the Middle East perhaps 3,000 years ago, when some unknown genius devised a collection of symbols keyed to the phonemes of his Semitic dialect.

However, to begin with the Alphabet, even at its most ancient, would be to start at the end of the story, for human beings were leaving visible records of their thought behind them long before they were phonemic analysts—even unwitting ones.

The first writers were also the first artists, and the walls of their caves were both art gallery and library. Their marvelously lifelike reindeer, bison, and rhinoceros; stick-figure shamans and medicine men; the child's Christmas-tree pattern, repeated over and over to denote a fir forest: these were done by brilliant artists for the sheer joy of it, and for another reason as well—the pressing need to shape a message.

It is hard for us to interpret the precise sense of many of these messages. Whether a given collection of images meant: "This is the hunt when we caught five reindeer," or rather "We are going hunting. We must catch at least five reindeer," is difficult to decide. But boast or prayer, the work of those unknown artists was an unmistakable message. A letter written in picture-writing.

This *pictographic* system was probably universal in earliest times. Crude as it may seem to us, it was capable of amazing expressiveness in the hands of an ingenious people. The Amerinds of North America developed this form of writing to a high degree of perfection, perhaps for the same reason they evolved systems of sign language: the large number of mutually unintelligible tongues and dialects spoken within a comparatively narrow range of territories.

It would be a mistake to think that such a system of pictography was limited only to the representation of concrete objects. Even at an early date the need must soon have been felt to express not only the idea of five reindeer, but the notion of five days, as well. Though a day is an intangible, a unit of time, it was found that a row of five suns conveyed the desired message quite unambiguously. It was thanks to such cleverness that a number of Amerind tribes were able to record in their own script copies of the treaties they signed with the U.S. government.

The generalization of such stylized figures to represent less tangible aspects of reality marked a new development in writing: the ideogram. The lovely, yet demanding, brush-characters of Chinese are examples of such an approach to writing. Though in origin pictures, over the millennia each character has become conventionalized and, in all but a handful of instances, utterly unrecognizable as the image of any object. We shall discuss in greater detail the various aspects of Chinese (and Japanese) caligraphy in chapter 13; it is enough here to point out that such ideographic systems represent in a single character *a notion or concept*. Though many characters do refer to concrete objects (*daughter, mountain, pen,* etc.), the reference is made with regard to the idea, or to the word (in which latter case, the term *logographic* is often used), rather than to a simple visual image of the object itself.

We may picture the next stage in the development of writing by imaginary examples based on our own language. Let us suppose that English itself were written in an ideographic script. Such a system would require thousands of separate characters, each assigned to a different concept. (This is the case in Chinese, with its upwards of 50,000 ideograms.) Would there be any means by which the immense battery of symbols might be reduced, if for no other reason than convenience?

There is—by means of systematized punning. We can see this quite clearly in our hypothetical ideographic English. Let us imagine that we wish to write out the phrase, "I see . . ." In the ideographs used heretofore, such an assertion might be depicted by (1) a symbol originally representing a man pointing to himself (thus indicating first-personhood), followed by (2) another character intended to show a hand placed above the brow (as when we gaze out over a long expanse of plain). In our *simplified* system, however, "I" will be represented by the character normally used to express "eye"; "see" might then be expressed by a conventionalized line of waves (the sea).

This may be the raw stuff of puns, and poor puns at that; but something very much like this has actually taken place among a number of peoples—ancient and contemporary. The result of such thoroughgoing puns is a *syllabary;* that is, a set of symbols, each of which represents the sound of one particular syllable. (Though the Japanese do use characters in much the same fashion as the Chinese, i.e., ideographically, they have also devised two separate syllabaries in which they could represent their language, if they wished to. The symbols themselves were originally Chinese ideographs, in fact; but in the *katakana* and *hiragana* they have come to stand for nothing but the sounds of the words originally expressed. Since all Chinese words are one-syllabled, the result is two scripts of syllables.)

Through the successive stages of writing we can already trace the slow approach to what we would consider an alphabet. The syllabary, in fact, is within a hair's breadth of being just that. It is only one more small step which is needed—the step which reduces each character to the status of an elemental sound, rather than the *grouping* of sounds which we know as a syllable.

Only one more, small step. But a step which, so far as we can tell, was taken only once in the world's history. The step which created every true alphabet which we know of today.

In retrospect, the invention was obvious enough; but hindsight comes cheap. Even with the most logical syllabary in the world, the feat of logical induction which could isolate the [b] from an entire family of characters representing "ba," "be," "bi," "bo," "bu," and so forth, would have been a feat of high originality. When we realize that the parent-system which this brilliant and anonymous alphabet-deviser had to work with was, quite possibly, Egyptian, our respect is even further increased.

For the priestly writing of the Nile was close to being the most confused script ever to burden a hapless people—though the Japanese system of *kanji* (Chinese characters) plus *kana* (syllabary) certainly runs it a close second. The most disconcerting thing about the Egyptian writing was that it actually consisted of three different types of system, each of which might be represented by one and the same written symbol.

There were the *word-signs*, to begin with. These were characters serving much the same function as do the Chinese; i.e., they represented an entire word (concept) within the language. Naturally enough, the number of these word-signs was very large. By a process of metaphorical and psychological extension, many of these characters acquired secondary meanings in addition to their primary significance; thus, the sign which represented "a place-mat for gifts" (primary), could also mean "flattery," "peace," "repose," "setting of the sun," and further derivative notions (secondary).

There were, as well, the so-called *determinatives*. It would be hard to find an equivalent for these symbols in our language, though perhaps the number code used in Roget's *Thesaurus* and standing for general logical categories serves a roughly similar purpose. These determinatives helped to classify the associated statement according to certain widely-inclusive principles: a squatting human figure (male or female), for instance, warned that the characters following represented human names; a pair of legs referred to acts of motion; a rectangle with a gap in one side indicated that buildings were the subject of discourse; a wavy line (representing hills or waves) gave notice that foreign lands were to be dealt with. With the passage of time, the use of these determinatives became extremely widespread, so that in the last days of Egyptian writing few words indeed were unaccompanied by an explanatory symbol.

Last—and least—were the *phonetic signs*. There were only about one hundred of these characters, and in appearance there was nothing to distinguish them from the word-signs or determinatives, and that was precisely the confusion in the practice of Egyptian writing. A *given symbol might be used as word-sign, determinative, or phonetic sign*. In actual use, the situation was not so completely confusing as all that, for interchangeability was limited; it was rare when a phonetic sign was used as a determinative. But there was nothing to prevent the Egyptian scribe from using a large number of phonetic symbols in a word-sign manner, and an even larger number of word-signs as determinatives.

But though there were only a small number of these common-usage symbols which were solely phonetic, it was this comparative handful which was destined to play a leading part in the story of worldwide civilization-to-come. Of the hundred signs which the Egyptians could use as representative of sounds, a little less than a quarter were chosen to become the ancestors of our ABC's.

The exact story of how twenty-odd Egyptian signs became our alphabet must remain vague and uncertain in its earlier chapters. What does seem to be certain, however, is that the original users of this new *alphabet* were Semites—speakers of tongues akin to present-day Arabic and Hebrew. Whoever—and whenever—these unknown Semitic alphabetizers were, they responded brilliantly to the Egyptian riddle of the pyramids (and presumably bills-of-lading and mortgages as well).

Apparently something like twenty-two of the Egyptian phonetic signs were taken from the one hundred existing, and were used to represent the characteristic phonemes of some Semitic tongue. The precise signs taken is still a matter of conjecture, dispute, and investigation, though there are intriguing resemblances between certain signs of the Egyptians and the earliest Semitic symbols which have come to light. Thus, the broken rectangle which was an Egyptian determinative for "structure," may have been ultimately adapted to the form which one finds in early Semitic inscriptions, standing for the [b] sound. The general Semitic word for "house" begins with [b], and the Egyptian word's meaning, upon translation into Semitic, may have prompted the use of the symbol for the initial sound of the Semitic equivalent. Even in school primers today we do much the same: "A is for aardvark," "B is for ball," etc.

It is very possible, however, that the original Semitic adaptations from the Egyptian originals were not used as a true alphabet, but rather as a syllabary. In speaking of the Egyptian phonetic characters, we used only a vague descriptive term, because they were not *letters* in any modern sense of the word. More than half the hundred stood for two consonants. So that a single character, for instance, might stand for *hn*.

It should not be imagined that the Egyptian as a matter of course went round his city pronouncing words such as *bt, ks,* or *nk,* however. Such purely consonantal clusters—though occasionally met with in words like the Berber *ttss,* the Russian *zdravstvuitye,* and the English *strength*—are most commonly the specialty of Grundoon, the Groundhog Child, of Walt Kelly's *Pogo.* It is simply that we do not know what vowels were used in conjunction with the consonants indicated by the Egyptian symbols. (Even to the present day, modern Hebrew writes the consonant only, leaving the interpolation of vocalics to the reader's imagination and knowledge of the language.[14])

Even the symbols—twenty-four of them—which represented only a single consonant may have had a standard vowel associated with them while Egyptian was still a living speech whose writing had such ambiguity. Though not represented as such, the vowels may well have been understood in juxtaposition with the phonetic signs. If this be the case, then even the phonetic symbols composed merely an imperfectly syllabic system.

There is some tenuous evidence that in fact such was the case. David Diringer in his *The Alphabet* mentions the possibility that the early Semites may have at first used their newly-invented alphabet as a syllabary, rather than as a collection of phonemic signs, since there existed in many of the variants—and still exists today in Hebrew—a specific mark of punctuation which indicated the absence of a consonant-associated vowel. If there had been no early implication of some vowel's presence with the written consonant, so the argument runs, there would have been no reason to indicate specifically the absence of one.

Whatever the early status of the Semitic consonantal system, it did in time become a true alphabet. That is, its signs grew to represent the basic phonemes of the language for which it was used as a script. Because of the nature of Semitic tongues, however, it was never felt necessary to use specific characters to represent purely vocalic values (see chapter 13), though the semi-vowels "y" and "w," as well as other vocalic consonants ("r," "l," etc.) were included in the alphabet.

In time this system of consonants came to the attention of

14 Save in children's books, whose audience still knows the spoken language only imperfectly; poetry, where knowledge of exact vowels for rhyme purposes is vital; in the case of rare words, where excessive ambiguity might result; and in Holy Writ, whose uttered values *must* be set down explicitly.

certain recently (only half) civilized invaders of the northern Mediterranean. *Their* language was not a Semitic tongue, however, and a purely consonantal script was insufficient for their needs. Vowels were a necessity in the adequate transcription of their speech. Conversely, certain sounds which were to Semites distinct (i.e., separate phonemes), were to these *Greeks* mere positional variants of one and the same consonant. A handful of "extras" was therefore pressed into service as vocalic symbols, and in altered forms have come down to us as the familiar A, E, I, O, and U.

It was only to be expected that in the process of borrowing, certain alterations should have been made (above and beyond the limited transformation of consonants into vowels). The most obvious change was that in the order of the letters. This can be most easily seen by setting forth the approximate order of the consonantal (Semitic) alphabet:

#	B	G	D	H	W	Z	KH	T	Y	K	L	M	N	S	*	P	S
1	2	3	4	5	6	7	8	9	10	11	12	13	14	15	16	17	18

Q	R	S	TH
19	20	21	22

Though unfamiliar in form, most of the consonants set forth—in the present-day "square" Hebraic form—have relatively familiar values. There are, however, definite exceptions: (1) and (16) for example, are here represented by # and * since they represent definite Semitic phonemes which normally have no distinct value in Western tongues. (1) was the "glottal stop" produced by a sudden release in tension of the vocal cords—used in certain dialects of English between two vowels in place of [t], as in "Brooklynese" for "bottle." (16) was an *extremely* throaty guttural, which still survives in contemporary Arabic as the sound called "hamza." There were, furthermore, three sibilants whose precise nature we are still unsure of, but which probably clustered uncertainly around a trio of phonemes more or less resembling our *sh*. (Even in Old Testament times there were dialectical distinctions marked by some divergences, as seen in the *shiboleth:sibboleth* mentioned in *Judges xii:6*.)

During the first days of Greek literacy there was considerable variation in the form and value of the individual letters, as is only to be expected in any pioneering age. Even in the earliest period, however, it was possible to divide the numerous sub-families of Grecian script into two broad groups: the Eastern, and the Western. Eventually the two became reconciled in the alphabet of Classical times, which represented the following sounds:

a	b	g	d	ĕ	z	ē	th	i	k	l	m	n	x	ŏ	p	r	s
1	2	3	4	5	6	7	8	9	10	11	12	13	14	15	16	17	18

t	ü	ph	kh	ps	ō
19	20	21	22	23	24

Before this reconciliation of Eastern and Western forms, however, certain outposts had been established on the Italian mainland by Sicilians (whose island had earlier been colonized from Greece proper). These settlers from Greater Greece (as Sicily was then known) used a variant of the Western Greek alphabet; either directly, or via the Etruscans,[15] this set of letters became the basis of all present-day Western European scripts.

The earliest Greek alphabets had failed to distinguish between long and short "e," and long and short "o"; the pairs *ĕ* and *ē*, *ŏ* and *ō* developed only after a Western Greek alphabet had spread to Italy. This is why *E* and *O* are the sole forms in the West today, since this "home country" innovation was not passed along to the western colonies, to say nothing of the barbarians whom the colonials had educated. The letter *upsilon*, which had in Greek the front-rounded value of "u" in French "lune" (represented in the IPA alphabet by [y]), was altered slightly in shape and used for the rounded back vowel similar to our "oo"

---

[15] Such a book in fact exists: Diringer's magnificent *The Alphabet*, already north of present-day Rome. Their alphabet was Western Greek in type, however, and the then-illiterate Romans may have received their letters from Etruscans second-hand, rather than directly from speakers of Greek.

in "soon." Thus "V" was born (originally used indifferently for [u] and [w]).

"H" was originally used by the Greeks to represent a "rough breathing"—in all probability quite similar to our own familiar [h]. In the amalgamation of varied alphabets which produced the Classical Greek script, however, this form lost its aspirate character and was impressed into service as the symbol for long "e." In the Roman descendant of the Western Greek alphabet, however, it managed to keep its original value throughout much of Europe.

(The full story of the Alphabet, its travels and adventures, its good fortune and bad, would take the resources of an entire book itself, and one longer than the present volume.[16] Where relevant to a particular tongue further details will be mentioned in chapters to come; but the remainder of this chapter can sketch in only the briefest of outlines.)

The Roman alphabet kept a historical continuity in the multiple rebirths of Latin as the modern Romance tongues. With the spread of Christianity to the Celts and Teutons, these folk, too, accepted the letters of Rome; though differing handwritings favored by these groups produced the "Irish hand" still found as book print in the Gaelic-language volumes of modern Eire, and the "black letter" still used (though decreasingly so) in German written and printed matter.

The Greeks are responsible for another family of written forms however; not merely those of the West. The quaintly half-familiar letters we may notice on Soviet, Bulgarian, or Yugoslavian postage stamps are a living reminder of the Slavic debt to the Hellenes.

A number of the *Cyrillic* letters (whose name commemorates St. Cyrill, a Byzantine-Greek apostle to the Slavs, and traditionally—with St. Methodius—a bestower of alphabets) are familiar to us on the basis of our own alphabet. Thus, of the 32 letters of the Russian alphabet, *A, K, M, O* and *T* could be identified by

---

[16] Such a book in fact exists: Diringer's magnificent *The Alphabet*, already mentioned.

anyone knowing only the Roman letters. Many other forms are only thinly disguised variants of letters well-known to all those acquainted with Greek. A handful of additional letters has been shown to originate in modifications of Hebrew square-letters, while the remainder appear to be arbitrary inventions devised to account for sounds peculiar to the Slavic tongues.

We have seen how the Greek adaptation of a Semitic invention based on an Egyptian potentiality has managed to become the cultural imperialist *par excellence*. From the Australian schoolboy laboriously tracing out his first letters to the Turkish journalist writing an editorial; from a Greek-scholar reading the *Iliad* in the original to a Russian dutifully pursuing the intricacies of *A Short History of the Communist Party of the U.S.S.R. (Bolshevik)*; all are in some measure paying tribute to an act of ancient Graeco-Semitic inspiration.

But of course the Greek, Roman, and Cyrillic letters are not the only alphabets under the sun. Next most familiar are probably the intricate curlicues (so like shorthand in their general tenor) of Arabic. Today, "the Arabic alphabet" is a sadly appropriate name for that graceful script; for with few exceptions, the flows and swirls of this formerly pan-Islamic system of orthography are confined to the transcription of Arabic alone.

There was an earlier and a prouder day when the Arabic letters were the vehicle for many another tongue as well. (Even today, the Persian of Iran and the Urdu of Pakistan—both Indo-European languages, and hence kin to our own speech—are written in the cursive whirls and twists which are the legacy of the followers of the Prophet.) Until 1928, Turkish was written in Arabic characters, and it was only through the fiat of Mustapha Kemal that Latin letters came to the Osmanlis. Many a tongue of Central Asia—when written at all—was put to paper in Arabic form; but with Sovietization has come the Cyrillic (occasionally the Latin) alphabet.

Originally it was the Arabs themselves who took their letters with them as they brought the Crescent and the Sword. The sweet love-poetry of the Hispaniolized Moor was long written in a Spanish whose garment was the script of Muhammad; even the Jew living in relatively tolerant Muslim Spain often chose to commit his secular writing to paper in the letters (and often the language) of his Semitic cousins.[17] Many a South Slavic speech (Bulgarian, Serbo-Croatian, Macedonian) found an occasional home in Arabic letters, as did such disparate tongues as Pacific Malay and that descendant of Dacian Latin—Rumanian (often written in Cyrillics as well, before it came to rest in modern times in Latin garb).

The decline in the fortunes of the Arabic script can largely be attributed to the historically recent surge of colonization and industrialization: in short—Westernization. But though this process accounts for much, it does not tell all. Though Persian and Urdu may—perhaps—eventually adopt some variant of the Graeco-Latin alphabet, it seems far less likely that Arabic itself ever will (even discounting the factor of historical pride, which must be strong indeed). For the Arabic script is well adapted to the structure of a Semitic tongue, as one might suspect; its emphasis —like that of the Hebrew *aleph-bet*—is upon consonants.

Unfortunately, it is precisely this strong adaptation to the consonantal pattern of Semitic utterance which has often made for difficulty in the use of Arabic letters to transcribe languages, such as Turkish or Spanish, where much of the essential meaning is communicated through the vowels. (It is safe to say, for instance, that the three consonants *k-t-b* will have something to do with *writing* in Arabic or Hebrew; interpolated vowels or attached elements will only particularize. But there is little held in common by "bat," "bit," "boat," "about," "bow tie," "but," and "butte"; though phonetically and phonemically they all have the consonantal structure: *b* + *t*.)

One last characteristic has often made an alternative script seem attractive in comparison with the Arabic letters: the latter's

[17] The classic *Guide for the Perplexed* of Maimonides—Reb Mosheh ben Maimon, the RaMBaM—was written originally in Arabic; only later was it translated into Hebrew, then into Latin and other languages of the West.

intrinsic difficulty. Though the shapes and ligatures (joinings) of the Arabic alphabet are esthetically pleasing, they present a good deal of difficulty to the student—even to one whose language may be Arabic. The very ease with which one letter links with its follower (together with a historical emphasis on ornate calligraphy) has often produced artistic—but highly illegible—scriptorial masterpieces. Intimately related to this drawback is the presence of each of the more than 30 Arabic letters in four distinct forms: *initial* (used at the beginning of a word); *medial* (used between two other letters); *terminal* (used at the end of a word); and *isolate* (used when the letter is written alone). Permutation of these forms and the number of individual letters results in a total of more than 130 separate patterns which must be learned. The diversity of ligatures which are possible and which depend on preceding and succeeding forms adds in turn to problems of recognition and penmanship. A final difficulty lies in the marked resemblance which numerous letters have for one another, often differing only in the absence or presence of a specified number of associated dots.

If Islam had maintained its warrior energies at the peak they reached in an earlier millennium, it is possible that today we might write English—with difficulty—in the lovely script of the Muslim. But History took another turning many centuries ago. It is unlikely that the future lies with this exotic, fair, and eye-straining mode of orthography. Even if the accidental drawbacks it possesses were to be pared away—a not impossible task—the letters of Allah would still be too well suited to the tongue which first made them famous. Even if their shapes were changed, their logic would not be ours; for the plan of that alphabet is patterned to another way of speech, another set of sounds.[18]

18 We have shown something of the scripts most familiar to the West. For the story of that tremendous and improbable—yet true—migration of the parent Semitic alphabet east to India, one must turn to Diringer. As always, he tells the story vividly, though the Far Eastern chapters of this saga of letters are immensely complex. Suffice it only for footnote purposes that the scores of alphabetic scripts in the Orient owe their existence to the creation of those twenty-odd consonantal signs long ago, near the Mediterranean.

9

About *the* language

". . . Son of man, can these bones live?"
                              —*Ezekiel* xxxvii:3

ekwos, equus, eoh, ek, equestrian;

kmtom, centum, kant, satem, cent, sot, hundred.

WE do not know where they lived for sure. Guesswork often puts them somewhere in that vaguely defined land which marks the transition from Asia to Europe, near the low mountain-chain of the Urals that is the first high ground after a thousand miles of steppe. But no one can be certain. Their fishing villages may have huddled around the eastern shore of the Baltic; they may have lived on the plains of western Turkestan. We cannot tell. They lived and died before written history.

They were the speakers of "Indo-European," "Indo-Germanic," or "Aryan." The various names given their speech are our invention—not theirs. (If they were like many another primitive tribe, they may well have called themselves simply "The People," and their language "Peoplish.")[1]

All we can say with anything like certainty is that six to eight thousand years ago there were men who spoke a common tongue (or group of closely related dialects). And from that speech descended the languages spoken by half the people of the world today. Our own English is one such remote descendant.

[1] The Germans' name for themselves and their language—*deutsch*—originally meant nothing more than this.

155

"Indo-European" is the least misleading of the three names commonly given to that long-dead language,[2] and it is the term which we shall use throughout this book. Though not ideal, it gives at least an idea of the incredible spread of its offspring languages. *Every language of Europe* (except for a negligible four) is distant kin to Indo-European, and the languages of a majority of the peoples of India are also related. Hittite, spoken in ancient Mesopotamia, was an Indo-European language too; as well as the Tokharian spoken in central Asia and unearthed only in 1906.

We shall never be absolutely certain as to the finer details of Indo-European; it changed radically long before Man's creation of writing. It has been preserved only in the altered forms of its children, some of whom (English, for example) have changed almost beyond recognition, others (Lithuanian) remaining amazingly faithful to the image of their parent.

Without the evidence of the written word, without the testimony of documented history, how do we even know that some such language as Indo-European ever existed? It is a natural question to ask, and no less good for being obvious.

*   *

Let us imagine that you came into a small town and spent a week or so there. If, during the course of your stay, you caught sight of 9 or 10 different people, each with red hair, a snub nose, long jaws, and a cast in one eye, you would probably think them related. In such a village, where there would be church records of marriages and births, where everyone knew everybody else, it would be a simple matter to recollect Grandpa Postlethwaite and how all the Postlethwaites have always taken after him. Perhaps

---

[2] "Indo-Germanic" implies some special closeness to German, when, in fact Sanskrit and Lithuanian are probably closest to the original; "Aryan" implies no relationships, but has unfortunately acquired certain racial overtones, and the race of the Indo-European speakers—assuming they were of a single race— will always have to be an enigma.

he may be still alive, and can fill in all the details of family relationship. But even if he is gone, his parenthood is still visible and marked in his descendants.

Something like this is the story of how Indo-European came to be recognized. Just as one can be certain of the existence of *some* common ancestor in that small town—even if we never learn that his name was Postlethwaite—just so, men learned to notice similarities in groups of languages in Europe.

Unfortunately, the state of knowledge at the time when such similarities were committed to paper (the 17th century) did not encourage the speculation concerning relationship. Though word lists might be drawn up which showed resemblances between (say) German, Danish, and English; or Russian and Polish, nevertheless, these similarities were not attributed to a common origin, save in the case of the Romance languages—Italian, Spanish, Portuguese, French—where there were actual documents which could show how Latin had split into the various vulgar (common) tongues. There were no texts in an "Ancient Germanic," nor any mortgages written in "Old Slavic." (We know now that the break-up of these parent-tongues took place earlier than the splintering of Latin, at a time when the speakers possessed no alphabet, and before other, more literate societies could record the particular features of their language.)

Strangely enough, a rather good case could be made for the thesis that the truly scientific study of language owes its existence to the British conquest of India in the 18th century.

An English judge, Sir William Jones, who had already acquired a reputation as an oriental scholar, thought it advisable to learn the language in which the ancient and epic lawbooks of India had been written—Sanskrit. His subsequent writings on the language, together with his translations of numerous Sanskrit classics, marked him as a pioneer in ancient language. (Sanskrit had been the language of a true civilization when Latin was still the jargon of savages huddling behind the stockades of what was to become Rome.)

In time, he passed a knowledge of the language on to a young Scot—Alexander Hamilton[3]—working for the British East India Company. Hamilton in turn, taught the language to a young German, Friedrich Wilhelm von Schlegel—who wrote a book. And it was this book that was to be the first of a line of works which would make the German language indispensable for any student in linguistics for the next hundred years.

Uber die Sprache und Weisheit der Indier (On the Language and Wisdom of the Indians) appeared in 1808. In it, for the first time, a language was held up as being, at the very least, the equal of Greek or Latin in subtlety, power, precision—and complexity.

Schlegel's book was followed in 1816 by Franz Bopp's[4] *On the Conjugational Pattern of Sanskrit.* In these books, and others soon to follow by still other Germans, a convincing picture was presented of the basic similarities which existed between this long-dead language of ancient India, and the entire family of Teutonic languages.

The picture was made even more complete when it was shown that this similarity of structure and of vocabulary existed, not merely between Sanskrit and the Teutonic languages, but with other European tongues as well. The Romance and Slavic languages—even the Celtic—were shown to have basic affinities with this tongue in which nameless Brahmins had celebrated the virtues of Vishnu and the terrors of Siva.

What was one to make of this picture? Could it be all one huge coincidence? (Remember that these discoveries were made in a day when it was still thought that Hebrew had been the one language until the Tower of Babel incident.)

To give you some idea of what met the eyes of the astonished pioneers, here are the sort of similarities which revealed themselves to these Columbuses of language:

Sanskrit *vāk* = Latin *vox* (from which our "voice" originally came)

[3] No relation to our revolutionary war hero.
[4] Another German writer.

Sanskrit *pāt* = Latin *pes* = Greek *pous* = German *Fusz* = English
    foot
Sanskrit *jīvah* = Ancient Persian *jivō* = Latin *vīvos* = Greek *bios*
    = Russian *zhivoy* (English *alive*)

These similarities extended far beyond a mere concordance of
isolated words with related meanings; the very *patterns* by which
words were altered to indicate changes in meaning also showed
an amazing parallelism:

Sanskrit	*Greek* (the Doric dialect)	*English meaning*
pāt	pōs	foot (nom.)
padam	poda	foot (obj.)
padah	podos	of a foot
padi	podi	in a foot

That this similarity extended to verbs and not merely to nouns
may be seen in:

Sanskrit	*Biblical English*	*Latin*
bharami	I bear	fero
bharasi*	thou bear*est*	fers
bharati	he bear*eth*	fert
bhara*mas*	we bear	feri*mus*
bhara*ta*	you bear	fer*tis*
bhar*anti*	they bear	fer*unt*

* *The italicized letters represent forms common to each of the languages.*

Sir William was not slow to draw conclusions from these
similarities. In a letter which has become one of the milestones of
linguistics, he wrote that the resemblances between Sanskrit on
the one hand, and Latin and Greek on the other, were stronger
"both in the roots of verbs and in the forms of grammar, than
could have been produced by accident; so strong indeed, that no
philologer could possibly examine all the three without believing
them to have sprung from some common source which, perhaps,

no longer exists. There is a similar reason, though not quite so forcible, for supposing that both the [Germanic] and the Celtic, though blended with a different idiom, had the same origin with the Sanskrit."

Since those pioneer days, Sir William's conjecture has been amply confirmed. Subsequent and painstaking study of numerous languages, both ancient and modern, has shown that languages as apparently different as night and day did in fact spring from that "common source which . . . no longer exists." There can be no further doubt that English and Russian, German and French, Greek and Latin, Armenian and Welsh, are all distant cousins sharing common descent from a long-lost ancestor.

*   *

Admitting that such a long-lost ancestor existed, what was it like? What sort of language was it that changed in the course of time into so many others?

It was almost certainly a difficult language, as English-speakers would see it. (An ancient Brahmin, Greek or Roman, or a modern Lithuanian or Russian might not think so; but as we shall see, our language has changed more than most in the Indo-European family.)

It was a language burdened with *gender,* for one thing. Those readers who have painfully mastered the masculine-feminine-neuter of Latin or German can already begin to appreciate the troubles in store. Gender, which is strictly a grammatical idea, should not be confused with *sex,* which is a category implicit in the world around us; the two concepts often overlap, but are by no means identical.

In those gender-tongues which have survived (and almost certainly in Indo-European as well) many male creatures were masculine, many females feminine, and many objects without sexual distinction were neuter. However, the Latin *nauta* (sailor) was feminine in gender; the German *Weib* (woman, wife) is neuter; and the Greek *logos* (word) masculine.

This wholesale labeling of nouns in an arbitrary fashion led to one interesting result: although the words equivalent to *he, she,* and *it* might exist in these languages, they could not be used in what strikes us as a logical fashion. Thus, in German, one asks: *Was ist aus dem Weib geworden?* (What has become of the woman?) In answer, one must say: *Es ist ausgegangen* (*it* is gone out). Though German has a word roughly equivalent to "she" (*sie*), it can only be used when referring back to a noun of feminine gender; since a *Weib* (even the most womanly) is obstinately neuter, she must remain itishly *it*.

This sort of unsexing of individuals has its counterpart in an opposite tendency to personalize the inanimate helter-skelter. Taking one class of examples: many Indo-European languages have shown a trend toward the turning of abstract nouns (knowledge, beauty, honesty, length, roundness, etc.) into feminines. As a result, in Latin, German, and French (and many other related tongues) one says literally: "Ah, wisdom is precious, indeed she is."

(We discussed the problem of gender theoretically in chapter 4 of this book. As a particular feature it will recur in discussions of specific languages. Let it suffice for the time being that gender made for difficulty.)

Indo-European was also the proud possessor of a well-developed *case system*. Again, students of Latin or German will anticipate the nature of the difficulties which ensued. Whereas French, Spanish, or Italian use individual words to indicate the relationships between words, Indo-European used a system of endings.[5] Thus while these first three languages would say (literally) *the house of my father,* Indo-European said something similar to *house my-of father-of. House my-of father-of* would not be *quite* the equivalent, since (1) *my-of* and *father-of* were almost certainly not thought of as combined forms, but

[5] English has almost lost its case system—but not quite. See chapter 14.

rather as single words, and (2) the ending equaling *-of* was probably not a single word which could stand alone, any more than the *'s* of *father's* can.

In all likelihood, there were eight cases used in Indo-European:

(1)   the *nominative* case— indicating the actor within a sentence:
       The man sees the dog

(2)   " *genitive*   " — indicating the possessor:
       The friend *of the man*

(3)   " *dative*   " — indicating the "to whom" or "to which":
       She gave the bread *to the man*

(4)   " *accusative*   " — indicating the "receiver" of a verb's action:
       The sun warms *the man*

(5)   " *vocative*   " — indicating direct greeting:
       Where are you going, O *man?*

(6)   " *ablative*   " — indicating "motion away from":
       The letter came *from the man*

(7)   " *instrumental* " — indicating "means by which":
       He wrote *with the pen*

(8)   " *locative*   " — indicating location, "place in which":
       His house was *in the city*

This system of cases would present no real difficulty if the neat presentation set forth above told the story. Unfortunately, like similar tables in grammars of Greek, Latin, Russian, Sanskrit, and the like, it does not.

First of all, the endings differed in the singular and in the plural. This gives us 16 different endings to cope with at the onset. To make matters worse, Indo-European also had a dual number which indicated "two of" things. This dual number existed in all 8 cases (probably), so that the number of possible forms rises now to 24. With the existence of 3 different genders, the possible combinations become 72![6] Even here, however, the end is not yet in sight; for there were *declensions*—different classes of endings into which masculine, feminine, and neuter nouns could fall. Thus, though the total number of forms for any one given noun might *only* be 72, the sum of all possible combinations of all declensions may well have exceeded 500! It is small comfort to realize that the adjective was also forced to go through similar (though often not identical) maneuvers.

"Is that all?" the reader is probably saying as he wipes his brow. Far from it. So far, Indo-Europeanishly, we have only dealt with *things* (nouns); we have not even begun to speak of what they *do* (verbs).

As the reader may already have foreseen from discussion of the noun, the Indo-European verb was a cluster of complexities. Strangely enough, the principal notion expressed in it was *not* time. We, with our clearly marked distinctions between *run-ran, am-was, give-gave,* may find this exceedingly strange, but in all likelihood such was the case. Prior to *tense* (time of action) probably came the concept of *aspect*[7]—indicating the *kind* of action.

Thus there existed one basic form of the verb (such basic forms being known as *stems*) which expressed the idea of incompleteness of action; this stem, with attached endings indicating the subject and the number, gave rise to an *imperfective,* or *continuous,* aspect.

Another stem, again with appropriate changes, produced an aspect, the *aorist,* which stressed the *momentary* side of action.

Still another, the *perfect* stem, with changes, produced the aspect which indicated that a given state of affairs was the result of prior action.

[6] In actuality, the number at this point was probably somewhat smaller, since there may have been considerable overlap between masculine and neuter endings. A goodly number of masculine and neuter forms must have differed, even so.

[7] For examples of aspect in Indo-European tongues today, see the Slavic languages in chapter 12.

(There is also evidence that a future stem may have been used with some verbs; but it was probably not common. Even today, we often use a present form, the futurity indicated by context, or a helper-word: e.g., I am leaving for Europe tomorrow.)

English examples for the first three types of aspect (or equivalent stem) were omitted deliberately; English has no true equivalents. (A parallel was given for the future, since even in Indo-European this aspect was probably rather close to our ideas of tense, i.e., time distinctions.)

For the imperfective aspect, one might have written, "I running"; but this sounds like Pidgin English for a statement about present time. This is misleading, since the central idea here is one of duration over a period of time, with concommitant lack of completion of the action, rather than a statement of *when* the action was carried out. If the reader will make no attempt to insert an "am," "was," or "will be" between the "I" and the "running,"—*and not even think of them*—he will begin to have some idea of what a purely aspectual system is concerned with.

In like fashion, the aorist was used to communicate the idea of action at a point—rather than over an interval—in time. Unfortunately, the English *ran* or *run* by their very forms make unavoidable some notion of time. To imagine the true state of affairs, we would have to invent an imaginary form—*ryn,* for example—which indicated momentousness, once-and-for-all-ness, past, present, or future—all of them indifferently.

The perfect aspect is not quite so far removed from English usage: our three tense-forms, past perfect (I have stood), pluperfect (I had stood), and future perfect (I shall have stood), all have in common the idea of continuous action which leads up to a state of being which is, was, or will be, the result of the action.

Over the course of millennia this primitive system of aspects gradually evolved—in whole or in part, depending on the language—into a system of tenses, whose various forms indicated differences in time. (How and why this change took place must always remain a matter for conjecture.)

In addition to these purely verbal forms, Indo-European also possessed a host of "hybrids": gerundal and participial forms which were part-verb and part-noun or adjective, analogous to our "I love *running*" in which *running*—a gerund—performs noun functions, or "The *running* boy," in which the italicized word is a participle acting as an adjective. In English, these two verb derivatives happen to have the same form, but in Indo-European—and even in such a close relative of ours as German—the two are markedly different. And, of course, there was the familiar eight-case system. If these gerunds and participles were to serve as nouns and adjectives, they would have to be declined as such—and they were.

As might be expected in such a synthetic language, separate words were not used to indicate the subject of the verb in question. Like Spanish, Italian, Greek, and Latin, the endings attached to the various stems of the verb indicated whether it was *I, you, we,* or some third party, who was performing the act involved.[8] The conjugation of the Sanskrit "to bear" shown on page 159 of this chapter will give some idea of what the primitive Indo-European pattern must have been like. It is probable that in certain moods and/or aspects, at least, not merely the stem of the verb, but the very endings themselves must have differed.

If we could have actually heard, or seen written down, this ancient and long-lost tongue, one thing would have struck us as odd immediately. The absence of "little words." These *particles* as they are known technically, generally serve two purposes: (1) to express certain grammatico-logical relationships within a statement, and (2) to color the speaker's attitude, indicate credibility, or otherwise fill in the bare skeleton of linguistic actions. We shall never know whether or not Indo-European was rich in the latter sort of particle—this type of little word is notorious for its "here today, gone tomorrow" status;[9] but the grammatical par-

---

[8] Separate pronouns *did* exist, but were used only in positions isolated from the verb and, perhaps, for emphasis, e.g., "*I* (not you) did it."

[9] Even comparatively close languages may differ in this respect: Latin is poor in these affective particles, Greek supremely rich.

ticles were almost certainly noticeable by their scarcity. They were not widely needed.

Thus, equivalents for our prepositions—one class of grammatical particle—were used with a sparing hand; the case forms of the noun often did duty for them, as can be seen by re-examining our outline of the old Indo-European eight-case system. (We, too, often use the one remaining case left to us, rather than an equivalent preposition, preferring "Peter's father," to "the father of Peter.")

Adverbs, too, may have been less common than they are today. Often they must have been replaced by a different verb entirely. Though the Germanic peoples (and to a lesser extent, the Slavic) will make use of such form as *go up, go down, go away, go quickly,* etc., the Romance languages prefer the use of such unrelated and basic verbs as *mount, descend, leave, hasten;* and there is some indication that this reflects older usage common to Indo-European.

As we might expect from a language spoken under the rather unsophisticated conditions of 8,000 years ago, there was probably no, or little, use of the comparatively modern device of subordination. In its place, there may have been either the stringing together of sentences with *and*'s, or the simple juxtaposition of statements. In such a case, our, *I loved the girl whom I married* may have been expressed by, *I love the girl. (And) I married her.*[10]

*   *

We can not go much further in describing the language of that long-dead people. There have been dictionaries compiled in Indo-European, and even a fable or two composed in it, but such

[10] If Sanskrit is any indicator, the Indo-European speaker may have made use of another device as well to express subordinate relationships: the long clause-like, and serpentine, compound adjective:

I saw theyesterdayunwelllooking John for
I saw John, who looked unwell yesterday.

work is presumptuous indeed. The most that can be done in this field of historical lexicography is to deduce the most probable forms of basic roots, and prefix to them a sheepish asterisk— *ek^wos—in humble admission that the form is hypothetical.

They died too long ago for us to be glibly certain. Who they were, how they lived, what they thought, are things we shall never know. We have done enough—more than one could have guessed a few short centuries ago—when we have unearthed the bare bones of their language, and shown how it has come to rest on the tongues of scores of nations today. More than that we cannot tell, and it is unlikely that we ever shall.

Across the millennia we catch vague and distorted glimpses of them, but the vision of history is poor indeed at such range. That of linguistics is better, but even so, far from perfect. That something like what we call the Indo-European language was once spoken we can be sure of. The other details are a blur.

We may carry some part of their blood in our veins, but their flesh is dust in the wind and their names are forgotten.

✍ 10

Our German cousins

ik ben (Dutch)
du bist (German)
han är (Swedish)

Though Indo-European may be our long-lost ancestor, it is when we turn to the largely-contemporary Germanic family of languages that we come closest to home. It is a long, long trip to make, but whether we realize it or not—and most of us do not —English is merely a Germanic dialect which has succumbed much to the charm of strangers. (Not truly strangers; but at least kissing cousins as we shall see in the immediately succeeding chapters.)

It may seem rather strange to say that English owes its primary allegiance to the Germanic group; for to those of us who know neither a Romance nor (another) Teutonic speech, the languages descended from the Roman tongue are far more familiar. If we compare the two sentences:

Es ist unwahrscheinlich, dass an dieser Stelle jemals eine grosse Stadt gestanden hat, von der keine Spur geblieben ist,

and

Il semble improbable qu'il y a jamais eu à ce lieu une grande ville de laquelle il ne reste aucune trace, and then consider the rough translation:

It is (seems) unlikely that there had ever stood at this place a great city of which there remains no trace,

we must certainly conclude that the second version—the French —is far closer to our idiom than the original German.

Though we used the word "unlikely" in our tentative rendering, "improbable" would have served just as well—and would have been infinitely closer to our vocabulary than "unwahrscheinlich," which literally in our speech would be "untrueseemly." "Stelle" means little or nothing to us, but "lieu" calls up memories of the phrase "in lieu of" (in place of); while "ville" will conjure up associations with "village" and the idea of human habitation in general.

A little less obvious to the casual eye, yet plausible enough on further consideration, are "semble" with its distant echo of "seem"; and "reste"—not in the sense of "repose," but rather of "immobility": i.e., the thing rests where we left it.

But both the immediate and the casual eye would be wrong: we are "Germans" after all. This can be seen by the large number of simple words which English shares (often in altered form) with such languages as Swedish, Icelandic, Dutch, and of course German itself. In all of these tongues, "ja," with the *j* pronounced as our *y,* is the word for "yes." (Our word, in turn seems likely to be the result of fusion of an original "yea" ("ja" in other guise) plus an emphatic "swa" (Old English for "so"). In time "yea swa" fused into a single entity—our present-day "yes.") Such forms as:

ek hefi, jag har, ik heb, and *ich habe*

(Icelandic, Swedish, Dutch and German for "I have") are additional proof of historical kinship. In spite of the widespread similarities to the Romance tongues, in much of our acquired vocabulary the preponderance of basic Teutonic elements and resemblances in grammatical structure place English unmistakably in the Germanic camp. In terms of historical relationship,

French is a cousin, rather than a brother; though kin to English, it is no closer than, say, the Celtic languages *as far as common descent is concerned.*

The relationship between English and German is, by comparison, an intimate one. There was a time when the language of Luther with its "Wenn ich mit Menschen-und mit Engelzungen redete und hatte der Liebe nicht . . ." and ours ("Though I speak with the tongues of men and of angels and had not love . . .") formed a single tongue indeed. This is not, however, the place in which to discuss the evolution of English from its Germanic origins—chapter 14 of this book will be given over to a bird's-eye view of that series of changes which have made our language what it is. Here we shall content ourselves with a few observations on those peculiarities which make Teutonic tongues Teutonic.

*   *

There must have been something in the complexity of the original Indo-European verb which disturbed the primitive Germanic peoples greatly. There is, in fact, a theory propounded by Feist (a German) and Vendryès (a Frenchman), that the Germanic languages are the result of "pidginization" of Indo-European speech by the ancestors of the Germanic peoples, who presumably spoke some non-Indo-European tongue. This would account for the rather strange phonetic features characteristic of the Teutonic language-group, e.g. the substitution of [f] for [p] in words which have kept this original sound in other linguistic families. Compare the English "father" with the Latin and Greek "pater," the proto-Germanic "fisk" ("fish") with the Latin "piscus." The Feist-Vendryès theory is, however, speculative in the extreme.

Whatever the reason, the Teutonic verb became a thing of relative simplicity. In place of the wealth of verbal flexions distributed over a number of tenses, the Germanic verb possesses only two true tense systems: the Present and the Past. This simplicity is somewhat offset by the existence of vowel-mutating ("strong") verbs such as our *find-found* (German: *finden-fund*, Danish: *finde fandt*); but this class is a minority, and furthermore, a shrinking minority. (Over the centuries, numerous verbs have moved from this category—the past tense of *help* was once *holp*, for instance—to the weak class whose past forms are created by the addition of a syllable to the verbal stem.) The two-tense system of a typical weak verb is shown in the following table:

	German	Dutch	Swedish	Danish
I call*	ich	ik	jag	jeg
	nenne	noeme	kallar	kaller
I called	ich	ik	jag	jeg
	nannte	noemde	kallade	kallede

* "call" in the sense of "call someone something"; i.e., "name"

All other tenses in Teutonic languages are *compound;* they are formed by using helper verbs to eke out the small battery of autonomous forms which do exist. Thus, in company with the English, "I have seen,"

> ich habe gesehen (German)
> ik heb gezien (Dutch)
> jag har sett (Swedish)

Future tenses of the phrase are similarly compound in nature:

> ich werde finden (German)
> ik zall vinden (Dutch)
> jag skall finna (Swedish)

Though the *sense* (future) of these phrases is the same (in English, "I shall find") there is a differentiation in the meaning of the auxiliary verbs used. The English "shall," the Dutch "zall," and the Swedish "skall," all have their origin in a verb which implied obligation or purpose. The German "werden," on the other hand, had connotations of process—of "undergoing-ness"; for the verb "werden" (the infinitive) in its pure state means "to become." If one were to read a good deal of psychology into these distinctions—an extremely dangerous venture—one might say that the English-Dutch-Swedish *I am obliged to* . . . used as a future imply some different sort of attitude toward the world-at-large than does the German *I become.* . . . Quick and easy psychoanalysis-via-language might be tempted to posit a certain passivity to the German, who regards futurity as a becoming, in comparison with his fellow linguistic Teutons who regard it as an active obligation. Yet it was the "I become go" German who proceeded to set a good portion of Europe under dominion; his "I shall go" brethren were those who sought merely for room to breathe.

In spite of idiomatic differences between the means of expressing futurity, all these Germanic compound futures (that of English included) are recent developments. Though Present and Past were sharply distinguished, the Future was originally left at the mercy of present-tense-plus-context. Even today such usage is congenial to the Teutonic languages: "Ich gehe morgen," and its English equivalent, "I'm going tomorrow," are both illustrations of the Germanic tendency to regard what-is-to-come as a legitimate periphery of what-is.

This use of present for future tenses may strike us as natural, but this is only evidence of the essentially Germanic roots of our language. No Frenchman in his right mind would be guilty of such a locution as "Quand je *pars* [present tense] demain"; if saying "When I leave tomorrow," his statement will be: "Quand je *partirai* [future] demain." The fact that we regard such sentences as: "When I shall leave tomorrow, I shall do as you asked," as strange is only the memento of a long-gone day when English (and other Germanic tongues as well) had no future tense whatsoever.

We may make the excuse to ourselves that the "tomorrow" in such sentences is sufficient indication of futurity. This is a plausible view of the matter, and one taken by Chinese, which does not use a separate tense form for statements relating to future time. But by these very same standards of sufficient indication, a sentence of the type: "I am going yesterday," should be equally legitimate. The adverb of time makes the notion of pastness fully explicit. That, in fact, we do not regard such sentences as permissible, is merely evidence of the fact that Germanic tongues (among them, English) have always had a past tense; the Teutonic habit of present-for-future is thus a reflection of historic poverty—not proof of logical analysis.

This simplicity of verb forms is a characteristic held in common both by the Northern (Scandinavian) languages of the Teutonic clan, and by the Western (German, Dutch, and English); it is continued in the formation of the passive voice (which in Latin was a separate form: *amor, I am loved*—in distinction to *amo, I love*).

Thus, Germanic tongues express passivity by means of various auxiliary (helper) verbs used in conjunction with the past participle, as in our, "It *is taken.*" Unfortunately, there is rather little uniformity in the choice of the auxiliary chosen. The Scandinavian tongues prefer the verb *bliver* or *blir,* whose original sense was "to remain" (compare the German *bleiben* which is not used in passive formations). German and Dutch use *werden* and *worden.*[1] English, of course, employs the verb "to be."

There are two interesting exceptions to this generally uniform pattern of tense formation among the Teutonic languages: (1) the Scandinavian flexional passive, and (2) the German-Danish pseudo-passive.

We have mentioned the Norse use of *bliver* (or *blir*) as an equivalent for our "be" in such locutions as "I am loved" or "he will be elected," but as a glance through Scandinavian literary work will soon show, there is an alternative. Rather than saying, *Jag blir smickrad* in Swedish for "I am flattered," one

---

[1] We can see here a structural similarity to the formation used in creating the future. Compare the German *ich werde lieben* (I become to-love, i.e., I shall love) with *ich werde geliebt* (I become loved, i.e., I am loved). The difference lies in the substitution of the past participle for the infinitive.

may use the "-s passive"—*Jag smickras*. This terminal -s, with passive meaning, extends throughout the entire gamut of possible forms; it replaces the final -r of the present tense, and is attached to other forms:

jag smicklas	(I am flattered)
jag smicklades	(I was flattered)
jag har smicklats	(I have been flattered)
jag skall smicklas	(I shall be flattered)
etc.	

in contrast with:

jag smickla	(I flatter)
jag smicklade	(I flattered)
jag har smicklat	(I have flattered)
jag skall smickla	(I shall flatter)

This "-s passive" would appear to be a marked exception to the rule of Teutonic verbal simplicity, yet—historically, at least—it is not. It is the remnant of an earlier construction in which the reflexive pronoun ("himself") was used instead of a passive construction. As we have already seen in our discussion of grammatical voice in general, many languages use such forms as "he hurt himself," or "the door closes itself," for "he was hurt," "the door was closed." The original Scandinavian pronoun—of the approximate form *sig,*—became incorporated into such utterances as "Han smicklade sig" (he flattered himself) and through human laziness became nothing more than a final [s] sound. (This is a usage completely paralleled by the Russian final "-s" in reflexive statements, often with passive meaning (concerning which see chapter 12). There is also a "pidginized" version of Portuguese—Papiemento—in which something faintly analogous has occurred: *the man's house* is expressed by "o homems casa" instead of the standard Portuguese, "a casa do homem"—*the house of the man*. This is not, as was first thought, a borrowing of the English possessive flexion; but a contraction of "o homem, su casa"—*the man, his house*.

The pseudo- and true-passives of German and Danish have already been mentioned in chapter 4 (p. 60). It remains here only to touch upon the queerly conventionalized nature of their compounding, in Danish in particular. The pseudo-passive, as in German, is constructed with the local equivalent (*være*) of "to be." Since this construction is in keeping with English-speaking habits, we do not find it strange; it is in building the true (i.e., present time) passive, that Danish usage strikes us as odd. For in description of current action, the Danes will use the verb *bliver* (remain), to express "is" in such sentences as "The door is opened." This verb, with its connotations of stasis and rest, seems ill-chosen to express the activity of a truly passive (rather than statal) utterance. The German *werden* (become) appears better suited to the dynamism of the honest-to-goodness passive—preferable even to the rather neutral *"be"* or *"être"* of English and French, and certainly more appropriate than the *"bliver"* of Copenhagen.

Such judgments, however, are only another instance of reading too much historical evidence into the extant state of a language. Although "bliver" still does mean "become" when used as a verb in its own right, as an auxiliary it means only what the construction is *accepted* as meaning—a verbal particle distinguishing a process-passive from a description of state-of-being. If this seems outlandish, let us remember that our everyday verb "to be" can take on functions sharply divorced from its basic notion of identity. When we say, "he is good," *is* has lost most of its concrete meaning, and acts only as a conventional juncture between pronoun and adjective. Though the root meanings of "to be" and "to exist," are highly similar, "he exists good" is simply not English.

The principal difficulties which verbs of the other Teutonic languages present to the speaker of English are with regard to *word-order*. The Scandinavian tongues present no especial difficulty, except for placement of the Northern word for "not"— *inte* (Swedish), *ikke* (Danish)—in subordinate sentences. "I said that I had not come," would be, in Swedish, "Jag sade att jag inte hade komma": literally, "I said that I not had come."

Otherwise, the languages of Sweden, Denmark, and Norway are much like the speech of Biblical times. Since the progressive tenses of our tongue, (*I am going, you were going, he will have been going*) formed by the use of "be" are absent in these languages of the North, one says "I take the train to Stockholm," rather than, "I am taking. . . ." As in the language of the Good Book, these Scandinavian languages (like German and Dutch) also turn about verb and subject when an expression of time or place is used to begin the sentence. To a Swede, Dane, or Norwegian, therefore, our King James form: "Then went he from the city," is normal, everyday usage.

This particular reversal is common to all Germanic tongues, save English—and even in our language it survives in certain stereotyped expressions like "Then came the news," and "Down fell the pine tree." There is another kind of turnabout, however, which is peculiar to German and Dutch alone: so-called "subordinate word-order."

This type of re-ordering is produced after certain subordinating conjunctions (whence its name), of which "after" (in German, *nachdem*), "while" (*während*), and "because" (*weil*) are representative examples. The net effect of these subordinating conjunctions is to throw the verb to the end of the clause in which it occurs. Thus, the German would say, "Er liebte sie, *weil* sie so ganz schön *war*"—"He loved her *because* she so utterly lovely *was.*" This convention extends to instances in which compound tenses are employed, in which case the auxiliary takes up the final position within the clause: "Er glaubt das, weil sein Freund es gesagt *hat*"—"He believes it *because* his friend it said *has.*"

In an earlier day, this casting-back of verbs after certain—not all!—subordinate conjunctions was not the rigorous matter it is today in standard German; but the custom is now so firmly established in standard usage that it is impossible to read even a simple passage of German prose, or understand educated conversation, without taking account of the delayed verb. This is particularly true because the most common subordinating conjunction of all—"dass," equivalent to our "that"—is one which possesses this verb-postponing ability. One must say "Ich sehe, *dass* die Stadt sehr gross *ist*"—"I see *that* the city very large *is*."

Summarizing the types of word-order which can occur in German (or Dutch), we may list them as follows:

(1) *Normal word-order:* "Der Mann sieht den Hund" (The man sees the dog). Similar to English.
(2) *Inverted word-order:* "Morgens sieht der Mann den Hund" (In the morning sees the man the dog). Used whenever any element—most commonly expressions of time or place—is placed first in a sentence.
(3) *Transposed* (subordinate) *word-order:* "Nachdem der Mann den Hund sieht, geht er immer in die Stadt" (After the man the dog sees, goes he always into town). Used after certain conjunctions. ". . . geht er . . ." is in inverted order since some element other than "der Mann" (grammatical subject) begins the sentence.

Two further idiosyncrasies mark the German and Dutch verb; but though both have been the cause of much agony among students of the languages concerned, they fall into a rational pattern when considered together. *Position of non-conjugated forms* and *separable prefixes* have caused far more trouble than they ever should have.

Non-conjugated forms are those, such as infinitive and past participle, which are not directly connected with a noun or pronoun subject. In German and Dutch these forms are placed at the end of the clause or sentence, even in *normal* word-order. One therefore says, in German,

"Ich will nach Hause *gehen*"

and

"Er hat jenes Buch *genommen*";

"I wish home to-go," and "He has that book *taken*," respectively. This terminal position is also taken by non-conjugated forms in sentences whose conjugated portion takes *inverted* word-order. Thus: "Gestern *wollte ich* nach Hause *gehen*," and "Oft *hat er* dieses Buch *genommen*"—"Yesterday *wished* I home *to-go*," and "Often *has he* that book *taken*."

It is only in *transposed* (subordinate) word-order that this rule is broken, and even here the non-conjugated part takes up the next-to-last position: "Ich war ernst gestern als ich sagte, dass ich nach Hause *gehen wollte*," or "Man sagt, dass er oft dieses Buch *genommen hat*," would have English word-for-word translations: "I was serious yesterday when I said that I home *to-go wished*," and "They say that he often that book *taken has*."

Mark Twain and others have poked a good deal of fun at these shy, retiring habits of the German verb, but in spite of an initial strangeness one can become accustomed to them without too much trouble. After all, Henry James, William Faulkner and—on another level entirely—certain writers in the social sciences provide pitfalls of their own to the unwary.

The problem of separable prefixes would be no problem at all to the English-speaker—if it were not for the resistance set up in the mind by the problems of word-order mentioned immediately above. For something very much like these prefixes makes up a good portion of the idiomatic liveliness of our own tongue. Such sentences as our:

"I look over (*i.e.*, *peer over the surface of*) the table,"

"I look the table over" (*inspect it*), and

"I overlook the table" (*fail to catch sight of it*),

are perfect examples of what would be, in German or Dutch, considered particularly baffling instances of verbs with separable prefixes.

The form, "overlook" would be considered primary, since it approaches the typical, infinitive, structure of such verbs as, "zusammenlaufen" (German) or "samenloopen" (Dutch), which both mean "run together," in the sense of "converge." *But only non-conjugated forms are thus run together as unitary forms.* "Zusammenlaufen," "übergehen," "abnehmen," are the typical infinitive forms[2] of verbs meaning "to converge," "to ascend," and "to decrease"; the only other forms of these verbs which possess this unitary character are the past and present participles (e.g., "abgenommen"—"decreased" or "taken away," and "abnehmend"—"decreasing" or "taking away").

Otherwise, Dutch and German separable verbs are rather like their English counterparts. "Ich gehe weg" matches perfectly with our "I go away," both in sense and in word-order. (What give us trouble are the non-conjugated forms: "Ich werde weggehen," "Die beiden Flüsse sind zusammenlaufend." Our linguistic habits find, "I shall away-go," and "Both rivers are convergent [i.e. 'together-running']," uncongenial.)

The apparent exception to this rule of conjugated parts remaining separate is an apparent one only. Under conditions of transposed (subordinate) word-order, there is also a joining-together of prefix and verb; thus: "Er sagte, dass die beiden Flüsse zusammenlaufen"—"He says that both the rivers together-run." This seeming anomaly, however, can be seen as nothing more than obedience to the rules of transposed word-order itself. The verb *must* come last. If one were to say, "Er sagte, dass die beiden Flüsse laufen zusammen," it would be the adverb portion of the total form, rather than the verbal kernel itself, which would take up the end position. The apparently exceptional behavior of conjugated forms under conditions of transposition may thus be seen as actually a regularity in the language.

By and large, there exist in German or Dutch no such regular rules of gender as given in rules of verbs; it is largely impossible to tell from the endings of nouns whether they be masculine, feminine, or neuter.[3]

It is the form of the definite article which labels a noun: *der*

---

[2] A redundant "zu" (to) may be inserted after certain verbs; "Ich will ubergehen," as contrasted with "I wünsche überzugehen"; "I want to desert" vs. "I wish to desert." Compare the English, "I must *go*" with "I am obliged *to go,*" for a similar alternation in forms.

[3] There are some rules, such as nouns ending in *-schaft* (e.g., *Freundschaft*—"friendship") are feminine. However, these rules apply only to a limited number of words.

(masc.), *die* (fem.), and *das* (neut.) are the nominative-case equivalents of our "the" which define the gender of the following noun. (*Die* is also the form used before all plurals.)

We spoke of "nominative-case equivalents" because German, like Latin or Russian, possesses an unmistakable case system —though one which is only a sad remnant of the complete battery of forms discussed in the previous chapter. Here too, as with gender, it is primarily the definite article which identifies the case. There are only a handful of distinctive endings left to the body of the noun itself.

There remain only four cases, in German, of the original Indo-European eight. When combined with the three genders and the common plural, this reduced system gives rise to twelve possibilities, illustrated by the table of definite articles below:

	Masc.	Fem.	Neut.	Common Plural
Nominative:	*der*	*die*	*das*	*die*
Genitive:	*des*	*der*	*des*	*der*
Dative:	*dem*	*der*	*dem*	*den*
Accusative:	*den*	*die*	*das*	*die*

Although there are twelve possibilities in theory, we can easily see that because of an overlapping in forms, there are actually a far smaller number of separate and distinct linguistic (and written) elements; *der* is nominative-masculine, genitive-and-dative feminine, and genitive-plural; *des* the genitive for masculine and neuter; *dem* the dative for masculine and neuter; *den* the accusative-masculine and dative-plural; *das* nominative and accusative neuter; and *die* feminine and plural for both nominative and accusative cases. There are, in fact, only five distinct forms (*der, des, dem, den, die*) to apply to twelve theoretical functions.

This duplication of forms does not present any great difficulty in those instances where one and the same form serves a common case-function between genders or numbers, e.g., the masculine-neuter *des* in the genitive, and the *die* common to both feminine and plural in either nominative or accusative. (The worst that can happen is that one may be uncertain as to the gender of a given noun; *des Hauses* might thus, in theory, be formed from an imaginary masculine-nominative *der Haus,* rather than from the actually extant *das Haus.*)

True confusion becomes a possibility when a given form serves to perform a variety of case functions *within* a given gender or number. *Den Garten sieht der Mann,* in spite of its unusual word-order—conversational German would normally say: *Der Mann sieht den Garten*—is fairly unambiguous; *Garten* is singular, therefore *den* can only be the masculine accusative— not the plural dative; *Mann* is masculine, so *der* must be the nominative. The meaning of the sentence can be nothing else but, "The man sees the garden."

But what of such sentences as, *Die Frauen lieben die Männer?* Does this mean, "The women love the men," or, "The men love the women"? Both nouns are in the plural, and *die* represents both nominative and accusative. Furthermore, unlike Latin, Russian, Polish, and other, more completely case-observant tongues, there is nothing in the form of the nouns *Frauen* and *Männer* to indicate which is the subject, which is the object, of the sentence.

This sort of ambiguity can arise quite frequently in German, since an inspection of our table of definite articles shows that only the masculine has forms which distinguish nominative from accusative cases. More properly, this sort of ambiguity *could* arise quite frequently; in fact, it is rare, for German relies almost as strongly on word-order as does English. (The word-order used, granted, may appear somewhat strange to us; but it is as conventionalized as our own, according to its own lights.)

Thus, though *die Frauen lieben die Männer* might in theory (or in poetry) have either of the two meanings given above, in actual speech (and in all but the most mannered prose) the sense of the statement is: "The women love the men"—following the same convention of word-order used in English. Even in clauses

where the construction differs from English usage, every attempt
is made to place the subject before the object. In transposed
(subordinate) constructions, for example, this would be the recasting of the independent statement: *Man sagt, dass die Frauen
die Männer lieben*—literally, "One says that the women the men
love." To convey the opposite meaning, Germans would normally
reverse the position of the two nouns: *Man sagt, dass die Männer
die Frauen lieben.*

The one extremely predominant case-ending which belongs to
the noun itself is the genitive *-(e)s* of masculines and neuters.
Except in the case of proper names (e.g., *Peters Hut*—"Peter's
hat") the noun so inflected is generally accompanied by the *des-*
form of the definite article, or by some other word also bearing
the *-(e)s* ending (e.g., *der Freund dieses Mannes*—"The friend
of this man," "This man's friend").

This particular inflection is familiar to us both in form and in
function. Our possessive *-'s* is historically identical with it, the
apostrophe in current use often marking the former location of
a long-vanished *-e-* found in earlier stages of our language. The
one unusual feature of the German case-ending is that it is not
normally used with feminine nouns, or with plurals of any
gender; it is strictly a masculine-neuter trait in the singular. One
may say *das Haus des Offiziers* (or *des Offiziers Haus*)—"The
officer's house"; but *Dame* will indicate possession only through
the form of its definite article in such expressions as *das Haus der
Dame*—"The lady's house." Even "the house of the men," where
the masculine noun is plural in number, forgoes terminal flexion and is content with *das Haus der Männer.*

This genitive *-(e)s* aside, there are no longer conjugational
inflections of the noun with any vitality still current in German.
All dative plural nouns, whatever their gender, add a final *-n*
(*den Männern, den Weibern*) which distantly echoes the form
of the dative plural article. Certain one-syllabled masculines and
neuters *may*, in addition, take a final *-e* in the dative singular
(*der Mann* vs. *dem Manne, das Hirn* vs. *dem Hirne*); and certain nouns of this class must carry this ending when frozen in

certain idiomatic expressions (*zu Hause*—"at home"). Both the dative-plural -*n* and the masculine-neuter -*e* are, however, today only fossilized remnants of a much earlier day in the history of the language, when noun-flexion was a far more vital—and formidable—grammatical device. (Compare the modern German noun, for instance, with its counterpart in the English of a thousand years ago—Anglo-Saxon.)

*   *

From earlier discussion of languages with well-developed case and gender systems, we know that adjectives were forced to keep pace with the changes undergone by their associated nouns. This phenomenon of *concord* is exhibited in Teutonic languages, as we might expect, in a rather muted form consistent with the reduced flexional apparatus of these tongues.

The Scandinavian languages have three possible forms in which an adjective may occur: (1) root, (2) neutral, and (3) general. Both root and neutral forms occur only before singular nouns preceded by the indefinite article. In *en ung hund* ("a young dog"), the adjective is in root form since *hund* is classed in Swedish as a common noun; *ett ungt barn* ("a young child") contains the neutral form (with suffixed -*t*) since the language of Sweden places *barn* in the neuter category. The general form of the adjective is characterized by a terminal -*a* (in Swedish) or -*e* (in Danish) and is used before *all* plurals, and with those singular nouns—common or neuter—preceded by such words as "this," "that," "my," "your," "his," "our," etc. Thus—to choose Swedish examples once more—this general form would be used in *detta unga barn* ("this young child"), *min goda bok* ("my good book"), and *goda hundar* ("good dogs").

The Dutch adjective is simpler still, existing only in two forms: predicative (the root form) and attributive. The predicative adjective occurs in those contexts which explicitly posit some quality of the subject; this is most often the case when noun (or pronoun) is separated from the adjective by some part of the verb "to be," though other verbs may also establish predicates on occasion. Predicate position occurs in such English sentences as: "He is *handsome*," "She seems *bored*," "He became *rich*." "He is *old*," is expressed in Dutch by "Hij is *oud*"; for the predicate adjective takes no ending. When the adjective is used in an attributive position, however—as in the English, "The *pretty* girl"—Dutch usage requires addition of a final *-e*; "de *oude* postbode" ("the old postman") in contrast to "hij is *oud*."

Like Dutch, German too leaves its predicate-adjectives bare and unadorned; but here simplicity stops. As we might expect, German flexion is rather a complex affair.

A complete tabulation of attributive adjectival forms in *Hochdeutsch* will be found in any grammar of the language; we must content ourselves here with a sketch of the underlying logic which gives rise to them.

Like Caesar's Gaul, German adjectives—in attributive position—can be divided into three parts: *strong, weak,* and *mixed.* Strangely enough, the strong forms are the ones most rarely met with, for they are used only when no other word precedes the adjective itself. (Consider the relative scarcity of such phrases as, "nice boy," "good fellow," and the like in our own language.) Since it is normally the function of the "other word" (often the definite article) to indicate case relationships, in its absence the unaccompanied adjective must take the job upon itself. Hence the salient characteristic of the strong declension of adjectives is: it mimics the endings of the definite article. This can be seen clearly in the following presentation of *gut* ("good") in its strong forms as an accompaniment to *Mann:*

Nominative:	*guter Mann*
Genitive:	*guten Mannes*
Dative:	*gutem Mann(e)*
Accusative:	*guten Mann*

The *-er, -em,* and *-en* endings serve in place of the missing *der, dem, den.* (The genitive form, *guten,* is exceptional, and modern. At an earlier stage one said (and wrote) *gutes Mannes;* this form still occurs in proverbial expressions.)

Under only one set of circumstances is use of the strong adjective common: in conjunction with nouns in the plural. In German, as in English, one has far more occasion to use such phrases as, "nice people," "expensive cars," "pretty women," than to employ the corresponding forms with singular nouns. The strong declension in the plural (common to nouns of all three genders) is thus encountered with a good deal of frequency. Here too, *gute, guter, guten,* and *gute* recall the final elements of the missing plural article (*die, der, den, die*).

The weak adjective declension is decidedly more common in German. Its only two endings are *-e* and *-en,* and it is obvious that they can do little to characterize the twelve possible combinations of case-number-gender which may occur within the language. They do not have to, for the weak declension is used only after some other word which—like the definite article—can adequately specify the grammatical relationship desired. The syntactical status of *Mann* in

> *der gute Mann*
> *des guten Mannes*
> *dem guten Manne*
> *den guten Mann*

is quite unambiguous, thanks to the presence of the definite article; nothing is demanded of the adjective itself, and it contributes that with gusto.

The *mixed* declension is a halfway-house, found only after a limited number of words (e.g., *ein*—"a(n)," *mein*—"my" etc.), and only *some* of the forms of these words mark the status of the noun. As its name implies, the mixed declension is composed of forms drawn from both the weak and strong categories; where the preceding word possesses an ending which can express the grammatical function of the following noun, the intervening adjective "rests on its oars" with weak endings; when forced to do work of its own, through the failure of the foregoing word to specify, it appears in strong guise. Note the following example:

Nominative:	mein	gutes	Haus
Genitive:	meines	guten	Hauses
Dative:	meinem	guten	Hause
Accusative:	mein	gutes	Haus

In the genitive and dative cases, *mein* possesses distinctive endings which label the noun (*Haus*) beyond any possibility of mistake; *gut,* therefore, takes on the *-en* ending appropriate to the weak declension. In the nominative and accusative, however, *mein* lacks definite terminations which would distinguish subject from object. (The forms *meines* and *meines*—which would be self-sufficient—do not exist in German with the adjectival sense of "my.") In these instances, the strong endings *-es* and *-es,* in faint reminiscence of *das* and *das,* take up the burden of meaning.

*   *

A single chapter within a book can give but a bird's-eye view at most of an entire language family. In these pages we have darted down at random to catch a glimpse of some of the odder —or craggier—features of the Teutonic landscape. There is much which, of necessity, we have scanned or ignored completely. Gothic, for instance, that *Eastern* Germanic tongue which died out in the Middle Ages, but left behind it a lovely translation of the Bible. Features of that otherwise-lost language tell us much that would only be guessed at concerning the early history of the Teutonic tongues.

Then too, though we have touched on certain features of the Scandinavian branch of the Teutonic family, we have largely neglected Icelandic—that arch-conservative of languages, which has marked time for a thousand years. Its speakers can still read the Eddas: works written within a century or so of the Norman Conquest. It is as though there were still somewhere in the English-speaking world an enclave which used the Anglo-Saxon of King Alfred's day. Icelandic and English are the only members of the Germanic clan which have preserved the once-wide-spread "th" sounds (*th*is, *th*istle) which in more changeable Teutonic modes of speech have become *d* and *t*. Icelandic still keeps the letters which Anglo-Saxon once had, *etha* and *thorn,* to represent these sounds. *Etha* has even been taken into the International Phonetic Alphabet (voiceless "th" being marked by the Greek *theta*. This is not the only conservative trait which the language possesses; like modern-day German and like Anglo-Saxon, Icelandic has kept a four-case system and the various adjective declensions which its flightier Norse brothers have stripped down to mere vestiges.

In any discussion of the Germanic tongues, we must say a few words about their sound systems and the spelling conventions which set them off from one another. We have already mentioned, in passing, the change in Indo-European consonants which was made by the first speakers of Old Germanic. This change, taking place at an extremely early date, is common to all Teutonic languages; but there was a second change which took place about 1200 years ago which was far more limited in its range: the so-called High-German Consonant Shift.

This shift, which seems to have originated in the Alpine region, radically altered the phonetic apparatus of certain dialects of Western Germanic, and set them in a class apart. Thus, [t] (which had been [d] in Indo-European) became [ts] at the beginning of words and [s] in the middle or final position; [p], formerly the Indo-European [b], moved to [pf] initially, [f] medially or terminally. This High German shift characterizes modern standard German alone of the Western Germanic tongues, and may be illustrated by the following pairs of words (English of course did not take part in the change):

Modern German	English
Zeit*	tide
zehn	ten
zu	to
Zunge	tongue
besser	better
essen	eat
Fuss	foot
was	what
Pfennig	penny
Pfeffer	pepper
Pfeife	pipe
Pflanze	plant
Affe	ape
hoffen	hope
laufen	lope
Schlaf	sleep

* *"Z" is a German spelling-convention; it is* pronounced *as* [ts].

These were not the only changes, of course. Initial [d] became the High German [t]—compare the English *drink* with the modern German *trinken;* [s] before consonants such as [l], [m], [n], [p], and [t] became [ʃ]—English: (*to*) *sleep, smug, snow,* etc., German: *schlafen, Schmuck, Schnee.* Furthermore, final [k], thanks to the High German Shift, became that typically German sound [χ], resembling the Scotchman's "ch" in Lo*ch* Ness or "braw bri*ch*t ni*ch*t"; *book-Buch, make-machen, cook-kochen,* all exemplify this particular change.

Two points are of general linguistic interest in this series of changes: (1) the changes are regular—the alteration is not limited to three or four individual words but is carried out in all utterances of a given phonetic class; and (2) they may occur simultaneously, in *Pfeffer* for example, the first [p] shifts to [pf], the second to [f]. Thus, *Zeichen* ("sign") by a double substitution and a change in vowel becomes the English *token*.

This series of 8th century changes puts modern standard German at two removes from the parent Indo-European dialect; in this sense, German has evolved further than the Scandinavian tongues, or the West Germanic Dutch and English, for none of these languages has made this additional change in its phonetic apparatus.

For High German one may outline the following three stages of development: Indo-European (*dant-*), Germanic (*tand*), High German (*Zahn*). These successive changes may be regarded as a series of sieves which progressively narrow the linguistic classification of Indo-European languages in the West. *Dant-* is the Sanskrit root form of the word for "tooth"; languages such as Latin (and its descendents), Greek, and the Celtic tongues have preserved this stage of phonetic development. The Germanic languages—all of them—have introduced the shift to [t] (*tand* is the Dutch for "tooth"). Of these Germanic tongues, one particular sub-group has introduced further novelty, in turn altering the resultant [t] to a [ts] (German *Zahn,* with the same meaning as *tand*).

These High Germanic changes are what often conceal a very real identity in form between the German and the equivalent English word; we see the resemblance of Dutch *groeten* and English *greet,* but the essential similarity of German *grüssen* is somewhat less obvious. The Swedish *tecken* bears a greater likeness to our *token* than does the German *Zeichen,* though historically, German and English are more closely kin, being members of the same West Germanic sub-family, in distinction to the North Germanic Scandinavian languages.

Upon seeing such a Dutch phrase as "Ik heb het voor mijnen vriend gemakt," and comparing it with the English "I have made it for my friend" and the German "Ich habe es für meinen Freund gemacht," there is often a tendency for the English-speaker to regard the language of Holland as merely a sort of pidgin-hybrid of *Hochdeutsch* and English. This, of course, is an utterly wrong-headed way of regarding the matter. It is simply that "Dutch" is a West Germanic tongue which has—like English —avoided the High German Consonant Shift.

It is this type of situation which emphasizes the unreality of an arbitrary distinction between languages as opposed to dialects. For historically, the Indo-European languages are *all* dialects, Germanic tongues one group among many. Within the Germanic sub-family, the diverse languages have only the status of minor variations.

It is often customary to regard a mode of speech as dialectical if there is mutual intelligibility between the standard language and the dialect itself. This may be a secondary criterion, but the primary means by which a given mode of speech has been assigned dialectical or standard-language status has actually been a political one. The differences between Danish, Swedish, and Norwegian, for example are far less than those which separate Cantonese and Mandarin—two dialects of the Chinese language. In fact, the three Scandinavian varieties of speech are dialects of a single language—Old Norse—which existed not much more than a thousand years ago. It is only thanks to the independence of the three nations concerned that we regard their national forms of language as relatively independent. In like manner, Dutch is a language because it is a Low (non-High) dialect of West Germanic which has achieved formal status as the accepted variety of speech within the confines of a nationally sovereign border.

But the actualities of human verbal activity cut across the legal fiction of frontiers. Within Germany there are many people to whom standard (i.e., High) German is a language acquired only —if at all—in the schools. These speakers of Low German, *Plattdeutsch*—call it what you will—are considered to speak a dialect of German though it would be difficult for one whose native speech was standard German to understand them; while a Hollander would find that their language was basically his own. Theodore Storm who is best known for his writings in the standard language of Germany—his *Immensee* is unavoidable in second year German—also composed a number of poems in the Low German of his native Holstein. A Dutchman would think Storm's:

Mit golden Schiin to't Finster rin

(in High German: *Mit goldnem Schein zu's Fenster (he)rein*) a rather misspelled dialect of his own language's way of saying: *with golden shine in through the window.* Klaus Groth's opening line in *En Vergissmeinnicht:*

De Dag de graut int Osten

(*the day is graying in the east*) could be transferred practically intact into the language of Holland.

In connection with this "political" definition of Dialect and Language, it is interesting to note that before the unification of the English and Scottish crowns, there was truly a Scots language (and by this we do *not* mean Scots Gaelic). It stemmed from a common source with English and there was a high degree of mutual intelligibility between the two (as there is between Dutch and many varieties of German). But Scotch had a national identity and prestige of its own. William Dunbar (1465–1520?) could write great poetry in this tongue without any feeling that his idiom was dialectical, as in his *Lament for the Makaris:*[4]

> *I that in heill was and gladness*
> *Am trublit now with great sickness*
> *And feblit with infirmitie . . .*
> *He [Death] takis the knichtis in to the field*
> *Enarmit under helm and scheild.*
> *Victor he is at all mellie . . .*
> *I see that makaris amang the lave*
> *Playis here their padyanis, syne gois to grave;*
> *Sparit is nocht their facultie:—*
> *Timor Mortis conturbat me . . .*

And of course if Canute *had* managed to unify his Norse and English kingdoms, perhaps English might be thought of today as a rather interesting West Germanic dialect in a kingdom

4 Makaris = "Makers" (i.e., Poets).

whose best writers wrote in some unimaginable form of Icelandic
. . .

The intrinsic sounds of the Germanic languages (their phonemes) are by and large comparatively uniform. English has its
"w" and "wh" ([w] and [ʍ] in the IPA); Dutch its guttural "g"
[ɣ]; Danish its glottal stop [']; Swedish and Norwegian their
systems of musical intonation. But though there are individual
peculiarities to each variety of speech, there is a decided likeness in the general principles by which these related tongues
assemble their basic elements into syllables and their syllables
into words. There would be little danger of confusing the
Swedish *tacksamhet,* the Danish *Taknemmelighed,* the Dutch
dankbaarheid and the German *Dankbarheit* (all equivalent to
our *thankfulness, gratitude*); but they do show a generic similarity, and in more than the *-het, -hed, -heid, -heit* endings which
they use to form a large number of abstract nouns (cf. knight-
hood, God*head*).

If we use C to stand for any consonant and V to represent any
vowel, we may set forth the commoner phonetic patterns characteristic of the Germanic languages. A frequently-encountered
pattern is *CVC*, as exemplified in the Swedish *hål* and the German *Loch*. Another class consists of abstracts of the general
formula CVCV (Danish *Varme,* German *Wärme*). Two-syl-
labeled words whose first element is of a roughly prepositional
nature are often of the type *VCCVC* (these are characteristically
Germanic): *andel, eenheid, Abfall.*

There are, of course, other patterns of this sort; the actual
analysis of them proves extremely complex, difficult, and time-
consuming. When one takes into account alternative possibilities
and permitted substitutions, the results are usually formidable
quasi-mathematical expressions filled with plus and minus signs,
brackets and parentheses. Thus, the two-syllable, typically Germanic words mentioned immediately above (*andel, eenheid,* etc.)
are only one particular sub-type; many of the initial quasi-prepo-
sitional elements used in analogous words have a beginning con-

sonant (*Durchfall, vertrek*). To encompass these two variants in one formula, we would have to make use of an expression:

$$C \pm VCCVC$$

in which the $\pm$ indicated that, within the sound structure of the languages concerned, it was possible to use or to forgo an initial consonant.

Languages are particular about what vowels and consonants they will allow to enjoy one another's company. Our little . . . *CVCVCVC* . . . formula was a gross oversimplification as we can see if we think of the spelling and pronunciation of the German *Knie* and English *knee;* the Germans do pronounce their initial consonant, for the initial [kn] is a permissible cluster in German. Though this was once the case in English as well, we have since lost this particular combination at the beginnings of words (though not internally: *knock-kneed*), and the "k" survives only as an orthographic remembrance of things past.

Whatmough[5] cites a formula which has been devised to represent any one-syllable English word. Though the expression can be modified, at its simplest it presents well over ten separate terms, many of considerable complexity.

As we might guess, one thing which is characteristic of the Germanic family is an acceptance of consonant-clusters. The English "strength" or the German "verschwinden" would strike the average Italian, Indonesian, or Japanese as being fully as unpronounceable as the Russian "zdravstvooeetye" seems to the ears of an English-speaker. Like the Slavic linguistic family, the Germanic shows a good deal of internal homogeneity in contrast to the diversity of phonetic pattern shown within the Romance group—a diversity which is all the more surprising in light of these tongues' recent differentiation from the unity of a common idiom, Latin. (Recent *linguistically,* for the 1500-odd year span since the beginning of the break-up of Latin is short

[5] Whatmough, J.: *Language: A Modern Synthesis,* St. Martin's Press (New York), 1956; p. 246.

when measured against the span of Old Germanic's disintegration.)

*   *

In taking leave of these non-English Teutonic tongues, we shall list some uniquely characteristic traits which may help the reader distinguish one Germanic language from another.

In speech:

> *Icelandic* is characterized by the frequent occurrence of an "een" sound—this is one common form of the Icelanders' postposited article *the;* the presence of both the voiced and voiceless "th" sounds and an often-heard "oor" ending make for a reasonably certain identification.

> *Swedish* has a lilting musical pitch (which it shares with its near relative Norwegian); the occurrence of *"inte,"* in particular, distinguishes Swedish from any other Scandinavian tongue.

> *Norwegian,* like Swedish, has musical pitch—but the *inte* particle will never be heard. The word for "not" in Norwegian is always pronounced *"ikke."*

> *Danish,* unlike Swedish or Norwegian, *lacks* musical pitch. Instead it often has the glottal stop—a "catch in the throat" such as begins each syllable of our utterance *uh-uh* (i.e., "no") as distinct from *uh-huh* (meaning "yes"). The absence of both "th" sounds as well as the absence of the "een" and "oor" endings eliminates confusion with Icelandic.

> *Dutch* is marked immediately by the presence of "het" meaning either *the* (neuter) or *it;* "niet" meaning *not;* and of the *voiced* variant of the German and Scots "ch."

> *German* can be distinguished from Dutch by a clearly-articulated "die" (pronounced "dee") or "das" ("dahss"); by "nicht" standing for "not"; and by the phonetic groupings "shm-," "sht-" and "shp-" at the beginning of words.

It is even easier to tell one of the Germanic languages from another when they are encountered *in writing:*

Swedish is immediately identified by *och;* if this word can not be found in the written material, the frequent occurrence of *-a* and *-an* at the end of words will establish identity. One further clue: *ö* will always identify Swedish provided the only words in the text capitalized (except for names of persons) occur after a period (i.e., provided they occur at the beginning of sentences).

Norwegian, in writing, can be pinpointed by the combination *ae* (or *æ*); this, however, is according to the new spelling rules established in 1938. To be absolutely certain of the identity of the language, look for the joint occurrence of *å* and *og,* or either *å* and *og* with such frequent endings as *-e, -en, -et.*

Danish uses the combination *aa.* This combination may be found also in Dutch (or in Finnish—see below); but *aa* together with *ikke* and/or *og* is uniquely Denmark's.

Dutch can be identified with certainty by such words as *het* and *niet.* If these can not be found within a given text, the combinations *aai, ooi*—and in particular, *ij, eeuw, ieuw, uw*—serve to make the identity of the language unmistakable.

German may be singled out beyond any question by such written forms as *der, die, das, dem, zum* and *zur. Ein* (either in this root form, or as *einer, einem, einen*) is also unique.

Icelandic can be easily identified by the endings *-inn* or *-ur* (postposited forms of the word for "the") as well as frequent accented vowels (*á, ú*). *Important:* An upper- or lower-case "d" with a bar through the upright; or a letter which looks like an up-and-down line with a loop projecting to the right. Anglo-Saxon also had these two letters (*etha* and *thorn*) but modern English has discarded them.

One further clue: if capital letters are found at the beginnings of words with great frequency *within a sentence*—then the language is either Danish or German. Both these languages capitalize all nouns, not merely those which are the names of persons. This hallmark, when used in conjunction with the others listed above, can often remove the last traces of uncertainty.

Finnish is not a Northern Germanic—or even Germanic—language, though the location of Finland often leads to classifying its language in the Scandinavian group. In fact, Finnish is not even Indo-European: its closest kin are Estonian, Hungarian and Turkish. The language may be identified by the frequent occurrence of the double-vowel *-ää-*, as well as such clusters as *-ii-* or *-y-* followed by any double consonant. The presence of *ja* —which is Finnish for "and" (it does not stand for "yes") is also highly indicative, especially if the word does not occur at the beginnings of sentences.

*　　　*

Much that might have been included in a discussion of Teutonic languages has been omitted here; four-volume grammars can be—and have been—written about any one of them. Certain additional features will, however, be discussed in telling the story of that rather odd member of the clan—English. In touching on those Saxon roots and Norse imports which are so basic to our own language, we may cast further light on certain details here left in shadow.

Though English is kin to the Germanic languages of the Continent, we have stressed many of those characteristics which our tongue no longer possesses (as well as certain traits it never had). For with all the individual differences which sunder the Teutonic languages of Europe, nonetheless they have more in common with one another than any has with English. In the thousand-and-more years since King Alfred's time, our language has moved far—and the journey has been down a road that is all our own.

✐ I I

Our romantic second cousins

Roma
i Romani
los Romanos
os Romanos
les Romains

FOR centuries, people who speak English have had a unique feeling when their thought turned to Rome and post-Imperial Europe. It is not the sense of direct continuity felt by the historically-aware Frenchman, Spaniard—or most of all, Italian—who knows that he is in some fashion a latter-day Roman. Nor do we have that feeling of offering a stranger's love and admiration for the warmth and culture of the Mediterranean world which often marks the northerner (Goethe was a prime example) sensitive to the changes and fortunes of Time.

Not being citizens of the tradition nor respectful and awestruck visitors from beyond its borders, speakers of our tongue have been for at least half a millennium, psychological amphibians. The blood of the southern lands flows through us; we have made it part of the very fabric of our history—and yet is the product of a transfusion. It was a life-saving procedure almost certainly, and we feel somewhere at the back of our minds an appropriate gratitude.

Something of this emotion doubtless stems from admiration of that one Civilization which bound together the ancient world with roads and laws. Two thousand years after his death, the children of barbarians still read the words of Caesar in school-rooms from Glasgow to Melbourne; Cateline tries Cicero's (and students'?) patience in Capetown and Los Angeles. But there is something more than respect for the Empire. The Romans were not an amiable people, yet our feelings are tinged with warmth and color.

Part of it doubtless stems from the adventure and courage of the earliest missionaries—half-forgotten paragraphs in history books that tell of St. Patrick's crossing from Brittany, St. Augustine (*not* of Hippo) preaching to the heathen.

Though our language is ultimately Germanic, we have met and bred with many peoples—*become* many peoples—and taken many great traditions to our heart. Though the Norman Conquest left scars which took two centuries to heal, somehow the cruelty of the invader—himself Teutonic, and only three generations settled in France at the time he struck Britain—never became a stick with which to beat the dog of "un-Englishness." There was a curious absence of permanent rancor in the aftermath of this in-cursion. Roland and Olivier at Roncesvalles, Carolus-Magnus, Charles-le-Magne, Charles-the-Great, Charlemagne, even the reigning (though usually absent) Richard Lion's-Heart: all these became the stuff of love and legend to Saxon Johnson and Celtic Mallory, as well as Norman de Montfort.

Our language and history show a divided allegiance: half-Germanic, semi-Romance; yet in spite of our strong roots in Germanic sources, it is heroes such as Horatius at the Bridge and Roland fighting in the Pass who are best-known and most congenial to our spirit. Though we may admire the sinews of Siegfried (and even more the courage of Beowulf), they still touch us with a hint of the strange and unwelcome. This is even so of the definitely-Christianized Parsifal who redeems the image of the Grail.

Our love turns southward for its objects in the teeth of all arguments by Saxonists. Though the shape of our speech in its essentials may be that of Arminius (Hermann), boasting of the ambush he carried off against the XXth Legion—most of us still find ourselves wishing that those legionnaires had won.

Whatever the vices of that empire and its people—and Carthage sown with salt was one of the earlier examples of genocide —*something* put down roots which bore good fruit. From the bits and pieces of what had once been the Empire came the beginnings of a new society. From it many another people drew the raw material from which they fashioned the image of chivalry and high courage.

The best of that dream manages to keep itself alive (though precariously in these days), and from time to time we still find ourselves wondering about that twilight world. A world which in many spots was not even aware that it had died to a re-birth, still less conscious of a new dawn coming. What of the men who lived in that world? What of those people who—in some lands at least—knew that the Empire had died, and that they had once been of it?

It is imperfectly that we know of them; but the picture emerges fragmentarily through chronicle and legend, scrap of parchment, and distorted story.

They were not the nine-foot heroes of tradition in the beginning—men must be long and safely dead before they grow that tall. They were not noblemen, for the senators had died or dwindled back in Rome; they were the often-poor, the none-too-clean and unlettered who established the foundations of—sometimes battled their way into—a later hereditary nobility. Many, if not most, of them were soldiers, farmers and—in the infrequent towns of a dying time—shopkeepers. They were those who had lived or were living through the dissolution of what had once been an entire world.

*   *

It is impossible to say how many of these Romans actually carried any trace of the blood of Latium in their veins—quite probably only a minority of the population. Certainly the number of pure-bloods must have been vanishingly small in the days of a dying, and later dead, Empire. Even during the Augustan Age, many of the best citizens of the Imperium were Hispanic or Gaulish in ancestry (and sometimes birth). All the more certain that in those latter days, when Rome was an allegiance of heart rather than law, men of that vanishing or vanished world should be men of the neighborhood who held dear a memory that had once seemed to their great-great-grandsires an alien imposition. (Even today, our own soldiers have often enough taken German or Japanese wives; but our army—unlike the Roman—does not enforce a minimum twenty-year period of service, nor encourage its veterans to settle down for life in the country of occupation.)

As Rome splintered at is peripheries, three fates offered themselves to the abandoned orphans of civilization:

Where the armies fell back, leaving civilians and a handful of veterans and their half-breed families to make out as best they could (as in Britain or along some of the German border), the remnants doubtless stared uneasily into the dark of forests or up into the hills that fell back into deepening haze. Their fears were justified in one way or another. The landscapes held full quotas of fear and savages. The waifs of empire—they themselves, their children, or at most their grandchildren—were either killed or absorbed. Depending on time, circumstance, or the tactics of geography, they either died in the villas and towns which were second-rate imitations of those in Italy, or they intermarried. A century later, the only trace left of them was the ruins of burnings and a handful of oddly-distorted words which some expert might have recognized as having once been Latin. (Eventually, those Roman words which had suffered a sea-change found their way back into the forests and the hills, to become part of the speech of the Welsh *Silures* or Germanic *Alemanni* who may never have been—or seen—half-breeds— and had certainly never known of any such thing as a town. *Sagitta* ["arrow"] became the modern Welsh *saeth, cupidus* ["miser"] turned into *cybydd;* the forest-dwelling German cared not at all about the burning of the *latifundia* [the great farms more like agricultural factories than anything we would consider homesteads], but somehow *Wein* [*vinum*, "wine"], *Keller* [*cella*, "cellar"], and a number of other words made their way into the tongue of these barbarians.)

In Dacia, where the troops had settled *en masse* and managed to preserve a solidarity of spirit and organization—though isolated from their home in the West—the language and something of the culture survived. There could be nothing like an indefinitely-preserved purity, of course. The modern Rumanian vocabularly has much in it of Slavic and Turkish which either co-exists with, or has supplanted, the original Latin base. There are even a number of grammatical constructions which seem to be modeled on (or borrowed from) Slavonic tongues. In spite of all these touches of the strange, however, this descendant of the speech of the eastern legions bears in all of its fiber the marks of a Roman birthright.

There were others, though; those who somehow sustained a stronger tie with the Rome that was, thanks to the accidents of time and place (though Rumania is still well conscious of its outpost status as a representative of the West along a rather alien frontier). It is with these last, these relatively favored children of the Empire, that this chapter will principally deal. Which of those circumstances favored a flourishing of a new culture—one *strongly* flavored with the memories of Rome? And what became of the language of the Seven Hills?

What became of the culture is the subject of our familiar medieval and modern history; what became of the language, we can hear in trips through Italy, France, Spain, and Portugal (with a side-excursion to Sardinia).

There are documents still extant which give us a rather good idea of the fate of post-imperial Latin. Prize examples lie in the history of the Latin-speaking portion of that kingdom which was ruled by Charles the Great. Alas for good intentions! We suspect that it was Charlemagne himself who—though respecting the ancient tongue—helped to kill the language of the Caesars as a recognizable idiom.

In 786, scandalized at the state into which the *lingua latina* had fallen, Charles decreed that from that time forward all sermons and addresses delivered to the people within the churches were to be given in grammatically-correct Latin. It is almost certain that in this rather pathetic ordinance, Charlemagne was *not* demanding a return to the language of Classical times—presumably the very memory of that tongue had been forgotten, not to be summoned to consciousness again until the time of the Renaissance and a love for things truly ancient.

Rather, Charles' image of correctitude was based on the language of the Church Fathers; a language which would have struck senatorial orators as decidedly lower-class in its preference for prepositions and compound tenses as against case-expressed relations and unitary synthetic indications of time. (See chapter 4, page 48.) Yet even this Latin—the Latin of Tertullian, Augustine, Jerome, and all the saints' posterity and eventually to be immortalized as the Vulgate (the "common" tongue)—was beyond the capabilities of the honest monks and priests of that later era of the Frankish kingdom. By the time of the birth of a new age, the language of Rome had moved far from its (even Vulgate) synthetic origins, as can be seen in the wording of the following bill-of-sale:

Constat nus at alliqua fimena nomine Nautlindo, vindemus tibï pecia de maso probrio jures meo.

Such forms as *nus, fimena, probrio* show how far the phonetic patterns of Classical Latin had been altered (*nos, femina, prop-*); *maso* would never have occurred to a Roman of Augustus' day, though *mansio* might later mean "dwelling"; while *Nautlindo* and *de maso probrio* simply show that any real sense of particular case endings for individual nouns had been lost (many prepositional phrases having been introduced even from the days of Julius Caesar).

Charlemagne's insistence on a higher standard of grammatical —even if nothing more exalted than Vulgate purity—was quite probably the final straw. The relatively learned men—the clergy

—of Francia could expound doctrine in the version of Latin which they had learned in a dying day, and naturally they could speak the still more "debased" variant of Romanic which was the everyday vernacular of the countryside. This last was the language they had known since childhood days. But a return to the ideal standards of the second, third, or fourth centuries A.D.? That was asking far too much. Forbidden the Latin they knew, it is likely that they fell back upon the dialect natural to themselves and their audience.[1]

Whatever the cause, Charlemagne soon had to admit defeat. In 813, less than a generation after his original edict, the Emperor of the Franks was forced to accommodate himself to the reality of his age. In a second declaration, Charles reversed himself. Clerics were now ordered to speak to their flocks in the *lingua romana rustica,* rather than the *lingua latina.* By this act, Charles the Great conceded that the language of the people in his western provinces (for those in the East spoke an early German) was no longer something which could even by a stretch of the imagination be termed Latin.

We first come upon an unmistakable example of this newly acknowledged "rustic Roman" in the Strasbourg Oaths (842) sworn by Loduvigs and Karlus (two of Charlemagne's sons: in modern French their names would be *Louis* and *Charles,* in German, *Ludwig* and *Karl*) in a mutually protective alliance against Lothair (French, *Lothaire;* German *Lothar*), still another of the fecund Frankish monarch's offspring.

Karlus, overlord of the Romanized portion of his father's realm, swore his oath of honorable support in *lingua tudesca* (the German of the time), so that his brother's troops might understand him. In this early German he promised that:

[1] Before this retreat to the common speech, it is interesting to wonder just how much of the Vulgate sermons was understood. Presumably a good deal, since even the best-intentioned of listeners will be immune to a totally-unintelligible address. The gap between everyday speech and what was still considered to be Latin (although Vulgate), was probably not too much greater than the difference between Chaucerian and Shakespearian English—i.e., a marked, but not insurmountable, one.

In Godes Minna ind thes christianes Folches ind unser bedhero Gehaltnissi, fon thesemo Tage frammordes, so fram so mir Got gewizci indi Mahd furgibit, so haldih thesan minan Bruodher, soso man mit Rehtu sinan Bruodher scal, in thiu Thaz er mig so sama duo, indi mit Ludheren in nohheiniu Thing ne gegango, the minan Willon, imo ce Scadhen werdhen.

In modern (High) German this would run:

Um Gottes Liebe und des christlichen Volkes und unser beide Heil, von diesem Tag vorwärts, so weit mir Gott Wissen und Macht verleiht, so unterstütze ich diesen meinen Bruder wie man mit Recht seinen Bruder soll, vorausgesetzt, dass er mir dasselbe tut, und mit Lothar in keinen Vertrag eingehen, der ihm, meines Willens, zu Schaden werden.

In English:

For the Love of God, and for that of this christian Folk and both our Healths [well-being], from this Day forward, as God give me Knowledge and Might, I shall uphold this one, my Brother, insofar as one may with Right one's Brother, provided that he do the same for me, and with Lothaire shall I enter into no carryings-on that will do him [i.e., Louis], any Hurt, of my own Will.[2]

It had been Loduvigs, however, as the elder of the two, who had sworn the oath first. Whereas Charles' version has the virtue of comparative rarity—Germanic prose of that era being almost non-existent—Louis' declaration is part of a continuum leading from the Latin of Tacitus to the French of Sartre. His language shows the acknowledged fate of the once-imperial tongue within a few decades of his father's fruitless attempt to save it:

Pro Deo amur et pro christian poblo et nostro commun salvament, dist di in avant, in quant Deus savir et podir me dunat, si salvarai eo

---

[2] This rendering of the Old German is unidiomatic, but is used deliberately to keep something of the word-order and the Germanic vocabulary of the original "tudescan." A similarly forced translation of the "rustic Roman" of Louis' Oath—the contents of which are substantially the same—is given in what would be (in our language) an unnaturally Latinate wording.

cist meon fradre Karlo, et in aiudha et in cadhuna coso, si cum om
per dreit son dradra salvar dift, in o quid il mi altresi fazet et ab
Ludher nul plaid nunquam prindrai, qui, meon vol, cist meon fradra
Karle in damno sit.

The world and the Empire had changed indeed, and without
realizing it, the men whose language this was were no longer
men of Rome; what was to them the *only* language, would have
been a pidginized, half-intelligible jargon to the legionnaires of
another, nobler day. In the earlier idiom of the Imperium, this
declaration would have run:

Pro Dei amore, et pro christiano populo, et nostra communi salute, ab
isto die in posterum, quantum Deus sapere et posse mihi donat, sic
salvabo ego istum meum fratrem Carolum, et in adjumento et in
quaque causa, sicut homo per rectum fratrem suum salvare debet,
dummodo ille mihi alterne faciat, at ab Lothario ullum placitum
nunquam prehendam quod meo voluntate isti meo fratri Carolo in
damno sit.

In our tongue (with as Romanized a choice of words as one
can possibly bend to the task):

For the love of God, and for [this] christian people, and our common
salvation, from this day in advance, in the quantity of sapience and
power that God donates to me, so shall I save my brother Charles,
both in aid and in any cause such that a human with rectitude his
brother may save, if in like mode he do me the same, and with
Lothaire shall I enter voluntarily into no agreement which to him
[Charles] would do damage.

*   *

We have already mentioned, in an earlier portion of this book,
that the Romance languages have simplified their nouns even
more than has English; *their* possessive forms (with the exception
of Rumanian) being formed invariably with the aid of a preposition (*de, di, da*) whose central meaning is "of." Considering

the complexity of the original Latin noun, with its six forms in the singular and six more in the plural, we may legitimately wonder how such far-reaching simplification came about.

A careful look into texts written in the older forms of French or Spanish, together with an elementary knowledge of Latin inflexion and a liberal supply of linguistic intuition, will give us the needed clues. In older French documents particularly (for they are the most plentiful), we find a very peculiar situation indeed: the so-called "law of the reversed -s."

According to this rule, -s is *not* the unique mark of plurality, but rather is the termination of many nouns *in the nominative singular* and *the accusative plural*. Thus, given *one* cat and *one* king, this law—when transposed into English—would give rise to such statements as:

> A cats looks at a king (*Li chats regard le roi*)

and, the situation reversed:

> A kings looks at a cat (*Li rois regard le chat*)

or, with two or more felines and monarchs each:

> The cat look at the kings (*Li chat regardent les rois*)

and

> The king look at the cats (*Li roi regardent les chats*)

There is, in other words, a "cross-over" declension of the noun, which may be summed up in the following diagram:

	Singular	Plural
Nominative form	-s	—
Non-nominative form	—	-s

Although this double use of -s may seem rather confusing, the rationale for it can be seen in the light of noun-endings commonly encountered in Classical Latin itself.

There was a large class of masculine nouns whose nominative singular ended in *-us*. This so-called "second declension," containing such often-used words as *amicus* (friend), *locus* (place), *modus* (method, means), and the like, in time became a *norma-*

tive system; that is, it provided a standard form to which other, less frequently used (i.e., "irregular") nouns were attracted. One such subsidiary group which soon merged with the normative class was the *neuter* second declension noun. If we compare it with its masculine counterpart, we can see how strong this power of linguistic gravitation must have been:

	amicus (friend)	*donum* (gift, offering)

SINGULAR

Nom.	amic*us*	don*um*
Gen.	amici	doni
Dat.	amico	dono
Acc.	amicum	donum
Abl.	amico	dono

PLURAL

Nom.	amic*i*	don*a*
Gen.	amicorum	donorum
Dat.	amicis	donis
Acc.	amic*os*	don*a*
Abl.	amicis	donis

With the exception of the nominative singular and plural, and accusative plural forms, the two sub-declensions are identical.[3] Small wonder that it was often difficult to say whether a given noun was masculine or neuter. And since [m] is a closed-mouth hum—almost weakly vowelish insofar as phonetic persistence is concerned—the neuter nominative form found itself doomed to early extinction.

*   *

For some unknown reason—perhaps the speech habits of the pre-Roman Gauls, but *only* perhaps—the Latin-speakers of what

---

[3] A similar resemblance of masculine and neuter forms will be noticed in German declension of the noun (see the preceding chapter), and in Russian and Greek (chapter 12). Chapter 13 offers a possible explanation for this likeness.

later came to be France held onto the [s] of the now almost
universalized masculine -*us* with peculiar tenacity; it was the
intermediate *vowel* which decayed. Thus, *murus* became (in
the nominative) *murs;* the -*i* and -*o,* together with the weak
-(*u*)*m* of the non-nominative cases in the singular withered and
finally vanished, leaving only the -*s* or equivalent alternatives
shown in the table on page 206. For analogous reasons (though
the process was somewhat more complex in details), -*s* was left
as the generalized *oblique* ending in the plural. (The accusative
-*os* of the fused masculine + neuter declension—formerly restricted to the masculine members of the group—was probably the
base from which this form evolved, but the dative and ablative
plurals in -*is* common to both once-distinct genders must have
helped to reinforce this tendency.)

This trend to a cross-over declension was probably also marked
in the Iberian peninsula; the sets of Hispano-Latin dialects which
became Spanish and Portuguese doubtlessly went through much
the same process as Old French. There was one striking difference, however: *the final vowels were preserved.* Where Old
French had -*s,* —, —, and -*s;* the older forms of Hispanic has -*os,*
-*o,* -*o,* and -*os.*[4]

The next step in the evolution of these western "new Latins"
led to what we today consider the normal course of events; rather
rapidly -*s* or -*os* fell from use entirely in the singular, and was
extended to the subject (nominative) form in the plural. By
this, -*s* became a unique mark of plurality, divorced entirely from
any notion of case function in either number. This transition is
illustrated in the following table:

	SINGULAR		PLURAL	
	Old Fr.	*Old Hisp.*	*Old Fr.*	*Old Hisp.*
Nom.	-*s*	-*os*	—	-*o*
Obl.	—	-*o*	-*s*	-*os*

[4] The shift from -*u*- to -*o*- in final syllables of Latin words took place very
early; only Rumanian, and certain Italian dialects, have preserved the original
sound—though as we shall see, it was these languages which lost the -*s* entirely,
even as a mark of the plural.

	SINGULAR		PLURAL	
	Fr.	Hisp.*	Fr.	Hisp.
All forms	—	-o	-s	-os

* "Hisp." = modern Spanish and Portuguese

Comparing these old and new forms, we might regard the result as a long-delayed winning of the battle by the oblique forms (-s and -os). Though the final -s in the singular had survived longer than other endings, it succumbed to human laziness. The only reason why it managed to preserve its existence in the plural was probably because of the convenience inherent in a distinct form which indicated more-than-one of a thing.

Preservation of this -s (and its later forced impressment into service as a sign of general plurality) did not occur in Italy itself, however. In the ancient Roman fatherland they kept allegiance to another system. We may view the logic of these Italians-to-be as dependent on the *nominative* forms. To this day, any Italian from Milan to Palermo finds an -s the sure hallmark of a newly-imported word.

Italian-of-the-future had lost the nominative -s very early in its history; together with the decay of other singular endings, this left only a final -o in the singular—one which may have been widely felt to be the last remnant of the original nominative form. This universal nominative may have led—through force of analogy—to the selection of the nominative in the plural, as well. Whatever the reason, Italian chose the suffix -i (see the plural masculine nominative on page 207) as its general masculine form: the Italian *amico/amici* matching almost perfectly the two Latin case-forms *amicus/amici*.

*   *

So far we have dealt only with the masculine and neuter nouns of the original Latin. But what of those which were considered feminine?

Let it be noted that many a feminine noun (ending in a sibilant) joined the slow exodus to a new, purely masculine-gender class (*lex*—"law," *dies*—"day," *res*—"thing"). But this group of aberrant nouns, though reasonably common, was still exceptional. The most typical class of feminines was that known as the "first declension" in Latin grammars.

Nouns of the first declension exhibited the following forms in the singular and in the plural:

puella (girl, maiden)

SINGULAR		PLURAL	
Nom.	puella	Nom.	puellae
Gen.	puell*ae*	Gen.	puell*arum*
Dat.	puell*ae*	Dat.	puell*is*
Acc.	puell*am*	Acc.	puell*as*
Abl.	puell*ā*	Abl.	puell*is*

It is easy to see how in French, Spanish and Portuguese this class could join the cross-over group: three of its four oblique plural forms already ended in -*s*, and there was not even the confusing presence of the sibilant in the nominative plural. Once the final -*m* of the singular accusative had decayed (and the genitive-dative -*ae* and ablative -*ā* had shortened and blended), there was left only the common ending -*a* to mark the singular number. In Spanish and Portuguese this final -*a* has been preserved (as it has also in Italian—see below), but in French it has long turned into a blurred or (most often) silent -*e*. The net result:

	SINGULAR		PLURAL	
	Fr.	Hisp.	Fr.	Hisp.
All forms	-e	-a	-es	-as

Italian again has kept faith with the nominative forms: a final -*a* is almost inevitably the signature of a feminine *singular*; -*e* of a feminine *plural*. Where Latin had the nominative forms *domina/dominae* (*lady/ladies*), modern Italian offers *donna/*

donne—the final *-e* definitely pronounced, as a sound midway between our "ey" and "eh." The original Latin accusative *dominas* simply never made headway. (French and Hispanic, having preserved the final *-s* in one function or another, could finally put it to use. But the Italians lost it very early in their linguistic career and saw no surviving examples of the sound which could lead them to employ it for some clearly-marked grammatical purpose—either to indicate case-plus-number, or [later] for number alone.)

The outcome of these series of changes has been this:

(1) A two-gender (masculine, feminine) system common to *all* Romance languages;

(2) In Spanish, Portuguese and French, the use of a final *-s* as the general mark of the plural for nouns of both genders;

(3) In Italian, a separate mark of the plural for each gender: *-i* substituted for the masculine singular *-o*, *-e* for the feminine singular *-a*.

Although we may regard this series of changes as a generalization of certain oblique forms in (2), and of nominatives in (3), there still remains a significant number of nouns which *all* the neo-Latins have shaped according to the pattern exhibited in the *oblique singular*. Most of these are nouns which in the original Latin were lumped together in the third declension—a grammatical category which served as a catch-all for masculines, feminines and neuters of various degrees of irregularity.

Thus, where the Latin forms were (for example):

> *amans* ("the fond one," "the lover")
> *imitatio* ("a copying")
> *libertas* ("freedom")

with the corresponding ablative singulars:

> *amante*
> *imitatione*
> *libertate*

Italian has *amante, imitazione, libertà;* Spanish *amante, imitación, libertad;* Portuguese *amante, imitaçao, liberdade;* and French *amant, imitation, liberté.* (The English *imitation* and *liberty* are closest in form to the French since it has been usual for us to borrow such abstract nouns, and the rules for their formation, from that language.)

The correspondences between these various national forms of the Latin original are remarkably constant, so that we may set up what amounts to a fairly trustworthy conversion-table:

LATIN	ITALIAN	SPANISH	PORTUGUESE	FRENCH	(ENGLISH)
-tio	*-zione*	*-ción*	*-çao*	*-tion*	(*-tion*)
-tas	*-tà*	{ *-dad* { *-tad*	*-dade*	*-té*	(*-ty*)

A knowledge of such conversion factors is of decided help in expanding one's working vocabulary in the various Romance tongues. It is often possible to work backward from a known English term and construct the appropriate equivalent in the languages above by altering the suffix to conform with local linguistic habits. We can be reasonably certain that *qualità, propulción, sociedade* and *infiltration* will be understood and accepted by an Italian, Spaniard, Portuguese and Frenchman, respectively.

Furthermore, it is often possible to combine these endings in one and the same word: *nationality* (*nazionalità, nacionalidad, nationalité*) is an example of a rather common abstract noun in which the neo-Latin equivalents of *-tione* and *-tas* coexist with ease.[5]

We have spoken of the Romance tongues and their simplification of noun declension. One member of the Romance group, however, has stood apart from this trend—though even here there has been a reduction in the number of forms when com-

[5] The same ending may even be repeated, as in *nationalization.* Such forms are based on the originally Greek model of a limited class of verbs ending in *-izein* (e.g. *baptizein,* "to dip into water," "to baptize"). From this grew a host of new verbs in *-ize* (or *-ise*) and the corresponding nouns in *-ization* (*-isation*) so common in English and in the Romance languages with appropriate phonetic alteration.

pared to the parent Latin. The language we speak of is that of the old Eastern province of Dacia: modern Rumania. In this land the Latin of the colonials has managed to preserve case distinction both in singular and in plural. There are, however, only two normally distinct forms in each: a nominative-accusative and a genitive-dative. As in German, these distinctions in case are usually shown by the form of the *article,* rather than by endings attached to the noun itself.

This statement could be argued, depending on what one considers "an ending attached to the noun," as distinct from an article. For Rumanian, like the Scandinavian languages, uses a *post*posited article, which is written (and pronounced) all of a piece with the preceding noun. To make decision harder, the noun remains invariant in its various case roles if accompanied by its "article ending," so that we have:

(nom.-acc.)   *satul*   ("the village," as subject or object)

and

(gen.-dat.)   *satului*   ("of the village" or "to the village")

in which the question of whether *-ul* and *-ului* are to be considered as true declensional endings becomes a difficult one to answer, since *sat* can exist in and of itself.

*   *

As a member in good standing of the synthetic clan (subclan: amalgamating), Latin observed the principles of *concord;* adjectives associated with a given noun were forced to echo the syntactic function of the noun with endings of their own, in many cases identical with those of the principal word. When speaking or writing of "the house of the good woman," Latin expressed the notion as *domus bonae feminae. Domus* we may leave to its own devices (we shall assume that it is nominative and singular); but "of the good woman" was more truly "of the good, of the woman" (*bon*ae *femin*ae). This sort of repetition could continue indefinitely, as in "the house of that good, wise, beautiful, and prudent woman" (domus ill*ae* femin*ae* bon*ae,* sapient*is,* pulchr*ae* et prudent*is*).

The "new Latins" as good children of a much-loved parent, have kept some memory of this tradition alive, but their piety to the past is of the most sketchy sort. It, too, is concord; but only with the stripped-down logic of their two-fold classification of reality (masculine-feminine, singular-plural).

At most, there can be four separate forms of the adjective, as in the following translations into the various Romance tongues of *new friend* and *new friends,* as compared with the original Latin:

CLASSICAL LATIN

	Masculine	Feminine
nom. sing.	*ami*cus *nov*us	*ami*ca *nov*a
nom. plur.	*ami*ci *nov*i	*ami*cae *nov*ae

MODERN ITALIAN

sing.	*ami*co *nuov*o	*ami*ca *nuov*a
plur.	*ami*ci *nuov*i	*ami*che *nuov*e

MODERN SPANISH

sing.	*ami*go *nuev*o	*ami*ga *nuev*a
plur.	*ami*gos *nuev*os	*ami*gas *nuev*as

MODERN PORTUGUESE

sing.	*ami*go *nov*o	*ami*ga *nov*a
plur.	*ami*gos *nov*os	*ami*gas *nov*as

MODERN FRENCH

sing.	*ami* *nouv*eau	*ami*e *nouv*elle
plur.	*ami*s *nouv*eaux*	*ami*es *nouv*elles

* An exceptional plural ending used with -*eau* or -*au;* originally not an "x" at all, but an abbreviation for "-us," just as "&" was once a scribe's contraction of "et," the Latin word for "and."

The Romance verb, in contrast to the simplified noun, has kept true faith with the amalgamational nature of the original Latin. Since even in earliest days, Roman verbal apparatus was more complex than the Germanic, it is small wonder that to this day the "action-words" of these children of Rome exhibit more complexity than their counterparts among Teutonic languages. This greater complexity, however, refers only to their ability to compress into a single vocable that which is expressed in Germanic tongues by use of auxiliaries; where German must say *Ich werde genommen haben* and English *I shall have taken,* Latin sums up with *sumpsero*—and even French has its *j'aurai pris.*

There has been some simplification of the modern Romance verb, but it has been only partial. One obvious set of changes has taken place in the so-called "perfect tense." In Latin, a form such as *amavi* still had much of the old Indo-European aspectual flavor. It was truly perfect in the sense that the principal connotation was one of completed action—but not necessarily action whose force extends to the present time, as is the case with the English *I have loved her* (and still do) in contrast to *I loved her* (once upon a time).

Since there was no such invariable nuance of duration up to the present in Latin perfects, they were often used where English would use the simple past, providing that the act was regarded by the speaker as accomplished or viewed in its totality: *librum legi* may be translated as either *I read* or *have read the book,* depending on the emphasis we are concerned with in English.

What we may *not* do is translate this two-word sentence by *I was reading the book* or *I used to read the book,* for these English phrases express essentially *imperfective* ideas: (1) continuous, extended action, or (2) habitually repeated action. For statement of such aspects of reality, Latin had another tense, the "imperfect" with a totally different set of personal endings. (Either of the two English imperfective sentences at the head of this paragraph, for instance, would have been expressed in Latin by *librum legēbam.*)

Over the centuries, Vulgar Latin acquired the habit of confining the perfect forms to use *only* as expressions of accomplished action; they lost even the possibility of indicating continuance-to-the-present which they had once possessed. That is, the perfect became nothing more than a simple (but perfective-flavored) past —the so-called "past definite" tense. Thus, we have the following definite-tense forms in Italian, Spanish and French, as compared with the Latin perfect from which they evolved:

LATIN	ITALIAN	SPANISH	FRENCH
amāvi	amai	amé	(aimai)*
amavisti	amasti	amaste	(aimas)
amavit	amò	amó	(aima)
amavimus	amammo	amamos	(aimâmes)
amavistis	amaste	amasteis	(aimâtes)
amavērunt	amarono	amaron	(aimèrent)

* French forms are given in parentheses since, except in the South and West, they are never used in conversation or in any but the most formal writing. In speech and informal composition they have been completely supplanted by the modern perfect: e.g., *j'ai aimai* is used indifferently as the equivalent of either *I loved* or *I have loved*.

The old pluperfect (*amaveram—I had loved*) and future perfect (*amavero—I shall have loved*) also fell from use. All, in time, were replaced by compound forms based on the verb *to have* plus the past participle of the verb.[6] The result is a perfect correspondence of structure between the past perfects of most Romance verbs and their English counterparts—e.g., It. *ha letto*, Sp. *ha leído*, Fr. *il a lu*, and Eng. *he has read*. The identity is also continued in the pluperfects; but since the new Latins have simple future tenses (see below), they require one less separate word in the *future* perfect forms: compare *avra letto, habrá leído* and *il aura lu* with *he will have read*.

The Classical Latin future and conditional forms failed, too, to survive in the hurly-burly of everyday speech; rather than the literary *amabo* (*I shall love*) the common folk of the Empire

[6] A few French and Italian verbs use the verb *to be* instead; compare the French *je suis arrivé* with the obsolete English *I am arrived*.

made use of circumlocution. *Amare habeo* (literally, *to-love I-have*) was popular in all parts of the Imperium except for Dacia in the East, where *amare volo* (*to-love I-want*) became the idiom of choice. These new, analytic constructions did not last indefinitely, however. The various forms of the verb *to have,* phonetically weak and placed after the main verb as they were, degenerated more or less rapidly into a set of flexions for a new synthetic future, completely unrelated to the Classical Latin tense. Compare the present-tense forms of the three Romance forms of *to have* with the corresponding futures built upon an infinitive base *to speak:*

	ITALIAN	SPANISH	FRENCH
"I have, you have," etc.	ho	he	ai
	hai	has	as
	ha	ha	a
	abbiamo	hemos	avons
	avete	habéis	avez
	hanno	han	ont
infinitive:	*parlare*	*hablar*	*parler*
"I shall speak, you shall speak," etc.	parlerò	hablaré	parlerai
	parlerai	hablarás	parleras
	parlerà	hablará	parlera
	parleremo	hablaremos	parlerons
	parlerete	hablaréis	parlerez
	parleranno	hablarán	parleront

The Rumanian for "I shall speak," would be *voi vorbì,* however, in which the first word is a much-altered form of *volo* (*I wish*). It is interesting to note that this construction is an exact parallel to English in such phrases as *you, he, they will speak* which in origin had the primarily volitional coloring of *you, he* or *they will* (i.e., *are determined*) *to speak.*

The classical synthetic passives vanished for good and were

replaced by analytic forms. In this instance, however, the new constructions were not newly-devised circumlocutions, but legitimate classical forms warped to a new purpose. Whereas a Roman matron might have hopefully said *amor* to mean *I am loved,* and reserved *amata sum* for *I have been,* or *was, loved;* her many-times great-granddaughter applied the formerly perfect-passive to a present situation. *Amata sum* in its various Romance guises (It. *sono amata,* Sp. *soy amada,* Fr. *je suis aimée*) came to mean nothing more than simply *I am loved.* (If it had been a man speaking, the verb would have remained the same, but the participle—obeying the rules of gender concord like any other adjective—would have assumed the forms: *amatus, amato, amado* or *aimé.*)

In addition to the present, past-definite, past-imperfect, future, conditional, pluperfect, present-perfect and future-perfect tenses, the Romance languages are moderately well-equipped with subjunctive forms. All of the new Latins possess simple forms for the present and past subjunctive, while Spanish and Portuguese have a separate future subjunctive as well. Furthermore, there are compound perfect and passive subjunctive forms, derived from the present, past and (in Spanish and Portuguese) future tenses of the subjunctives for *to be* and *to have.*[7] The net result of this has been that, though the Romance noun offers next to no difficulty (except for memorization of gender) to the English-speaking student, facility in use of the many verb forms comes only after considerable effort.

*   *

While speaking of verbs, this would seem to be an appropriate point at which to say a word or two concerning the pronouns usually so closely associated with the action-words.

[7] Colloquial French has added to the burden with its "super-compound tenses" (*les temps surcomposés*). To stress the notion of completion as strongly as possible, one may add a participle to an already-extant perfect tense: e.g., *quand il m'a eu donné le livre* (literally: *when he has had given me the book*) instead of *quand il m'a donné . . .* (*when he has given me . . . ,* or in English, *when he gave me*).

Almost all of the Romance languages have remained quite faithful to the old Latin (and Indo-European) principle of omitting subject-pronouns except when needed for emphasis or to avoid ambiguity. Thus, Latin (ego) *amo,* Italian (io) *amo,* Spanish (yo) *amo,* Portuguese (eu) *amo,* and an equivalent Rumanian form also without pronoun, all represent the English *I love.* But French is (as in many other ways) exceptional in its approach to verbal expression; it uses the pronouns which denote subject as invariably as does English. One may *not* say simply *aime,* but rather *j'aime* (the universally contracted form of *je—* j'—being used before verbs which begin with a vowel). As we shall see, French has departed most radically from the Latin in its system of sounds; this might be guessed simply from the gap which divides *ego* of the Latin from the Gallic *je* bridged by such ancient transitional forms as *eo, jo.*

But even when Latin *did* feel the need of expressing its pronominal subjects, a difficulty was immediately encountered in the third person, for there simply were no pronouns—even usually-omitted ones—which had the meanings *he, she, it, they.* When forced to be explicit, Classical Latin would "fudge," using derivatives of *is* ("this" or "that") with the feminine *ea* and neuter *id;* or of *ille* ("that one"), feminine *illa,* neuter *illud.* "They" was translated, according to the gender of the noun replaced, by *ei, eae, ae,* or *illi, illae, illa.*

The various forms of *is* died early in the history of Vulgar Latin, but *ille* and its relatives found their opportunities well-nigh unlimited. As subject pronouns of the third person they still flourish in all Romance tongues today: It. *egli, ella, essi, esse;* Sp. *él, ella, ellos, ellas;* Port. *êle, ela, êles, elas;* Fr. *il, elle, ils, elles;* Rum. *el, ea, ei, ee.*

And though the primary significance of *ille* as *that one* (or *those ones*) eventually died by the time the Romance languages were actually in the process of formation, something of the originally demonstrative meaning still survived. Thus it was that *ille* in its various forms came also to represent the various *object* pronouns of the third person, both direct and indirect. The rules concerning their formation and use are too complex to be described in detail, but a mere recapitulation of their forms is convincing: *them,* as direct object of a verb is *li* or *le* in Italian; *los* or *las* in Spanish; and *les*—for both genders—in French. The indirect objectival forms ("to them") are as clearly related to the original *ille* as are the words which express direct objects; and unlike English which uses distinct forms for singular and plural —*him, her, it* vs. *them*—the Romance singular forms are quite obviously related to their corresponding plurals. Portuguese is particularly revealing in its demonstration of the essential unity of these various forms:

	SINGULAR	PLURAL
Subject Pronouns	*êle* ("he")	*êles* ("they" masc.)
	ela ("she")	*elas* ("they" fem.)
Dir. Obj. Pronouns:	*o** ("him")	*os** ("them" masc.)
	a* ("her")	*as** ("them" fem.)
Indir. Obj. Pronouns:	*lhe* ("to him or	*lhes* ("to them" masc. or
	lhe her")	*lhes* fem.)

* As we shall see, Portuguese has a distaste for "l" in the medial position, and has dropped it universally; originally the forms here asterisked were *lo, la, los,* and *las.* In Spanish—a half-brother to Portuguese—*la, los, las* still survive. Spanish *lo,* however, has given way to the form *el,* taken from the beginning half of the Latin *ille.*

As if not called on to do enough already, this overworked Latin vocable came to serve still another function—one ignored by the Classical parent-tongue entirely. The old demonstrative was also used as a *definite article.*

In Classical Latin, as in modern-day Russian, Polish and the other Slavic tongues aside from Bulgarian, there was no word expressing the nuances of meaning carried by our word *the.* *Homo* (like the Russian *chelovek,* Polish *czlówiek* and Serbo-Croatian *chovek* or *čovek*) was the equivalent of that which we would express as *man, the man,* or *a man.*

Since *ille* managed for a while to keep to itself something of its old indicating force, even while it began to serve as a pronoun, it was easy for the Roman-speaker-in-the-street to catch the habit of prefixing nouns with the appropriate form of the demonstrative. No longer did *ille* have the sharply-defined meaning of *that;* the word had blurred in signification. What it did indicate was that the noun mentioned was in some sense particular in that it had been mentioned but a short time ago or the context of discussion focused the listener's attention on it.

No longer were the speakers of Latin content with *homo* or *femina* alone and unadorned. One spoke of *ille homo* or *illa femina, illi homines,* or *illae feminae.* New locutions sprang up which unmistakably meant "that" or "those." *Ille* in its various combinations of gender and number, and in the guises it took in the nascent Romance languages, came to be felt as that new psychological entity: *the.*[8]

(In like manner, the Romance tongues also evolved an *in*definite article. As in most languages which have such a word, this article sprang from the numeral *one,* and is still identical in form with the original number. English is exceptional in having a separate set of forms *a[n]*; but in Anglo-Saxon times the two related meanings were still expressed by the same set of phonemes. Just as the Germanic *ein, een,* and *en* are simultaneously numeral and article, so too are *un, une, uno, una* in the Romance linguistic orbit.)

The net result of differentiation and generalization in the use of *ille* and its descendants has been that throughout the entire family of Latin-born tongues, a limited number of phonetic forms has spread to assume a host of functions. Even within a single language, one and the same word may act as both object-pronoun and as article (subject-pronouns usually being differentiated in some way or other); while a comparison of one Romance lan-

---

[8] In those languages which do possess a definite article, it seems almost invariably the rule that it evolves from a pronoun whose meaning is approximately "that," and which often serves in addition as the form for the third-person pronoun. Such is the case in the Germanic tongues: *der* (and its variants) is now the article, but was once the general demonstrative. Homer's use of the language shows a similar stage in earlier Greek with the often pronominal use of *ho*; while the Bulgarian postposited article can also be shown to have developed from the general Slavic demonstrative.

guage with another reveals an even wider degree of overlap. Thus, *les* which in Spanish can serve only as the form expressing "to them" is in French the plural article ("to them" being denoted by *leur*).

*   *

We are fortunate with regard to the history of the Romance languages; Latin disintegrated relatively late in time, and the Romans were literate. We therefore have ample written documentation of the structures and probable sounds characteristic of the parent-tongue. Some degree of literacy persisted, and as the neo-Latin vernaculars emerged as vehicles of poetry and prose, we have found the transitional records of the drift from Classical usage.

We have already discussed at some length these new tongues' peculiarities of structure; in closing let us note certain consistent idiosyncrasies of phonetic and orthographic pattern. In addition to giving a general notion of the linguistic shape of the language, such comparisons will make identification of any one of the Roman tongues certain.

In speech:

> *Italian* has developed a marked aversion to the numerous (though comparatively simple) consonant clusters of the parent Latin; so that we have such contrasts as *observāre—osservare* ("observe"), *septem—sette* ("seven"), *flamma—fiamma* ("flame"), *placēre—piacere* ("to please"). In the latter two examples we can see how the consonant + [l] has shifted to consonant + [i] (in which the [i] usually becomes a "y-glide" before the succeeding vowel—"fyamma," "pyachaireh" would be approximate equivalents in English spelling).

> More important is the process by which Latin consonantal groups gave rise to Italian double consonants. These are not merely conventions of spelling, but are truly different from their single counterparts, and are distinct phonemes; i.e., often

the only distinction between two words is that of a single or double consonant—e.g., *sete* ("silk") and *sette* ("seven"). Continuants, such as [n], [s], [f], etc., are pronounced over a slightly longer period of time; stops, such as [p], [t], [k], are held back slightly before utterance. Although these doubled consonants are not phonemic in English, they do exist: *penknife* and *book-case* give perfect examples of the true Italian double [n] and [k] sounds, respectively.

The net effect of these changes has been to make Italian a language rich in vowels and well-equipped in single and double consonants, but a tongue largely barren of those consonantal clusters widely found in many other Indo-European languages.

In the matter of vowels and vowel-combinations, Italian is still remarkably close to Latin. There has been strangely little shifting of values. One transformation, however, is uniquely characteristic of Italian, and identifies the language beyond any possibility of doubt: the "woh" group. "Woh" is an approximate representation of how this diphthong strikes the American or English ear, but it is transcribed in Italian as *-uo-*. This set of vowels is the offspring of what was, in the Latin, stressed *-o-*, as may be seen in the following Latin-Italian pairs: *focus* ("hearth")—*fuoco* ("fire"); *domus* ("house")—*duomo* ("cathedral"); *novus—nuovo* ("new").

This triad of peculiarities—(1) high incidence of "hesitant" double consonants, (2) post-consonantal "y glide," and (3) frequently heard "woh"—is an almost certain guarantee that the language heard is, in fact, Italian. Further confirmation lies in the sound-groups "-ootoh" and "-yahmoh" (spelled *-uto* and *-iamo*); these are frequently-used marks of the past participle and first person plural ("we"), respectively.

Spanish lies somewhat further from the old Latin pattern than does Italian. Double consonants are not phonemic in Spanish, except for the extended *-rr-*, which serves to distinguish otherwise identical utterances: *pero* ("but") vs. *perro* ("dog"). One sound which is, among Romance tongues, a Spanish monopoly is the guttural [χ], the "ch sound" of Scots *loch* and German *ach!*; in Spanish, however, the sound is represented in print by *g* (before *e* or *i*) or by *j* (before any vowel whatsoever).

Another common Spanish phoneme is the "soft 'l,'" spelled as *-ll-*, but *not* a true double consonant. In Standard (i.e., Castilian) Spanish, this sound resembles the *-lli-* group in our *million, scullion,* so that *llover* ("to rain") is pronounced approximately "lyohvehr." In Latin American Spanish, however, the phoneme has shifted so far that it is indistinguishable from the simple "y glide," spelled in Spanish—as in English—with the letter "y." For this reason, confusion in orthography often results among the semi-educated: *yover* being used for *llover,* and *llo* for *yo* ("I").

Spanish vowels have, by and large, remained rather faithful to the original Latin scheme, but there have been two almost universal shifts which are peculiar to the language: from stressed Latin *-o-* to Spanish *-ue-*; and from stressed Latin *-e-* to *-ie-*. The contrast between *focus/fuego, locus/luego,* and *novus/nuevo;* and between *sempre/siempre, serpens/sierpe,* and *tenet/tiene* gives a good idea of this characteristic and regular shift. This pair of shifts occurred, however, only when the Latin *-o-* and *-e-* occurred in the stressed syllable. In unstressed syllables, the Spanish vowels stand unchanged; this accounts for the "radical- (i.e. root-) changing verbs" so familiar to students of Spanish: *puede* ("he can") vs. *podemos* ("we can"), *viene* ("he comes") vs. *venemos* ("we come"). Such conservatism in unaccented syllables also explains such apparent irregularities as neu*vo* ("new") as against *no*vedad ("a novelty," "a new thing").

Portuguese might be in some sense considered an old-fashioned Spanish. Actually, of course, it is a sister Iberian dialect of Latin, with as much right to claims of individuality as any of the Romance tongues; but it has preserved many features of the transitional Vulgar Latin which Spanish has since altered, e.g. the Spanish *o* to *ue* and *e* to *ie* shift already mentioned.

One change in the original Iberian pattern does serve to mark Portuguese alone. The final *-s* which is the sign of plurality in noun and adjective has shifted slightly, so that it now possesses the blurred value of the "s" in "sugar," or its voiced counterpart, the "s" in "pleasure." This blurred variant is characteristic of what is in other Romance tongues a final [s] generally, and can be heard in such verbal forms as *cantas* ("thou singest") and *cantamos* ("we sing").

Portuguese is also marked by a richness in nasalized vowels and diphthongs—even more so than is French. Thus, where Spanish has *son* ("sohn"—"they are") Portuguese has *são* with the same meaning; the Portuguese word is pronounced more or less as our "sow"—but like "sow" when spoken through the nose.

In addition to its many nasals, Portuguese abounds in many "indistinct" vowels, reminiscent of our English "oo" in "foot," "u" in "but," and "a" in "sofa."

The combination of (1) frequent terminal "sh" or "zh," (2) many nasal vowels or diphthongs, and (3) many indistinct vowels, is a fairly certain indication that the language heard is Portuguese. P.S.: The identification is all but certain if the listener notes a rather frequent occurrence of semi-isolated "oh," "ah," "ohsh," or "ahsh," (spelled *o, a, os, as*); these are the masculine and feminine, singular and plural, forms of the Portuguese word for "the." No other language has these particular forms.

French is a true maverick of the Romance clan, as the reader has probably guessed from the gap which separates Latin *ego* from French *je*. The number of changes which have occurred to transform the sounds of Caesar into the pronunciations of Voltaire and—later—Sartre are too many to number here. Whereas Italian, Spanish, and Portuguese have undergone certain limited alterations which mark them off from Latin, French has suffered wholesale phonetic catastrophe. The particulars of the slaughter could be given—and are often detailed in a good historical French grammar. But within the compass of a book whose aim is discussion of Language at large, there is little space for the chronicling of such thorough destruction; enough to point out that from the Latin *Augustus* (meaning the month of August) have come the Italian *agosto,* the Spanish *agosto,* the Portuguese *agosto,* the Rumanian *august*—and the French *août* (pronounced either as "ah-oo" or simply as "oo").

Identification of French rests most primarily upon negative evidence: there are none of the terminal -*o*'s or -*a*'s characteristic of Italian, Spanish, or Portuguese. French lacks the "ts" sound which, as we shall see, is common in Rumanian.

Given these points of negative evidence, what remains to show itself? Item: the high incidence of *middle vowels,* many of which approach the values found in such English words as *sofA, hUrt, fUr, Allow.*

Another trait often found in French pronunciation is the "uvular 'r' ": a sound produced far back in the throat and reminiscent of the sound produced by a quick gargle.

Highly indicative is a prevalence of "z" sounds; these are the products of the final -*s* which is in French—as in our language —the mark of the plural. But since the -*s* is silent in French *except before a following word beginning with a vowel,* at which point the [s] becomes a pronounced *z*- attached to the following vocalic utterance, the mark of plurality in French speech may truly be considered as an exceptional prefixed *z*-. Thus, *les fruits mûrs* is pronounced roughly as *lay fruee mur,* while in *les aptitudes utiles* the final -*s*'s become initial -*z*'s: *lay zaptitude zutile.*

Given these three clues: a guttural "r," frequent middle vowels, and initial *z*-sounds, the "constricted 'u' " is an almost certain verifier of French as the language heard. This sound, represented in Classical Greek by the letter upsilon and in modern German by *ü*, is almost impossible to describe to those who have never heard it; but there is a rather simple rule by which anyone can pronounce it himself: purse the lips as though to pronounce the -*oo*- in *tool,* and with the lips in this position, pronounce instead the -*ee*- in *feet.*[9]

Rumanian in spite of geographical isolation, has kept far closer to the sound-pattern of Latin than has French. There are comparatively few sounds peculiar to the language which do not exist in some other Romance tongue. The presence of many words ending in -*l* is indicative, and -*lui* and -*lor* make identification positive. The internal consonant combinations -*pt*- and -*mb*-, though not uniquely Rumanian, occur in that language more frequently than in any other Romance tongue.

Rumanian possesses one vowel (in script indicated by either *â* or *î*) which no other Romance language has; it is thought that

---

[9] Historically, this particular vowel has shown itself to be rather unstable, moving in many languages to the simple -*ee*- [i]. Welsh and Greek once had this sound but have lost it, though they keep its memory alive in their spelling. Compare also the English *foot:feet* with the more conservative German *Fuss:Füsse.*

it may have been borrowed from the Slavic tongues, since a highly similar vowel still exists today in Russian ("ы") and in Polish ("y"). It is almost impossible to characterize it except by describing it as an extremely guttural "ih," something like the "y" in *rhythm,* but even throatier. It is as much more guttural than the "i" of *hit,* than that sound is when compared to the "ea" of *heat.* Once heard, the sound is unmistakable.

In writing it is extremely easy to distinguish the various children of Latin from one another, for each of them has evolved a distinctive orthography of its own. There are a large number of consonants, and a smaller number of vowels, which have values common to more than one Romance tongue; but the combinations of these elements, together with accents and diacritical marks, provide rather simple means of identification:

> *Latin* itself, though no longer spoken outside the councils of the Church, is still to be found in documents. In carefully-printed texts, the *macron*—a line over a vowel, indicating length—is presumptive evidence of Latinity (amāre). (The *breve,* which marks a short vowel, is less frequently used, but is found occasionally where ambiguity might otherwise result, e.g., eă. Occurrence of such endings as *-ens, -is, -iis,* and especially *-ibus, -arum* and *-orum,* confirm the identification.

> *Italian* is marked by such combinations as *zz, gl, gh, scia;* by an initial *s* followed immediately by another consonant (e.g., *spiegare*—"to explain"); and by the use of one accent mark (`) which occurs *only* over the final vowel in a word of more than one syllable having final stress (*città*), and over a few monosyllables (*già, più, può, chè, dà, nè,* etc.). The noun endings *-zione* and *-tà* (as mentioned earlier) are found only in Italian, as are the verbal flexions *-are, -ire, -ato, -ata, -uto, -uta, -iamo, -anno.* The absence of *-s* as the mark of plurality is also significant; only Rumanian of the other Romance tongues shares this aversion to *-s.* And as we shall see, there are marked traits which can distinguish it from Italian in other ways.

> *Spanish* can be identified immediately by the character *ñ* (as in *cañon*) and by the use of exclamation points and question

marks *in pairs*, one each preceding the sentence and turned up-side down: e.g., ¿Es verdad? ¡No es verdad! ("Is it true?" "It is not true!") The only accent mark used in Spanish is the reverse of the one employed in Italian: (Spanish (ʹ) vs. Italian (ʼ). The word *y* (meaning "and") is frequently found, and is characteristic only of Spanish. The typical noun endings for many abstracts are *-ción* and *-tad* (or *-dad*). The forms of the definite article do not—with one exception—overlap those found in any other Romance tongue: *el* (masc. sing.), *los* (masc. plur.) and *las* are characteristic of Spanish and Spanish only. (*La* is the *feminine* singular article not only in Spanish, but in Italian and French as well.)

Portuguese has two unique consonant combinations, *nh* and *lh,* not used by any other language of the West. The *nh* is pronounced in the same fashion as the Spanish *ñ* (compare Port. *senhor* with Sp. *señor*); *lh* is a palatalized *l* (i.e., an *l* with a hint of a y-glide following). Portuguese *does* use the diacritical mark (˜) to indicate nasalization,[10] but only over vowels or diphthongs. Therefore, such words as *maçã* ("apple"), *feijões* ("beans") and *carvão* ("coal") can be only Portuguese.

Since Portuguese did not take part in the *o* to *ue*, *e* to *ie* shift characteristic of Spanish, many words in a Portuguese text will seem like a cross between Latin and Spanish forms: Lat. *novus,* Sp. *nuevo,* Port. *novo*; Lat. *locus,* Sp. *luego,* Port. *logo.*; Lat. *serra,* Sp. *sierra,* Port. *serra*; Lat. *nive* (obl.), Sp. *nieve,* Port. *neve.* Thus, the land which the Spaniards found at the tip of South America and named *Tierra del Fuego* ("Land of the Fire") would be known in Portuguese as *Terra do Fogo.*

Portuguese uses three different accents (ʹ, ʼ, and ^) which it shares with French, so that these are not distinctive. The language does not use initial, inverted question marks and exclamation points as does Spanish. Typical of Portuguese are the noun endings *-ção* and *-dade,* corresponding to the Spanish *-ción* and *-dad* (*-tad*). The forms of the definite article are uniquely Portuguese and provide sure identification of the lan-

---

[10] In Spanish, called a *tilde*; in Portuguese a *til.* Both words mean "a speck," or "blemish."

guage: *o* (masc. sing.), *a* (fem. sing.), *os* (masc. plur.) and *as*
fem. plur.). This initially-vocalic article can combine with a
number of prepositions, most usually with *de* ("of"); "of the"
can therefore be expressed in four different ways, depending on
the gender and number of the following noun: *do, da, dos, das.*
CAUTION: the article can also combine with the preposition
em, and *em* + *o* = *no*. This does not, of course, mean "no," or
"not" as it would in Spanish. The Portuguese negative is *não;*
no means "in the."

The verbal flexions of Spanish and Portuguese are almost
identical; a final *-am* or *-em*, however (third-person plural), is
Portuguese only.

French words have spread to so many other languages that it
is probable that the reader already has a number of criteria,
conscious or subconscious, by which he identifies them. However, the familiar three accents (´, `, ^) and the *cedilla* (¸)
placed under a *c* to give the letter an *s*-sound (*garçon*), are *not*
sufficient evidence, since Portuguese also uses them; this combination of features is, at most, information which eliminates
impossible identifications.

There is one character—not too often encountered—which is
almost solely French: the "dieresis *i*"—an *i* with two dots at the
top, side-by-side: *ï*. (This character is needed since the French
vowel-group *ai* represents not a diphthong ("ah" + "ee") but a
single pure vowel varying within the limits of our English "ay"
and "eh." For words such as *naïve* and *Saïgon* to be pronounced
"nah-eev" and "Sah-ee-gõ," the dieresis must be used; otherwise
they would approximately sound as "nave" and "Say-gõ."

The archaic spelling conventions are the best guide to identification of written material: words ending in the groups *-eau,*
-eaux, or *-aux* can be in no other language but French. The
negative particle *ne* (usually as the first half of the two-member
phrase *ne . . . pas* bracketing some third word), and the preposition *à* ("at," "to") *with its accent*, are peculiar to the language of Voltaire and Camus; as are *du* and *des* (combined
forms of *de* ("of") and the definite article), *au* and *aux* (analogous constructions formed with the preposition *à*).

The French versions of the abstract endings for nouns already mentioned are *-tion* and *-té,* as in *liberation* and the famous *liberté, égalité, fraternité* of Revolutionary times. Since French final vowels have largely withered away, or at least suffered widespread attrition, a Romance language in which most words end either in a consonant or in *-e* is almost certain to be French; high incidence of *-o* or *-a* indicates the probability of Italian, Spanish or Portuguese.

Characteristic verbal flexions in French are *-ons* or *-ions* (first person plural), *-ez* or *-iez* (second person plural), and *-ent* or *-aient* (third person plural).

Rumanian, though least well-known of the Romance languages, is strangely enough the easiest to identify. This descendant of Dacian Latin uses a number of diacritical marks utterly unknown in any other neo-Latin tongue—and rare even outside the Romance clan. A cedilla under the letter *t* (pronounced "ts" as in *viţel*—"the calf") is common in Rumanian, and used only by that language, as is the breve *a* (*ă*) in such words as *plouă* ("it is raining"), *răsărit* ("east").

Rumanian still preserves fragments of the old Latin case-system which show themselves in the various forms of the post-posited definite article. Certain of these forms—some nominative-accusatives in the feminine singular and masculine plural—are not distinctive to the untrained eye; but the extremely frequent *-l, -lui, -lor, -aua* and *-elei* are unmistakeable.

The Rumanian forms of the Latin *-tio* and *-tas* are *-ţia* and *-tate* (*-tatea* with the article), as in *legaţia* ("legation") and *universitate* (*universitatea*).

Like French, Rumanian has eliminated many final vowels, but the process has not gone so far and Rumanian does not follow the Gallic custom of turning most of the vowels it *does* preserve into an *-e.* Final *-i, -ă,* and *-ea* are often met with.

Rumanian follows the old Latin (and present-day Spanish, Portuguese and Italian) habit of omitting subject pronouns in favor of verbal flexion. The Rumanian verb in the first-person singular usually ends in the consonant of the verb's stem (*înţeleg*—"I understand"), which makes identification difficult from this form alone. However, the endings *-m* and *-ţi* (*vorbim* —"we speak"; *vorbiţi*—"you speak"), are within the Romance group, solely Rumanian.

*   *

This has been one of the longest chapters in the book—longer even than that devoted to the Germanic tongues, directly ancestral to our own. There are reasons for this, of which perhaps the most important is that *the development of the Romance languages is the only case of widespread linguistic evolution which has ever taken place within the context of literacy.* This combination of (1) wide change and (2) documentary continuity is close to unique in the history of tongues. Indo-European had broken up into families and sub-families of tongues long before there was the dream of anything like a phonemic or quasi-phonemic script which could preserve the stages of change. And those languages which have evolved and differentiated while possessing a form of writing have changed but little; there are texts which show the rise of Danish, Swedish and Norwegian, or of English and American—but the changes have been comparatively slight, for there has not been time enough, and the written word exercises a curb on radical change by its very existence.

Rome was unique: an extensive empire with a single official tongue; an empire which died and fragmented—*but which managed to preserve even in its break-up the institution of letters.* History is fickle, books burn, and scribes may be capricious or just plain lazy. No system of chronicling is ever as good as historians could wish. Yet, in spite of the lacunae, the torn-in-half sheets of parchment, the monasteries burned or abandoned and the contents of their scriptoria lost—something more survived than we might have thought likely.

The new Latins sprang up. At first they were nothing more than the ungrammatical slang and subliterate street-corner usage of those who had never known any better and never would. In each corner of the fading Imperium, the people spoke as people always will: vividly, racily, and incorrectly. Their "bad usage" survived the last of the Emperors, lived a twilight existence side-by-side with an ecclesiastical cousin—Church Latin—and became in time the vehicle of poetry and prose. *The Song of Roland* was an epic in a new tongue, not doggerel in pidgin-Latin.

That we actually possess a continuum of evidence and document which joins Cicero with Cervantes, Voltaire, Manzoni, the author of the Portuguese *Lusiads,* and the authors of anonymous Rumanian folk-poetry, is—from the philologist's standpoint—the main feature of interest. But there is perhaps another thing which draws the English-speaker to these children of Rome; a subtle thing which can only be hinted at.

We read *Beowulf,* and we thrill to his conquest of Grendel in the Marsh. Our heart beats a little faster at the courage of this distant, ancestral stranger.

But he *is* a stranger, and it is this sense of alienation which lies at the heart of our curious love for Rome and the things of Rome. Our language at its deepest roots may be Germanic, but the last Teuton, the last Anglo-Saxon, to speak the English tongue died centuries ago. His sons may have been as pure in blood (whatever that may mean) as he; but their eyes had turned away from a single-minded vision of the forest and cold gods riding in a wintry sky. It was more than Christianity which came from the south. It was a breath of fresh air, another climate of the heart and mind.

Petrus was a poor and dirty, quite probably an unlettered, man. His world broke down around him, often so slowly that he never noticed its going. But he began another thing, and his five-and-ten-times grandchildren carried on that work which is Civilization. Petrus no longer, but Pietro, Pedro, Pierre or Petru, he made a new world—a world which caught up the island Britisher or Saxon by the scruff of his imagination and made him something new, something divided in allegiance yet rich in possibility for the future. That *Englishman* borrowed the name, changed it a little, and became someone whose name was Peter.

✐ 12

The grammar that was Greece—and *is* Russia

SOMEWHERE in the back of the intellectual's mind there probably lies, even today, a dimming picture of Athens: of white marble columns, friezes from which stand out in bas-relief splendid horses and still more splendid men; a fading image of impossibly high-browed philosophers wandering gracefully through some never-never *agora* of the mind while discussing the nature of Truth and Beauty . . . Archimedes sketching geometrical figures in the sand even as the unthinking Roman soldier's sword cuts through the Syracusan air . . .

And perhaps in that same intellectual's mind there is another picture as well: that of "Byzantine" Russia. Turnip-dome churches into which walk an ignorant, ragged peasantry; the crack of a knout across a serf's ribs; the mournful cadence of song in a minor key or unfamiliar mode; a French-speaking gentry only half at home in the language of their nation . . . the darkened, genius-ridden soul of a Dostoievsky or Gogol . . . a world living in twilight only fitfully brightened by sullen lightning . . .

These two images stand at opposite poles of sensibility; what could possibly join them? The clue lies in that one word *Byzantine,* for it was the Greek-speaking world of the Eastern Empire which moved along the northern shore of the Black Sea and up the rivers to bring the blessings of Civilization to the Slav.

It is probably only a matter of historical coincidence (though who can be certain?), but when SS. Kyril and Methodios first encountered the Slavic tribes, they almost certainly found a linguistic world that was not uncongenial with their own. As Thessalonians, the Saints were presumably bilingual in the Greek of the Empire and in the Slavonic of the tribes which surrounded their province. Even if they had not been so, however, there could have been worse situations for prospective translators—for the language of the Slavs, though superficially uncouth and differing much in vocabulary, was of good Indo-European ancestry (as was Greek) and committed to a fundamentally similar world-outlook.

Slavonic, like Greek, was a tongue of many cases; it was, in fact, even more faithful to the original Indo-European eight-case system than was the tongue once spoken by Plato. The Common Slavonic of the 9th century was blessed with vocative, nominative, genitive, dative, accusative, instrumental and locative forms (together with traces of a separate ablative which had otherwise largely merged with the genitive). In contrast, the Greek even of classical times had the first five cases only—and the language of Byzantium had almost certainly fallen off from the complexity of that earlier age.

In another sense, too, Slavonic was truer to its past, and remains so to the present day: the Slavic verb was—and is—dominated by the notion of *aspect*. Thus every Slavic verb is actually a pair of verbs, one *perfective,* the other *imperfective;* the distinction resting upon the concept of *completed* vs. *uncompleted* action.[1]

---

[1] As we have seen in the preceding chapter, this notion exists, in limited form, in the Romance (and earlier Latin) distinctions of "simple" and "imperfect" past tenses: compare the French *je parlai* and *je parlais* and the Latin *amavi, amabam*. Greek, too, had something like this in its perfect vs. imperfect tenses— "I have released" or "I finished the job of releasing" vs. "I released" with the implication that the action was necessarily incomplete. But none of these languages carried the distinction through with consistency in all tense forms, or even most of them; the aspects were solely a matter of refinements on expressions of the past.

Thus, to give a contemporary example, modern Russian has at least two forms for almost every linguistic entity which Western languages consider to be a single verb. A beautiful example of this can be found in Dostoievsky's *The Idiot* where it is pointed out that *Koloomb bîl stchastliv nye togda, kogda otkrîl Amerikoo, a kogda otkrîval yeyoh*—"Columbus was not happy in the discovery of America, but rather in the discovering of it."[2] But whereas this writer has attempted to give something of the perfective/imperfective flavor of the passage by a distinction between *discovery* and *discovering,* the Russian of Dostoievsky makes the nuance unmistakable by the use of two different verbs in their past tense: *otkrît'* and *otkrîvat'* whose past forms are the *otkrîl/otkrîval* of the transliterated text above.

In this particular instance, the distinction between the two different verbs lies in the insertion of *-îva-* to form the imperfective. Unfortunately, the Slavic tongues are capricious with regard to the means used in forming such pairs; the methods employed are limited, but can—and do—vary from verb to verb. The imperfective *dyelat',* for instance, forms its perfective by prefixing *s-* to give *sdyelat';* compare *Chto on dyelal?* ("What did he do?" or "What was he doing?") with *Chto on sdyelal?* ("What has he [gotten] done?" "What has he accomplished?").

And *s-* is not the only prefix which can be used. There are many others, of which *na-* is perhaps one of the most common: *ya pisal* signifies that *I was writing* or *I was going on with my writing,* while *ya napisal* bears the connotation that *I have* or *had finished writing* or *had written it all.*

Sometimes, with what seems to Western eyes as sheer perversity, Russian and other Slavic tongues use completely different verbs: *ya skazal* vs. *ya govoreel.* (If the reader wishes to resign from the contest, let it be pointed out that even our own language does something of the sort occasionally; the various forms *be, was, are, is* were almost certainly drawn from entirely

---

[2] The *î* represents a sound almost identical with the peculiar gutteral vowel of Rumanian transcribed in that language as *â* or *î*; there are many who believe that the Rumanians may have borrowed this sound from the Slavs in the first place.

different sources originally, and were doubtless once parts of completely different utterances. The same applies to *go* and *went*.)

Perfective and imperfective are, however, rather vague categories by which to classify active reality, and the Slavic languages often feel called upon to draw even finer distinctions. Thus, certain verbs have specifically *punctual* forms as contrasted with *duratives;* the syllable *-noo-* when inserted before the ending of certain verbs lends them the character of *point-activity* as in *skol'zeet'*/*skol'znoot'* ("to slip") where the latter verb has overtones of slipping at one single instant. Although this ending (*-noo-*) was once specifically punctual in meaning (done at one single instant) rather than perfective (completional), in the course of time a blending and overlap of the two notions has resulted. Similar fusing of instantaneous-completional categories has occurred in other Slavic tongues as well.

More important are the *determinate-indeterminate* "sub-aspects." Though there are only about fifteen verbs which have this supplementary set of forms, they present a very real problem to the student of Slavic, since the verbs involved are among the most frequently used in the language. Both members of the determinate-indeterminate pair are imperfective: e.g., *eettee* and *khodeet'*, both of which are imperfective forms meaning "to go under one's own power." But one says *eettee v Pareezh* ("to go to Paris") when there is the idea of "purpose"; *he is going to Paris* (presumably to do or accomplish something) would be expressed with the third-person singular of this verb. The ideas of abstract ability or appropriateness to perform the action, habitual practice of it, or of a "round trip," however, require the *in*determinate form. Therefore, such statements as *Since he is a wine-buyer, he goes to Paris, he is always going to Paris*, or *he is going to Paris* (and, as a matter of course, will be back) would employ the appropriate form of the verb *khodeet'*.

This distinction of indeterminate and determinate exists *only within the imperfective aspect,* as an additional refinement. Both of these sub-varieties of imperfective have a common form in their perfective, formed by prefixing *po-* to the appropriate determinate form. Thus, both

> *On shol*v Pareezh*—"He went (det.) to Paris," and
> **shol*—past tense of *eettee*

> *On khodeel** v Pareezh*—"He went (indet.) to Paris"
> ***khodeel*—past tense of *khodeet'*

have one and the same perfective form:

> *On poshol v Pareezh*—"He has (*or* had) gone to Paris."

We have given this example in the third-person singular, but it must be remembered that the Slavic languages treat these aspects and sub-aspects in many respects as though they were utterly separate verbs. (Some grammars refer to them as such, rather than as differing aspects of one verb.) Therefore, this triad of forms—determinate-imperfective, indeterminate-imperfective, and their common perfective—may exist in a variety of persons and tenses in singular or plural, as can any pair of unrelated verbs in the more familiar Western tongues.

Before we leave this problem of determinate and indeterminate forms, however, the reader must take this one caution to heart: the distinction between these two sub-aspects is not completely identical with our simple vs. progressive tenses. The English differentiation in aspect between *he is going* and *he goes* is primarily in terms of *actual* vs. *habitual*. To the extent that this English notion of *actuality* often coincides with the Russian idea of *goal*, it is legitimate to translate the Russian determinate by using the English progressive: e.g., *pteetsa lyeteet* = "the bird is flying" (for some specific reason) as against *pteetsa lyetyet* = "the bird flies" (since it is in the nature of the critter to do so—birds naturally *do* fly). However, there are many instances in which the English and Russian forms are *not* equivalents. In such a sentence as "He is going to Paris on his monthly trip to discuss business with the French branch offices," the Anglo-American progressive tense would be equivalent to some Russian *in*determinative on at least two grounds: (1) it is part of the habitual routine of the person spoken of, and (2) it is presumed that "he" will return.

*   *

To make matters even more complex, there is still another distinction drawn with regard to the verb "to go." The reader will notice (p. 236) that the determinative *eettee* and indeterminative *khodeet*[3] were originally translated as "to go under one's own power." This is the only satisfying translation of this family of verbs, since an entirely different set is used to indicate that one is being conveyed to one's destination.

Depending on determinacy or indeterminacy, together with perfectivity or its lack, one uses *eettee, khodeet'* or *poyttee,* so long as the person or thing is actually moving. Thus a man may be the subject of a sentence with any of these as the verb, so long as he is doing the walking. If, however, he is taking a train, driving a car, or riding horseback, these verbs can only apply to the train, car, or horse itself—for it is one of them that is the agent in motion. The man—as passenger, driver, or equestrian—is only "traveling"; he does not "go."

In Russian there is a family of verbs reserved for the expression of this notion of "traveling" as contrasted with "going"; in their infinitive forms they are: *yekhat', yezdeet',* and *poyekhat',* corresponding exactly with the "self-powered" forms *eettee, khodeet'* and *poyttee.* Though it may seem a bit out of the ordinary on first sight, the Slavic system is quite logical in its own fashion. A train may be heading for Paris, and a man may be riding in it. In such a case, the Russian will insist on using a separate verb to specify the motion of each: the train actually "is going" (*eedyot*) or "goes" (*khodeet*); the man "is traveling" (*yedyet*) or "travels" (*yezdeet*).

If, of course, the man were going to Paris on foot, then he might safely be the subject of the verb forms *eedyot* or *khodeet*.

[3] And hence, by extension, the common det./indet. perfective *poyttee.*

It is, however, rather a long trip to make from Moscow or Volgagrad (formerly Stalingrad). We may sum up this rather complex state of verbal affairs in a single diagram:

ASPECTS AND SUB-ASPECTS OF THE TWO VERBS
MEANING "TO GO" (IN THE INFINITIVE FORMS)

	Imperfective		Perfective
	Determinate	Indeterminate	(Common Form)
(inf.) "to go" on foot (3rd pers. sing.)	*eettee*	*khodeet'*	*poytee* (*po-eettee*)
	(*eedyot*)	(*khodeet*)	(*poydyot*)
(inf.) "to travel" (3rd pers. sing.)	*yekhat'*	*yezdeet'*	*poyekhat'*
	(*yedyet*)	(*yezdeet*)	(*poyedyet*)

Identically the same distinctions are drawn for that Russian verb-complex which literally means "carry," but which is most often translated as "take." Following the same arrangement as in the table above (but omitting the third person singular forms), the forms are:

	Imperfective		Perfective
	Determinate	Indeterminate	(Common Form)
"to take" (under one's own power)	*nyestee*	*noseet'*	*ponyestee*
"to take" (in some vehicle, etc.)	*vyeztee*	*vozeet'*	*povyeztee*

There are about a dozen other verbs (all implying the idea of going in one fashion or another) which possess a three-fold aspect: determinate, indeterminate—both of which are imperfective—and a common perfective. Only the two verbs above, however, draw the extra distinction noted here between self-powered activity and activity performed thanks to outside (mechanical or animal) assistance.

Aside from such exceptional verbs as these fifteen or so, the Slavic verb is actually a thing of relative simplicity. *It has, in reality, only three tenses:* a Past, a Future, and a Present. Both the past and future forms are double, since for each imperfective verb, there is a corresponding perfective.[4] The following paradigm of a typical verb—*peesat'*, "to write"—will give a good idea of the general Slavic system today (the particular example is Russian, but the principle applies to almost all the Slavic languages):

PAST

	Imperfective		Perfective
	ya peesal, peesala	1st pers.	*ya napeesal, napeesala*
	tî peesal, peesala	2nd pers.	*tî napeesal, napeesala*
Sing.	*on peesal* ⎫		*on napeesal*
	ona peesala ⎬	3rd pers.	*ona napeesala*
	ono peesalo ⎭		*ono napeesalo*
	mî peesalee	1st pers.	*mî napeesalee*
Plur.	*vî peesalee*	2nd pers.	*vî napeesalee*
	onee peesalee	3rd pers.	*onee napeesalee*

FUTURE

	Imperfective		Perfective
	ya boodoo peesat'		*ya napeeshoo*
	tî boodyesh peesat'		*tî napeeshesh*
Sing.	*on* ⎫		*on* ⎫
	ona ⎬ *boodyet peesat'*		*ona* ⎬ *napeeshet*
	ono ⎭		*ono* ⎭
	mî boodeem peesat'		*mî napeesheem*
Plur.	*vî boodyetye peesat'*		*vî napeeshetye*
	onee boodoot peesat'		*onee napeeshoot*

---

[4] It is equally valid to say: each past and future form of a given verb has both an imperfective and a perfective aspect.

For the present tense, however, there is only one aspect: the imperfective—

> *ya peeshoo*
> *tî peeshesh*
> *on*
> *ona* } *peeshet*
> *ono*
> *mî peesheem*
> *vî peeshetye*
> *onee peeshoot*

The reader will notice that the perfective future of the verb (*ya napeeshoo, tî napeeshesh,* etc.) would seem to be—from their endings—present-tense forms; they correspond in every detail (aside from the perfective prefix *na-*) with the present imperfective. If it makes the task of learning any easier, the student of Russian (or any other Slavic tongue) can consider the perfective future as "really" a present tense *used* as a future. Slavic logic is, however, inflexible. It is possible to complete something in the past—there is, therefore, a perfective past; it is possible that sometime in the future one will have completed something—ergo, a perfective future. But one cannot by any stretch of the imagination at the same time be doing a thing and be finished with it. In the present tense there can only be an imperfective.

The careful reader will also have noticed something decidedly odd about the past tense of the Slavic verb. The imperfective and perfective forms match one another nicely; but there is something rather strange about the *endings*. Why are two forms offered for *ya* ("I") and *tî* ("thou"), but only one each (two of them corresponding to the *ya, tî* alternatives) for *on, ona* and *ono?* And why again the sole flexion *-ee* throughout the entire plural?

The answer to this question is simple, but rather unusual. In the beginning these past-tense forms were not truly verbs at all, but verbal *adjectives* (i.e., participles). Historically, *ya peesal* (or *ya peesala*) means "I am the was-writing one"; *ya napeesal*, "I am the finished-writing one." These participal phrases gradually came to be felt as true tense formations—new participles growing up to take their place—but they bear one ineradicable mark of their origin. The Slavic past tense, like the adjective in any synthetic language, *must obey the laws of gender concord.* Just as the Romans spoke of *bona puella, bonae puellae, bonus puer* and *boni pueri* ("good girl[s]," "good boy[s]"); just so, the Russian past tense must indicate the gender or the number of the subject. A Russian man will say *ya peesal*; a Russian woman, *ya peesala.* By the same logic, in the third person the masculine-gender pronouns *on* ("he"), *ona* ("she") and *ono* ("it") are restricted by their very forms to one particular variant of the verb. Since the three Slavic genders in Russian have melted together into a common plural form, it is this generalized plural ending (*-ee*) which is used after all personal pronouns in the plural of Russian pasts. Though the actual details of flexion may differ from one Slavic tongue to the next, it is fair to say that the past tense in these languages is actually a forgotten adjective that everybody accepts as an honest-to-goodness verb.

In contrast to this relatively simple verbal system, the Slavic luxuriance of "verboid" forms is fully the equal of Greek or Latin in complexity. There are, for example, four Russian participial types: present, active and passive; past, active and passive. Thus, one may say in Russian, *chelovek, peesayooshchee pees'mo* ("the man who-is-writing a letter") or *chelovek, peesavshee pees'mo* ("the man who-was-writing . . ."), using the active participles to speak of time present or past[5]; furthermore, the Slavic tongues are blessed with passive participles which enable them to express in a single word what less highly-inflected tongues must describe in an entire passive-voice clause. In the two words *peesayemoye pees'mo* (or *peesannoye pees'mo*),

[5] Russian and the other Slavic tongues do have, of course, constructions analogous to our "the man who is (*or* was) writing . . ." which make use of a relative pronoun equivalent to *who;* but this participial construction is characteristic of literary language or elevated discourse.

Russian can sum up that which we mean by "the letter which is (*or* was) being written."

We have already mentioned that the Slavic tongues do not permit the perfective aspect to have a present tense (using its forms for the future instead). The participles show their kinship to purely verbal forms by following this dictum themselves. The active and passive participles of the *past,* therefore, can exist in both aspects—*peesavshee* and *napeesavshee, peesanniy* and *napeesanniy*—but the present participle is found only in the imperfective (*peesayooshchee, peesayemiy*).

Of course in the days of St. Kyril and St. Methodios—better known in the West as Cyril and Methodius—the Slavic family of languages was a good deal more complex than it is at present; the verb in particular still had many forms and tenses which it has since lost,[6] but which in that moment of cultural confrontation probably made it easier for the proselytizing holy men to enter the psychological and linguistic world of the prospective converts to Greek Orthodoxy.

We have dwelt at such length on the idiosyncrasies of the Slavic verb because it has become an article of faith among many who have been badly burned while trying to learn Russian or one of its cousins that the action-words of Eastern Europe represent an all but insuperable obstacle to learning. A glance at Latin, Greek, French or Spanish grammar should be enough to call that statement into question. With few exceptions, the Slavic verb is a simpler creature than its Western counterpart, and should present no surpassing difficulty *provided the student masters the principle of aspect.*

English can—and often does—express notions of aspect: compare *she burst into tears* with *she went on crying.* This notion, however, is largely secondary (see chapter 3, footnote 1) in our language; in Slavic, on the contrary, it is primary. Although we do have such expressions as "to burst into tears" or "to go on crying," we do not have to use them; we may simply say of the

---

[6] Save in Bulgarian, which has preserved many verbal forms which have been discarded in most other Slavic tongues.

unhappy woman above that *she cried*. Russian, Polish, Czech, etc. must by their very nature say something of *how* she cried, as well as *when*.

*　　　*

The Slavic noun presents few novel features to those who have ever been confronted with Latin or Greek; it is very much like the classical Western noun—only more so. In comparison with the five basic cases of Latin—nominative, genitive, dative, accusative and ablative, the modern Slavic tongues are well endowed. With the exception of Bulgarian (see below), they all possess the first four cases of Latin mentioned above (also present in Greek)—and in place of the ablative, two additional forms: the *instrumental* and the *prepositional* cases. (Like Latin, too, the Slavic tongues preserve vestiges of a formerly widespread *vocative:* a case of direct address. With few exceptions, this vocative has now merged in form with the nominative; even today, however, there is almost universal in the Slavic family a distinct vocative form for the word meaning "God." Thus, Russian has *Bog* in the nominative ("God so loved the world . . .") as against *Bozhe* in the common exclamation *Bozhe moy!* (literally: "My God," though often used where Anglo-American custom would employ "Good grief!" or "O Lord!"). The corresponding Polish forms are almost identical, *Bóg* vs. *Boze,* as are the like alternatives in other Slavic tongues.)

Two peculiarities of case usage within the Slavic clan should be pointed out, however, since there is little to prepare the prospective student for them even in the heavily inflected classical tongues of the West. These are oddities which relate to the use of the *genitive* and *instrumental* cases in certain syntactical contexts.

Although languages characterized by grammatical gender often ignore—linguistically—the biological category of *sex,* they are generally strong in their allegiance to *concord*. As we saw in the preceding chapter (page 213), words referring to *femina* ("woman") were obliged to echo that primary word's case and gender. The case used depended upon the nature of the statement made, but the grammatical gender was simply a matter of arbitrary word-classification; thus *nauta*—"sailor"—is also a feminine noun, and associated adjectives will surround it in obediently feminine guise, as well as nouns of the same gender class, *even if inanimate*.

It is at this point of division between the animate and the inanimate that the Slavic tongues depart from the classic synthetic pattern; for in spite of a masculine-feminine-neuter triad of genders fully on a par with that of Latin and Greek, the highly-inflected languages of Eastern Europe do insist on a distinction between the living and the lifeless, in one particular set of instances: the choice of an accusative which is identical either with the genitive or with the nominative, for masculine singulars and all plurals (since these two broad classes of noun have no uniquely accusative form of their own).

Thus, the Russian nominative *offitser* ("officer") has as its accusative *offitsera* (identical with the genitive) since an officer is a living creature. *Park*, as an inanimate, has the same form as the nominative, even when used as the object of a verb (i.e., nominative and accusative forms are identical). Since the plurals of *all* nouns (not merely certain masculines) lack a distinctively accusative form, this distinction between a "genitive-accusative" for the living vs. a "nominative-accusative" for the lifeless is universal when speaking or writing of more than a single object. A Russian, therefore, would see *karandashee* (nom.-acc.) "pencils"—but when looking at women (unmistakably animate) the word used would be the common genitive-accusative form: *zhenshcheen*.

The Slavic use of an *instrumental* case, though a novelty to speakers of contemporary western tongues, is not inherently a problem insofar as the "central meaning" of the case is concerned. As its name implies, this particular form of noun (or pronoun) is used primarily to denote instrumentality, "means by which." From the Russian *pyero* (–"a pen") is formed the in-strumental *pyerom* (–"with a pen") as in *Tyepyer ya peeshoo pyerom*, "Now I am writing with a pen." Students of Latin will recognize a familiar construction—though using a different case —from their knowledge of the ablative-of-means in *gladio pugnat*, "he fights *with a sword*." In Greek, this notion of instrumentality is expressed through use of the instrumental dative as in *horomen tois ophthalmois*, "we see *with our eyes*."

Closely allied to this idea of instrumentality in its purest form is the concept of *manner*. *He fights like a hero* is another way of saying that *he fights with the courage* (or *daring, fortitude*, etc.) *of a hero*. The Slavic tongues, therefore, often use the instru-mental form of a noun in such contexts; cf. the Russian *on sprazhayet gyeroyem*.

Notice that *on sprazhayet gyeroyem* could also have been translated as *he fights heroically*, by replacing the instrumental clause with an adverb. Thus the Russian *spat'* ("to sleep") *kryepkim snom*, literally: *to sleep by means of a strong sleep*, but in idiomatic English: *to sleep soundly*. (Compare, however, the regional American *to sleep up a storm*, with the same mean-ing.)

What does present a problem to the student of Slavic is the use of this case form after the verb *to be* as in *ya bil stoodyen-tom*, "I was a student" (Russian), or *on jest konduktorem?*, "Is he the (train's) conductor?" (Polish). This use of a non-nomi-native case is peculiarly Slavic, though the precise conditions under which it occurs (often being optional) are the province of specialized grammars.

*   *

One who begins the study of Slavic languages had better re-sign himself at the onset to the mastery of a well-developed sys-tem of cases, as has been the fate of any who have set about learning either of the "classical" tongues of our Western world.

There is, however, one Slavonic tongue which offers a pleasant and surprising contrast, a language which has stripped away its declensional apparatus as thoroughly as have French, Spanish or Italian. Unfortunately, the language is rather peripheral in both location and importance, and there are probably few who will set about learning Bulgarian to catch new gems of scientific literature or to master the intricacies of internal politics within the city limits of Sophia.

It is a pity, for the Bulgarian language is a true maverick of the Slavic group. Though it does keep the three-fold gender system common to all members of the family, it has succeeded in abolishing cases. The student of Bulgarian finds himself confronted by only two forms of any noun: singular and plural. The principle by which plurals are derived from singulars is vaguely reminiscent of the Italian; -*ee* is added to the final consonant of masculine singulars, while it replaces the final -*a* of feminines; neuters change final -*o* to -*a*, final -*e* to -*ya*. Where other Slavic languages depend upon noun declension through six cases in the singular and an additional half-dozen in the plural, often eked out by use of prepositions, Bulgarian uses prepositions only, as do the Romance tongues (except Rumanian).

Bulgarian is also closer to the Western way of things in another respect: it has articles, definite and indefinite. Whereas the Russian *chelovek* means *man, a man,* or *the man,* according to context, Bulgarian has distinct forms for each: *chovek, edeen chovek,* and *chovekut.*

The reader will notice that the Bulgarian definite article is—like the Rumanian—postposited. Historically, it had a similar development, being derived from a particle meaning "that one." Russian still preserves these as independent words, *tot, ta, to,* while Bulgarian has evolved new terms to act as independent demonstratives: (*tova, onova*). The indefinite article, as in Romance and Teutonic languages, is merely a logical extension of the word meaning "one"; its four forms are: masc. *edeen,* fem. *edna,* neuter *edno* and plur. *ednee.*

There is always some fly in even the best of ointments, however. Though the Bulgarian noun is simplicity itself, even to a western European, the *verb* has managed to fossilize a number of forms which have since died out in other languages of Slavdom. Since this has probably frightened away those few who might otherwise have been drawn to the language, it is likely that not many besides the eight million or so Bulgarians (and their descendants) will learn this in many respects admirable Slavic tongue. A pity—some of the most beautiful folk songs in the world exist within it.

*   *

Most of the concrete examples of Slavic usage in this chapter have been drawn from Russian, since in this day and age it is that language which has drawn to itself most attention of all the Slavic clan. The Armenian, the Uzbek, the Turcoman Tatar of non-Slavs, and the Ukrainian and White Russian within the Slavic fold—each may conduct his day-to-day business in his native tongue; he may have newspapers and books printed in it within the confines of his particular constituent republic of the U.S.S.R.; but if he wishes to advance to something beyond mere regional influence or fame, he makes sure that his play, poem, novel, research report, description of an experiment or whatever rapidly adopts the linguistic dress of Dostoievsky and Pavlov.

Even outside the legal borders of the Soviet Union, the Russian language has assumed a pre-eminent place everywhere within the Soviet sphere of influence: Toth Geza may write a medical paper of surpassing interest to appear in *Orvasi Hitalep,* the Hungarian version of the *Journal of the American Medical Association;* Liu Chih Pan may have an article in the Chinese counterpart of our *Journal of the American Mathematical Association;* but if they wish to be truly appreciated, there will be a summary at the back—in Russian. (And quite possibly in English as well; there may even be a *résumé* in French or a *Zusam-*

menfassung in German. But the Russian will be almost inevitable.)

Since from the practical point of view if no other—and one must admit a good case for Russian on the grounds of much fine literature alone—the language of the Russians is of paramount importance, this is probably the point at which to deal with one Russian (East Slavic) idiosyncrasy: the foible of the disappearing "is."

This vanishing of the present tense of "to be" is peculiar to the Russian branch of the Slavic family. Russian will agree with general Western usage in:

> *On bíl offitser**   "He was an officer"

and

> *On boodyet offitserom***   "He will be an officer"

* The nominative in Russian is normal in the past tense (*offitser*) if this is a permanent or habitual characteristic of the individual concerned; *on bíl offitserom* would imply that his being an officer was a temporary affair, perhaps as a hastily-called-up member of the army reserve.

** In the *future*, the instrumental form is today normal (*offitserom*); students of Russian literature will notice, however, that 19th century Russian often preferred the nominative.

but in the present, the verb is notable by its absence:

> *On offitser*   "He is an officer."

The only forms, in fact, which survive of the Russian verb "to be" in the present are *yest'* and (very rarely!) *soot'*; and even these survivals are invariably used only when the words on each side of "is" or "are" are the same—*dyelo yest' dyelo*,[7] and not *dyelo-dyelo*—so that the intervening particle shows that something more than mere repetition is intended. Otherwise, *yest'* is used only as a "demonstrative verb" in the sense "there is": *Yest' tol'ko odeen sposob dyelat' eto* = "There is only one way to do that."

[7] *Dyelo*—"matter," "affair," "thing"; in this phrase, "business," i.e., "business is business," or in French "les affaires sont les affaires."

This predilection for a verbless sentence is not a barbaric innovation of the Slavs; if anything, it is a conservative preservation of the customs of an older day. Thus, Latin could have "Dulce et decorum (est) pro patria mori," which we would normally translate as "Sweet and fitting (it is) to die for one's homeland." Even Greek—that tongue of tongues—could follow the same model as the Russian in its Hippocratic Aphorisms, so well known to the physician:

> *ho bios brakhüs*
> *hē tekhnē makrē*
> *ho de kairos oxüs*
> *hē de peira sphalerē*
> *hē de krisis khalepē*

which word-for-word is

> *the life short*
> *the art* (or *craft*) *long*
> *the appropriate time* (a) *fraction-of-a-moment*
> *the test dangerous*
> *the crisis painful.*

Somehow this looks less barbarous in the original Greek characters, either because we do not recognize them (as with the dirtier footnotes in Gibbon), or because there is such a heavily-laden charge of love and respect bound up with those half-exotic, half-familiar letters which have for so long borne the connotations of culture. In their familiar translation as:

> Life is short;
> Art is long.
> The time for treatment is but an instant.
> The experiment is dangerous and
> The crisis is full of hardship,

the words seem less alien; but this is not how they were written. The original words would be more homelike to a nameless Russian digging potatoes or building a moon rocket.

The use of *be* as an audible (or written) juncture between

the subject and the predicate of a statement is, after all, rather restricted in its spread. Many, if not most, of the languages of the world do not know it; with them, simple juxtaposition suffices. And after all, what is wrong with "he officer"? Is there really any danger of misunderstanding? Even in American newspaper headlines it is acceptable English to say:

PRIVATE CONSIDERED EQUAL OF OFFICER IN BRAVERY

because the reader is assumed to have sufficient intelligence to interpolate the missing parts of speech to make:

(THE or A) PRIVATE (is) CONSIDERED (to be the) EQUAL OF (an) OFFICER IN BRAVERY.

So, depending on how the reader wishes to regard it, modern Russian usage may be seen as either (1) a "pidgin-headline" language, or as (2) a survival of a nobler day in which men did not repeat what seemed to them the obvious. The other members of the Slavic family are, however, committed to the old Indo-European (and Greek, Latin, Italian, Spanish, Portuguese, and Rumanian) system: i.e., they blend—Polish is a good example—the subject-pronoun and the finite verb: *jestem kuzyn,* the Polish form, is completely analogous to the Latin *consobrinus* (or feminine *consobrina*) *sum*. To hold to the literal sense of the statement, both can only be translated as: *I-am* (the) *cousin*.

*   *

The task of telling one Slavic tongue from another is a difficult one for the American or for the Western European in general. Like the troublesome job (for the Caucasian) of telling one Chinese from another, all members of this particular family have a tendency to look alike to outsiders. The various languages which comprise the Slavic sub-family of the Indo-European group have kept rather close together, as one can see from a comparison of such words (some of which have been transliterated from the Cyrillic to the Latin alphabet) as:

praveel'nĭy (Russian)
poprawny (Polish, the "w" pronounced as our "v")
správný (Czech)

and

praveelno (Bulgarian)

all meaning "correct" or "right" (though not specifically in the sense of a direction).

See, too, such forms as:

slishat' (Russian)
słyszeć (Polish)
slyšeti (Czech)

and

slusha (Bulgarian)

which all have the common signification, "to hear," or

tyeplo (Russian)
cieplo (Polish, the "c" being pronounced as a palatal)
teplo (Czech)
toplo (spelled as such in Croat, since this Roman Catholic population uses the Latin alphabet; the Serbians—Eastern Orthodox—employ the Cyrillic script for essentially the same tongue)
toplo (Bulgarian)

all these closely-allied (or identical) words having the common meaning: *warm.*

Nonetheless, to the crafty ear and eye there are signs by which one may tell one member of this inbred clan from its cousin.

In Speech:

Russian is marked by the frequent presence of the endings -(*y*)*evo* and -*aya*, -*ovo* and -*ohye;* and like Bulgarian and Serbo-Croatian (Yugoslavian), Russian is marked by unpredictable stress-accent. If the spoken emphasis of sentences follows no easily-predictable pattern, and the characteristics mentioned above are present—the chances are that the language heard is Russian. P.S.: if a word which in Western usage would begin with "h" in fact begins with a "g" sound, then it is almost certain that the language is Russian: e.g., *gyeroy* for "hero"; *Geetlyer* for "Hitler."

Polish can be distinguished from Russian by its constant penultimate ("next-to-last-syllable") accent. Additional confirmation springs from an often-heard *-yegoh*, *-atch*, *yekh*, or *ūv* at the end of words.

Czechoslovak is relatively easy to identify: a consistent stress on initial syllables is uniquely Czech in the Slavic family, as is the occurrence of *long, but unstressed,* vowels towards the end of words. The presence of the genitive masculine-and-neuter-*ekho* (where *-kh-* has the guttural sound of the *ch* in Scots *loch*) serves to confirm the identification.

Serbo-Croatian (the language of Yugoslavia) may be identified in speech by the presence of a musical pitch, reminiscent of the sing-song heard in Swedish. The often-heard endings *-ohga* *-ah-oh*, *-ar* and/or *-atee* together with this musical pitch make the specification of the language reasonably certain.

Bulgarian, like Russian and Serbo-Croatian, has a capricious stress; its postposited article—frequent in occurrence, and heard as *-ut*, *-ta*, *-to*, or *-tyeh*, helps to distinguish it from other members of the Slavic family, as well as the *absence* of such typical Slav endings as *-evo*, *-ovo*, *-(y)ego*, *-(y)emoo*, *-(y)akh*, *-(y)am*, and *-(y)amee*.

In writing, the various Slavic tongues can be told from one another by the following traits: *Russian* uses the exotic Cyrillic alphabet, as do a number of other Slavic languages. This can confuse the foreigner, but the common neuter ending *-oe* is peculiar to Russian, as is the use of a letter which looks like a reversed capital N isolated between words (this character, pronounced *ee,* is the Russian for "and").

Polish, as befits a Roman Catholic Slav nation, uses a variant of our Latin script. The characters *ą*, *ę*, *ł* and *ż* (the hook placed below indicating a nasalization of the vowel that is today

uniquely Polish), and the consonant-combinations -*rz*- and -*szcz*-
are a certain label of Polish identity. The noun (or adjective)
endings -*iego*, -*iemu*, -*ac*, or -*iec* are confirmatory. But of all the
written characters used in the Latin-alphabet scripts of any
Slavic tongue, the "crossed 'l'"—capital Ł, lower-case ł—is absolute: once Ł or ł is seen (and they are commonplace in the language), there is no doubt but that the language is Polish.

Czechoslovak is really two languages: Czech and Slovak. But
the differences between the two tongues are so subtle that only
a native of the country can distinguish them. Since Czech of
these two sister-tongues—as close to one another as Lowland
Scots and Standard English—has provided the literary model,
the average reader can be content with identification of the
common Czech + Slovak model, which is the form usually seen
outside the borders of this rather small nation. An absolute
identification mark of the language is the ř (the mark ['] is
known as the *kricka*, pronounced "kreetska"). This ř is, in pronunciation, close to the Polish -*rz*- or -*ż*-, and can best be approximated by attempting to pronounce an American -*r*- and
a -*zh*- (as the "s" in "pleasure") simultaneously. The particular
sound may be heard in the name of the composer of the "New
World Symphony"—*Antonin Dvořak*. Additional identification
is supplied by the characters ů, ě, ň, š, and ř, as well as by the
use of *l* or *r* in a vocalic ("vowelish") position: *vlk, mrk.*

Serbo-Croatian (the language(s) of Yugoslavia) is in reality a
single tongue divided by two alphabets. Serb—the written form
of those who accept Eastern Orthodoxy—is written in a modified
form of the Cyrillic alphabet, *but it includes the Latin character
"J."* The combinations *lj*, and *nj* are characteristic of the Croat
transcription of the common language into Western letters.

Bulgarian can be identified immediately in print by the presence
of a letter looking like a triangle balanced on its apex upon a
tripod. This character was once widespread throughout the lands
which used the Cyrillic script, but is now confined to Bulgaria
alone. High frequency of words ending in -*TA* or -*TO* is also
indicative, since these are the written forms of the postposited
definite article, joined firmly to the preceding noun.

✐ 13

A niche in time

WE have come many pages and we have discussed many tongues; hopefully, understanding has been gathered along the way. Even so, that elusive creature, Language, has certainly escaped the neat pigeonholes into which we so often try to cram the immensity of any real thing. There is so much we have missed along the way.

Most of the world, for instance. Geographically, Europe is at best a peninsula jutting from the western flank of Asia. We have ignored the central body of that huge expanse of land itself—and as for that *other* Asiatic extension into the world-wide sea—India, we have touched on her only in historic commentary on the speech of our own limited parish. Yet, in the more than a thousand years since the death of Sanskrit as a truly living tongue, there have been changes fully as radical and remarkable as those which quickened the Romance tongues from the corpse of Classical Latin. First came the *Prakrits,* whose language corresponds in historical importance to the language of the Strasbourg Oath; after them, from them, rose the colloquial tonques of today: Bengali, Urdu, Hindi . . . and a score of others. Each can trace back its ancestry as definitely to a noble speech as can Italian, or Spanish, or French. Their pedigree is infinitely better established than that of the Germanic languages—our own included.

Yet such is the chilly logic of history that the modern Indians have had to make a great renunciation, or at least a great postponement. After the achievement of independence it was intended that Hindi—a child of Sanskrit, and written in the same Devanagari characters—should become the common tongue of intercommunication among the diverse linguistic stocks of the great Indian sub-continent.

But time and politics can be cruel, and have put an end to many a dream. (At this very moment they are doubtless slaughtering a handful of idealistic projects—and most of them are not linguistic.) The original deadline for the transfer of state business to Hindi was 1965, but that date has been set back, and will probably be set back still again. There are so many linguistic rivalries, for one thing. Though Hindi is spoken by the largest single fraction of the population, substantial portions speak such other Indo-European tongues as Punjabi, Bengali, Gujarati, Sindhi, and Marathi.[1] And of course, there are the *non*-Indo-European languages. It should be remembered that Sanskrit and its descendants are the languages of invaders. The traditional ancestors of the present Indo-European-speaking peoples of India were the "Aryans" who dispossessed another population then in tenancy of the land. Such folk as the Kanarese, Telugu, Tamil, or Malayalam do not take kindly to the idea of adopting as the official language a speech fully as alien to them as is English.

And, of course, English is already *there*. The governing and professional populations of this great and new country are largely at home—more or less—in that language imposed during the period of British colonial rule. Even if it is not their first language (and it is said that Jawaharlal Nehru was obliged to take a refresher course in Hindi itself), it is still the tongue in which

[1] The Urdu language, however, is something of a sore point, since it may with justice be described as a variant of Hindi with a large admixture of Arabic and Persian terms. Written in a modified version of the Arabic script, rather than in Devanagari, it can be termed the Moslem version of Hindi.

the educated can most easily make themselves understood to one another if their individual languages prove mutually unintelligible. One can be absolutely certain of the sincerity of those who demand the acceptance of Hindi (or some other Indian vernacular); but the question is How? and When?

Asia itself is a giant about whom it is dangerous to make any absolute statement, even one of definition. True it is that there exists that one huge mass of land extending from the Pacific westward to end in the jutting promontory of Spain. But to define within that one island the borders of "the Orient" is a hazardous task. Does the East begin at the low-lying Urals (which have been used to distinguish "European" from "Asiatic" Russia)? May we erect frontier-posts in the snows of the Caucasus? There is a gradual fading . . . an interpenetration. Most often, perhaps, the western lands of Asia are taken to be "the Middle East"—and the notion of *that,* in turn, based on the prevalence of Arabic. This, however, is a dangerous criterion to use; the tongue of the Prophet is fully at home in the north of Africa, throughout the Maghreb ("the West") which lies further west than Spain itself—or even England.

Whatever the precise borders of Asia, and they are most likely borders of the mind, there do exist the Lands of the East. Though each region of Asia has a unique identity within its own consciousness of history, all are fused in the collective awareness of Western Civilization into a gigantic land of the strange, the wise, the cruel, and the old.

The language of China is appropriate to such an image of the East: it has much of the strange about it, to our eyes; it has been the vehicle of wisdom; and it is assuredly very old. As for cruelty —the Chinese system of writing, the ideograph, provides agony in full measure even to the Chinese, to say nothing of the stranger. And one of those strangers was (and is, even today) the Japanese.

To those who are neither Chinese nor Japanese, the two languages seem to be similar, if not actually identical. This misconception is largely the product of chance glimpses at the written forms of the two tongues, rather than the result of any real acquaintance with these highly individual languages themselves. For the speech of Japan is no closer to that of China than is our language to that of Finland; each member of the pair is completely unrelated to the other.

The primary reality which joins these two Eastern tongues is a certain script—a script which by its very nature overrides and obscures all other differences, for it is a mode of writing which is non-alphabetic. The writing of China and Japan is a commitment of *ideas*, not sounds, to paper.

Originally this pattern of ink-on-paper was the creation of the Chinese. Probably it was almost inevitably so, for the Chinese tongue is uniquely suited to the principle of *one utterance = one written character*. Chinese is the language of the monosyllable *par excellence*. Though there is evidence that in ancient times Chinese was capable of words of more than one syllable, for the millennia since reliable history began the tongue of the *Ch'in* has been one in which only a combination of *consonant + vowel + consonant*[2] is permitted. According to the logic of such a phonetic system, it was not a difficult leap to the notion of a unitary symbol-to-the-eye which would represent a single utterance—in Chinese, a word, and by extension, an *idea*.

This system of writing was upheld and sustained by the very simplicity of the spoken language itself. Chinese has managed to abolish most—perhaps all—of those grammatical distinctions which hang upon a change in the *form* of a word. Thus *wo* can mean "I" or "me," "mine," or "to me"; all depending on the position of this syllable in the ordered sequence of vocables. Even plurality is denoted by a modification of the central core: *wo-men* ("I-many") is the term for "we." As in Malay, the plural of nouns is either the same as the singular (one word being used indifferently for both), or a word meaning "many" or "several"

---

[2] Occasionally a zero-grade consonant (i.e., no consonant at all) is found in the initial position: *a*, or *ai*. The allowable consonants in the terminal position are even more restricted—limited, in most dialects of Chinese, to either [n] as in *chen*, or "ng" as in *cheng*.

is suffixed. (On occasion, also as in Malay, the word is simply repeated.) There are no tenses to the Chinese verb; the kernel alone is used to denote the nature of the action described, and can refer to past, present, or future. If there be some real need to specify the time at which some deed took place, then an adverb of time ("yesterday," "today," "tomorrow") or a conventionalized term of tense-indication ("finish" = past, "now" = present, "come" = future) is used. Otherwise, the verb is universal. And in fact the word "verb" is a misnomer, for there are few creatures in the Chinese universe of language which can correspond to our parts of speech. All utterances being monosyllabic, there is certainly little opportunity for a specific grammatical marker to occur. There are, in Chinese, no real equivalents for the English *-ize* or *-ate*, German *-en* or *-ieren,* French *-ir* or *-oir,* Italian *-are, -ire,* or Russian *-at'* and *-eet',* to indicate verbs—nor are there, all the more so, endings *à la* Latin to mark person. There exist no such unmistakably adjectival terminations as *-al* or *-ive,* or such nominal ("nounish") endings as *-ation* or *-ity,* which unsystematically differentiate between the various linguistic categories which we have borrowed from Latin and applied to our own speech.

The Chinese syllable *shang* alone before a "verb," or isolated after such a verbal form, can act as *noun* ("the one above," i.e., *the ruler*); in *shang jen* ("the above man," *the superior person*), the syllable is what we would consider an adjective; in *shang mah* ("to upper a horse," *to mount a horse*) the same utterance takes the part of a verb; and when the order of terms is reversed —*ma shang* ("horse over," *above a horse*)—*shang* would be recognized by us as a pre- (post-)position.[3]

In such a tongue, the Chinese system of using a single ideogram (historically a picture of the thing or a plausible concretization thereof) makes relative sense; the invariant ideogram will mirror the unchanging spoken word—and the only problem

[3] As in *t'a shang shang, he climbs, climbed,* [*or*] *will climb, up,* one might remodel a Chinese sentence so as to make the same vocable serve both as verb and adverb.

for the speaker of the tongue will be the memorization of forty to fifty thousand separate signs, each standing for a single notion in the written version of the language.

Since Chinese is comparatively poor in consonants (even initially), the number of permissible syllables is limited—not much more than 400. Though one can—and does—invent a huge number of distinct ideographs to express the wealth of reality *in writing,* spoken Chinese makes use of two other devices: (1) *tones* are employed, and are characteristic of the Sinitic ("Chinesoid") languages; (2) *juxtaposition* is also used, which is by no means unique to the Sinitic group of tongues.

The tones are analogous to our English-speaking levels of speech, in such phrases as *Oh!* (surprise), *Oh* (comprehension), *Oh?* (questioning) and *Oh-h?* (dubious acceptance of a statement). This four-fold distinction (some dialects of Chinese use as many as nine separate tones) helps to mark one homophone from another; even so, there are overlappings of meaning, one given tone for a syllable often carrying a number of significations. This ambiguity, however, is comparable to our *so-sow-sew* homophonic plight, and the context of a statement helps to eke out the meaning of any given sentence. (Needless to say, each of the syllables, even spoken in the same tone, has a different character to represent it in writing.)

Juxtaposition helps to clear up some of the remaining possible misunderstandings which might result from similarity of sound, and also aids in the expansion of vocabulary; such a device is common to the Germanic tongues as well—our own included. Thus, Chinese may link its words for *lightning* and *voice* to make *lightning-voice* or "telephone"; the same process has produced the German *Eisenbahn* ("iron-path") and the English and American *railway* and *railroad.* Since this setting of one concept next to another may be applied to script as well as to utterance (as the device of tonality can not), it also plays a part in the writing of Chinese: the characters for *lightning* and for *voice* are also placed beside one another to denote Alexander Graham Bell's invention on paper, as well as in conversation.

This system of writing-by-concept may—and does—make for heart-breaking labor in the Chinese school. The Chinese Communists have recognized this, and have begun, tentatively, to use the Latin alphabet to transcribe the new "National Language." But there is one advantage which the ideographic system possesses: it binds together a wide variety of mutually-unintelligible varieties of speech. For, in truth, there is no such thing as a "Chinese language"; there are, as spoken realities, a handful of human manners of speech, some no more closely related to one another than are French and Rumanian, Swedish and English. Since, however, the same ideographs are used for a given concept, no matter what its pronunciation, two Chinese who could not understand a single word of one another's *speech* can read the same newspaper—if they have ever managed the task of learning to read at all.

When one moves to *Japanese,* however, the picture becomes gloomier. The language of Nippon is not monosyllabic, and its words—the verbs in particular—are capable of an inflectional complexity which would do credit to Russian.

Japanese treatment of nouns is relatively straightforward, though a trifle exotic from the Western point of view; the device which expresses relationship is the *post*position. Since Japanese lacks articles, such a postpostional scheme gives rise to such forms as *oka-ni,* "to the hill" (lit. *hill-to*) and *niwa-no,* "of the garden" (*garden-of*). These postpostions are also used with the (rarely-employed) personal pronouns to generate forms analogous to Western cases: e.g., *watakshi-no* (I-of, mine, my), and *watakshi-ni* (I-to, to me) are approximately genitive and dative, respectively. "In my garden" might be translated as *watakshi-no niwa-ni,* though in fact the Japanese look with a chilly eye on the use of personal pronouns, regarding them as occasionally unavoidable, but smacking overmuch of concern with personality. In normal use, "niwa-ni" would be considered sufficient, the question of in *whose* garden being determined by the context of statement. The habitual absence of pronouns makes for a delicacy and ambiguity of meaning which is untranslatable.

At its best, as in Lady Murasaki's *Genji-no Monogatari* ("The Tale of Genji"), the Japanese allusiveness of declaration makes for subtlety and charm; at its worst—the world of science, philosophy, and the realm of what-is—the pervasive lack of fixed structure makes for bafflement. "There exists a going" is an appropriately vague statement within the formalized context of social hierarchy;[4] in a world of timetables and production schedules, such indefiniteness can make for difficulties. Unmistakable and unambiguous denotation of *who* goes is vital.

And *when,* as well. For upon inspection, the Japanese verb proves to be a tenseless creature, as indifferent to time as it is to person and number. Such a verbal form as *mairimashita* is conventionally regarded by Westerners as an example of the past tense. In reality, it is a perfective; insofar as the act is seen as completed, it is often equivalent to our past. But the significant kernel of meaning inherent in *-shita* is the idea of "over-and-doneness," not of past time as such. *Mairimashō* is the "dubitive" form, marking uncertainty. It, too, is noncommittal in statement of time, but is usually translated as a future in the tongues of the West (for what man can be certain of what is to come?). *Mairimasu* might be described as an "assertive" form—there is no doubt about the going in question; as such, this form of the verb ending in *-asu* is generally held approximately equal to our present.

A feature of interest, and vaguely reminiscent of a Finnish construction, is the Japanese creation of *negative* verbs, in which *-en* takes the place of *-u* in the assertive mode: *mairimasen—I am not going, you are not going,* etc.

[4] Though, as we shall see, *some* indication of person is given. The humble form of "to go" is *mairu;* the egalitarian form is *iku;* and the form denoting respect is *irassharu.* The well-mannered Japanese generally uses the humble form of verbs when referring to his own actions, the respectful form in direct address. In this sense—though not their core-meanings—these variants provide some clue to *who is doing what for whom.* Similar alternates exist for nouns; often, as with "to go," above, entirely different words are used. Most commonly, however, a prefix is employed. *Uchi* ("house") is *my* house; *o-uchi* ("honorable house") belongs to *you.* See also the suffix *-yama* in *Fujiyama,* "honorable" or "noble" Fuji.

Learning spoken Japanese, at something beyond the occupa-
tion-Armed-Forces level, can be hard. Not only are there these
(to the Western mind) puzzling idiosyncrasies of impersonality
and manner; there are the numerous "sub-languages" of Japan,
as well. There are, for example, wide differences between the
men's language and the women's speech. (Even in English we
have something which distantly approaches this: "My dear, what
a *lovely* hat" could be said only by one woman to another;
"Where did you pick up that tie?" is man-to-man talk.) There
is the language of ceremony and deference, already touched on;
there is the language of chivalry—and there is "baby talk," a
simplified version of the language used when dealing not merely
with small children, but when connotations of civility, *politesse*,
or subtlety would be wasted on the hearer—as in dealing with
most foreigners. Since most soldiers stationed in Japan picked
up a curious mish-mash of women's speech and baby talk, their
use of the language was something hilarious to hear—to the well-
bred Japanese.

Worst of all, however, even to the dedicated student of the
language of Nippon, is the *written* form. It has neither the simplicity of an alphabet, nor the appropriateness of ideographs in
Chinese. As we can readily guess from the polysyllabic and inflectional nature of the language, Japanese is *not* well-suited to
the writing system of China—yet this is the script employed.
For important words—nouns, verbs, adjectives—the same ideographs are found in both nations.

Since these ideographs represent notions rather than sounds,
one might think that the Japanese would read them as the native Japanese equivalents.[5] Sometimes they do. But, again, often
they do not. The actual sounds in which a given text may be
read aloud depend on a host of psychological intangibles. Is the
writer appealing to one's informal, poetic, or specifically Japa-

---

[5] As is customary with the few ideographs extant in the West. We read "&" as
"and"; in French, Spanish, German and Danish, the same symbol would be
pronounced "et," "y," "und," and "og." Universally ideographic are the *numbers;* "1" equals "one," "un," "uno," "een," "ein," "odeen" etc.

nese nature? If so, then one pronounces the *kanji* (ideographs) in the *kun* (native Japanese) fashion. If, on the other hand, the intention or mood of the author is didactic, scientific, or characterized by high seriousness, then the reader employs the *on* (quasi-Chinese) pronunciation. Thus, a Chinese character pronounced *jen,* and meaning "man," or "person," may be found in Japanese pronounced as *jin* or *nin* (*on* convention) in the works of science, philosophy, or religion; in the reading of a novel or newspaper, however, the very same Japanese may then choose to vocalize that identical character by *hito*—the perfectly good Japanese word for the same idea. (Within the *on* system there are a number of variant pronunciations often possible, as in *jin* and *nin;* these often depend on the particular dialect of the original Chinese with which the character was first associated, or—more often—the period in history during which the character achieved wide use.)

In actual practice, the rules for choice of *kun* or *on* reading of the *kanji* are not nearly so simple as the bare outline above would suggest. A man of wide and deep erudition might pride himself in using *on* even in reading the latest news dispatches in *Mainichi Shimbun,* one of the great Japanese dailies. In contrast, a Nipponese whose psychological bent was strongly in the direction of local identity might well use *kun* even where most of his fellows would read the same ideographs in an approximation of 6th century Chinese.

There is one sense in which this bifurcation between Chinese and Japanese language (and culture) comes close to home. Just as one might consider the earlier history of the Anglo-Saxon folk in Britain as a progressive chronicle of civilizing-from-the-South, so we may view Japan as a cultural province of China. In English we have the choice between "sleeplessness" and "insomnia," "loss of memory" and "amnesia"—the native term connoting an informal level of discourse, the Greek or Latin word referring to the same phenomenon seen in a learned, medical light. The Japanese are frequently in the same plight; but their learned terms—analogous to the English *narco-*, *cata-*, *infra-*, *hyper*, *-oid*, *-itis*, *-osis*, *-ism* and *-ize*—are taken from the Chinese.

Perhaps the best-known of these in the Western world is the ending *-do* found in *judo* and *Mikado*. Historically, *-do* is merely the Japanese attempt at pronunciation of the *t'ao* ("the way," "the path") described by the Chinese philosopher Lao Tsŭ. In Japanese, however, the syllable has become generalized to mean "a method" or "a discipline" by which one reaches a certain goal; in this sense, *-do* might be likened to (the originally Greek) *-ology*, and is often employed in similar contexts, cf. *judo*, *bushido*—"fightingology," "chivalrology."

But even with the best will in the world—and in light of China's cultural superiority in the 5th and 6th centuries, the Japanese were sufficiently humble—the *kanji* could not solve all the problems implicit in the transcription of Japanese. There were those unfortunate *flexions*—a species of grammatical animal never known in China herself during the days of her cultural ascendancy over the only half-civilized Islanders. What was one to make of those awkward excrescences? The Celestial Writing might well account for *irassharu*, insofar as the general notion of "going" was concerned. But how to distinguish this form from *irassharimasen* or *irassharimashita?* To those silly Japanese, endings meant so much! They could not be content with a single, unchanging word. (And presumably, from the Chinese point of view, it would have been nice if the Nipponese could have managed with monosyllables, as well.)

The Japanese answer to this was the *kana's; katakana* and (later) *hiragana*. Each of these is a syllabary (See chapter 8, p. 144) consisting of almost 50 signs; this syllabic system is well-suited to the phonetic and phonemic character of the spoken tongue, since Japanese consists almost entirely of open syllables, i.e., syllables of the general form consonant + vowel or diphthong. (The only exception lies in an occasional final *-n*.) *Hi-ro-hi-to*, *bu-shi-do*, *ju-do*, *a-ri-ga-to* (as well as *ka-ta-ka-na* and *hi-ra-ga-na* themselves) are representative examples of the permissible phonetic patterns within the Japanese tongue. Even words taken from Western languages are adapted to this system: *ai-su ka-ri-mu* ("ice cream"), *nai-fu* ("knife"), *fo-ku* ("fork"), *re-so-to-ran* ("Western-style restaurant").

With the appropriate changes required by the nature of the language itself, the Japanese syllabaries (both representing the same gamut of sounds, but differentiated in use in a way similar to our distinction of lower case and capitals, or roman and italic) are fully capable of representing any word, foreign or native. Alas, such was the influence of China, that this comparatively simple notation has never taken true hold. There *are* books and periodicals written entirely in *kana,* but they are for "the lower classes."

And let us make no mistake, no matter how unfortunate was the turn taken by Japan a millennium-and-a-half ago, it was in response to a very real logic of circumstance—China was the immense truth to which the then-primitive islanders had to bend. They could no more have ignored the great civilization which spread, huge and unavoidable, along the great coast across the water than could the Britons have ignored Rome, or the Saxons the culture and arms of a Norman-bulwarked France. There have been attempts made at a thoroughgoing *kana*-ization of the written language, as there have also been impulses toward adoption of *romanji*—the Latin alphabet. Until now, both have foundered with the realization that any such move would utterly cut off the islanders of Nippon from any real intercourse with the greatness that was China. (Thanks to their common ideographic element, the two nations have been tied to one another by a partial written comprehension. A Chinese, by ignoring the flexion-marking *kana,* could catch some of the essence of a Japanese text; a Japanese, deferring to the rigorous word-order conventions of Chinese, could catch much of the sense conveyed by the ideographs of a book written in Peiping.)

However, there may be a new day a-dawning. The Chinese Communists have begun the introduction of a Latin alphabet—at present used as a sort of phonetic commentary in the establishment of a hybrid blend of dialects to be fixed as a nation-wide tongue. If this alphabetic transcription catches fire in the popular and literary imagination, and becomes a primary means of committing language to paper, the last *raison d'être* for Japan's preservation of *kanji* will have gone to dust.

It is a cliché of those partly-educated enough to know that the Japanese and Chinese do speak two different tongues, that their languages are indistinguishable. It is difficult to understand this, since in origin the two varieties of speech are completely alien to one another: Chinese being kin to the tongues of Cambodia, Laos, and Viet-Nam—and more distantly related to Tibetan; while Japanese is a flexional, agglutinating speech perhaps having common roots with Korean and even (though here, all suppositions end in guesswork) ultimately with Finnish, Estonian, Turkish and Hungarian.

Chinese is a spoken tongue of monosyllables and varying pitches, of "singsong" tones; Japanese is many-syllabled, and the syllables are spoken with little, if any, individual stress. A rippling speech, in which there is no marked accentuation, and with such terminations as *-shi, -ashta (-ashita), -asen -esko, -asho* and *-asen* must inevitably be Japanese. It can no more be the language of China than could a tongue with such endings as *-ovo, -eeshchee,* or *-ooyeh* (typically Russian) be English.

In their written incarnations it is somewhat more difficult for the foreigner to tell these two Eastern languages apart; but there are nevertheless unmistakable marks of differentiation. Chinese will consist only of those beautiful and complex printed or brush-stroked characters which represent notions. In any text in Japanese, however, there will always accompany these *kanji* the decidedly simpler *kana* forms, indicating the numerous flexions and postpositions not to be found in Chinese.[6] Of all the *kana,* perhaps the most frequent—and hence a safe touchstone—is the syllabic grapheme (written form) representing the postposition *-no* ("of"). In hiragana, this character resembles the numeral

---

[6] The *kana* of both types evolved at best guess sometime in the 600's or 700's A.D. as simplified versions of entire Chinese characters, but the characters used only to represent an approximation of the original, monosyllabic *sound.*

"6" fallen on its side to the right; in katakana, it is simply a diagonal stroke from upper right to lower left.

Moving westward along that figment of legal imagination, the Chinese-Indian border, one touches the land of Afghanistan—the land of the Afghans. The official tongue, that which the Afghans themselves speak, is variously known as Pushtu, Pushto, Pashtu, Pashto, Pakhsto or Pakkhto. An Indo-European speech of great interest to philologists and historians of language, its principal importance otherwise is to the Afghans themselves and to those diplomats and commercial travelers who must deal with this proud people in its own tongue. Within the borders of this nation, however, there are numerous enclaves from other linguistic communities: e.g., the Turcomanians, the Tadjiks, a number of speakers of Arabic—and the *Fars,* the Persians.

These last—who have been cast into comparative obscurity by the workings of time, the sword and geography—have a vastly greater importance than the attention commonly paid to them. These, the Farsis of History, both within the borders of Persia and without, have been a suave and yet mighty people whose language was once the vehicle *par excellence* of poetry, skeptical wisdom and science in the eastern provinces of Islam. As if in memory of the finely-drawn intelligence which it once expressed, even today Persian is a monument to human sense. Of all natural tongues on earth, Persian comes perhaps closest to that regularity of structure and form of which the creators of artificial languages have dreamed. Like English, Persian is a tongue with a double soul: though its basic vocabulary and its primary structure are Indo-European (and hence cognate with the tongues of the West), it has been heavily influenced by Moslem and Arabic. The learned vocabulary of Iran is Semitic in origin, as the words of high import in our speech are Romance or Greek. Persian would be a relatively easy tongue to learn if it were not for one obstacle, but that barrier is a forbidding one: the Arabic alphabet.

This Semitic script, well-suited perhaps to Arabic itself, has been discarded by the Turks. Their speech is not an Indo-European one, but as much as Persian or English, it finds the expression of vowels of overriding importance. That masterful, determined, and rather wicked old man, Mustafa Kemal changed the script used by his people as part of the program designed to turn Turkey into a modern European-type state. (He remade his name as well, changing it to Kemal Atatürk—"Kemal, Father of the Turks.") After consultation with a committee of linguists, a variant of the Latin alphabet was made official and mandatory by fiat. At one stroke the intricate, lovely, consonant-rich but vowel-poor script of the Koran went into the dustbin as far as the secular books, newspapers and edicts of the new Turkey were concerned. This Latinized Turkish is an easy language to recognize: it is the only tongue using the Western alphabet which possess both a dotted and an undotted "I"—in lower-case, *i* and *ı;* in capitals, *İ* and *I*. G and *ğ* (note the accent mark) are also characteristic of the language. Like Finnish (together with its extremely close kin, Estonian) and Hungarian, tongues of the same Ural-Altaic super-family, Turkish is addicted to the use of postpositions and postposited modifiers more or less closely blended with the preceding word; Turcoman—a Central Asian dialect closely allied to the Osmanli of Turkey proper—is in accordance with this principle able to produce a monster like *birilishturalmaidurman,* built up by accretions to the root *bir-* ("to give"). A reasonably close translation of this would run: "I am not able to make them to be given to one another."

We have touched on Finnish earlier, in dealing with the Scandinavian sub-family of the Teutonic group, mentioning certain of its written features which are revelatory (chapter 10, p. 196). Estonian is extremely close to it in structure and vocabulary, but whereas Finnish was strongly influenced by Swedish over the centuries, Estonian has acknowledged a debt to German, Lithuanian and the Slavic tongues. Nonetheless, the relationship between the two languages is intimate—comparable to German and Dutch—as can be seen in the following pairs of

words, the first Finnish, the second Estonian: *kutsua–kutsuma*
("to call"); *mies–mees* ("man"); *kaikki–kõik* ("everything");
isä–isa ("father"). Though the two cousin-languages are easy
for the foreigner to confuse, two Estonian forms distinguish them:
(1) the "O-with-a-tilde" (Õ, õ) and (2) the umlaut-U (Ü, ü).
The first of these letters is *not* a nasalized vowel by the way;
and the *Ü* in Estonian takes the place of Finnish *Y*, which stands
for the same sound as in the German *für*.

Hungarian is also a member of this agglutinating clan, and
similarly postpositionally inclined: *ház*, "house," *házban*, "house-
in" (in a house), *házak*, "houses," *házakban*, "houses-in" (in the
houses). Orthographically, Hungarian can be told from any other
language by the use of *long* umlauts—like pairs of accent marks—
over the vowels *O* and *U*. There are, as well, short umlauts over
the same vowels, the paired dots familiar from German (Ö, ö,
Ü, ü). Also common: -*cs*-, -*nyi* and -*zs*-.

One characteristic held by all these Ural-Altaic tongues is the
phenomenon of *vowel-harmony*. The characters used in their
various spelling systems reflect this unique quality of speech,
bringing the various endings into vocalic line with the vowel of
the root. Thus one may say in Turkish *dağlarımdan* ("towards
our mountains") in which back vowels chime with the -*a*- of
dağ-; in contrast, "towards our flowers" would be *çiçeklerimden*,
in which the vowels -*e*-, -*i*-, and -*e*- replace -*a*-, -*ı*-, and -*a*-, so as
to approximate the frontal values of the vowels in *çiçek*-
("flower"). Similarly in Hungarian: *ház*ban ("in a house"), but
*kesztyü*ben ("in a glove").

These Ural-Altaic tongues in one sense may be thought of as
strangers in our midst. Though we still regard the Turks as
only halfway European, the Hungarians and Finns have been so
much a part of the West, both culturally and politically, that it is
usually only the student of their languages who may think of
them as true aliens. A walk down the streets of Helsinki or
Budapest (this latter before the Soviet suppression of 1956)
would show nothing indicative of a once-Asiatic past. Yet to this

day the speech of these peoples remains a legacy of the steppe and the lands beyond that are the East.

*   *

We brought in mention of the Ural-Altaic super-family by stating that Turkish had discarded the Arabic alphabet. One sentence earlier we were regretting that Persian had not. This coolness toward the script of Islam would be bad manners indeed if it were not that it is the virtues, not the defects, of this form of writing which make it a poor choice for any non-Semitic speech. For both the Arabic *alif-ba'* and the Hebrew *aleph-bet* (two related scripts, though today so different in appearance) are *consonantal writing appropriate to a consonantal structuring of speech*.

By a consonantal structuring of speech we do not mean that Arab or Israeli speak without vowels, but merely that the vowels which do in fact occur play only a secondary role in the conveyance of meaning. The primary kernel of significance in Semitic tongues is a group of consonants (usually three) which in and of itself is unpronounceable. Thus, both in Arabic and Hebrew the tri-consonantal *k-t-b* conveys the notion of "writing"; Arabic has its *kitab* ("book"), *katib* ("scribe," "writer"), *yekteb* ("to write"), *kutiba* ("it was written") and myriad other forms; Hebrew its *k'tivah* ("writing"), *katuba* ("bill of divorcement"), *k'tov* ("to write").[7] The associated vowels—arranged in distinct and fairly regular patterns—are distributed before, after and/or within the consonantal framework in accordance with strict grammatical and syntactic principles. To the native reader, they came as "second nature." An explicit rendering of them on paper,

---

[7] As shown in the Hebrew pair *katuba:k'tivah,* where *b* and *v* alternate, a limited change of the consonants—not merely the vowels—is possible; but when such changes do occur, they are always between related and/or similar sounds: e.g., *tsahov* ("golden," masc. sing.) and *ts'huba* (fem. sing.); *kelev* ("dog") and *kalbi* ("my dog"); *panim* ("face") and *lifnay* ("in the face of" or "in front of"). *Panim* affords an example of the comparatively rare bi-consonantal cluster—*p*(f)-*n*.

except in comparatively rare instances where ambiguity would be possible, appears as awkwardly superfluous to the literate Arab or Israeli as some system of notation in our language indicating the various modulations of pitch. We supply these automatically from life-long acquaintance with our tongue; Arabs and Israelis do, too, and in addition they interpolate the appropriate vowels.

Thus, *within the context of a Semitic tongue,* this consonantal alphabet is entirely adequate. In one sense, the consistent addition of vowels would be a lessening of "efficiency," since it would involve the addition of extraneous matter; and as certain Semitic scholars have pointed out, the purely consonantal transcription makes clear at a glance the fundamental structure of the word, unobscured by the shifting and transient vocalic commentary. Of course, the absence of vowels makes matters somewhat more difficult for the student of Arabic or Hebrew who comes to the language from a non-Semitic speech-community, and grammars and elementary readers are generally printed with a system of subsidiary vowel-notation added. (These vowel signs—small dots, dashes and hooks placed above, below or at one side of the consonant, and not considered true members of the alphabet —are indigenous inventions, evolved to dispel chance ambiguities and to insure absolutely faithful transmission of sacred writ down the centuries.)

*   *

Four of the minor tongues of Europe (i.e., languages with a relatively small number of speakers) arrange themselves neatly into paired contrast: *Lithuanian* and *Lettish* (Latvian) show just how staunchly conservative a language can remain, even over millennia; *Albanian* and *Armenian* are witness to how widely speech can change. It would be a pardonable exaggeration to say that the first two tongues (the only surviving members of the Baltic linguistic sub-family) can be described as

"Sanskrit of the Twentieth Century." In vocabulary, sound structure, and grammatical system Lithuanian and (to a slightly lesser extent) Lettish have remained incredibly faithful to the old Indo-European pattern. Such phrases as the Lithuanian *Su Diev* or Lettish *Ar Dievu*, Lithuanian *dūmai* ("smoke," cf. Sanskrit *dhūmas*) or *katras* ("which," cf. Sanskrit *kataras*) would have been understood in India two thousand years ago.

Albanian and Armenian, on the contrary, were long thought not to be Indo-European at all. Such were the changes wrought by time, migration, and war that only the most penetrating analysis has shown these two tongues to be true members of that great family of languages to which our own belongs. Much of the vocabulary of these tongues has been supplied by non-Indo-European peoples, though the existence of such forms as the Albanian *ty* ("thou") and *na* ("we," cf. Latin *nōs*), Armenian *tasn* ("ten," cf. Latin *decem*) and *hayr* ("father") helped in the search for these languages' antecedents. Even Indo-European words re-borrowed at a later date in these tongues' histories have often been altered almost completely out of recognition. Who would associate the Albanian *mbreti* ("king") with the Latin *imperator* ("emperor"), or *mik* with *amicus*? A measure of the far-reaching changes undergone can be seen in the Armenian words for *two* and *three* (transliterated to our alphabet), *erku* and *erekh*. Historically these two words have developed from a pair of words related to both the Latin *duo, tre* and our two names for these numbers.

*   *

One language in Europe stands as an absolute riddle and constant challenge to linguistic genealogists: the Basque spoken in the Pyrénées on both sides of the Franco-Spanish border. A tongue whose structure bears no relationship to any other known (a legend has it that the Devil tried to learn it for seven long years—and failed), Basque apparently constitutes an entire fam-

ily of its own. The author is of the opinion that Basque is, in
fact, New High Cro-Magnon: a contemporary descendant of the
language spoken by those completely human cave men who produced great paintings in the south of France some 20,000 years
ago. There is no proof whatsoever to support such a belief—but
then again, there is absolutely no evidence to contradict it. Until
such time as someone succeeds in showing otherwise, the author
will keep this domesticated crotchet as a well-loved pet; a foible,
but—he trusts—a harmless one.

*   *

Of those three dark continents, Africa and the Americas,
North and South, one may say almost anything. The situation
is so completely confused and complex that almost any statement made with regard to Language in these regions will prove
to be true of at least one tongue in the area.

Excluding the Arabic-speaking North, perhaps the largest
single family of African tongues is summed up in the one word:
Bantu. The characteristic feature of these languages which never
fails to impress the prospective student is their concord-with-
a-vengeance. Not the puny three-gender concord of Latin, Greek
and Russian; when the Bantus wish to partition Reality, they do
a thorough job of it, and their languages may assign nouns to
as many as seventeen categories. Along with the concepts of
male and female (roughly analogous to the Indo-European
"masculine" and "feminine"), flexional status is often equally
given to such pigeon-holings as: round objects, objects considered continuous or indivisible, granular collections, small
objects, objects marked by wide spatial extent, etc., etc.

Within a given category the affixes—*pre*fixes—normally differentiate between the singular and the plural (and sometimes
indicate specific numerical distinctions other than simply *one* vs.
many: the so-called *dual*—which also occurs in Greek and
Sanskrit—indicates *two* of a thing). Thus, *Bantu* itself means

simply "men"; "man" is *Muntu*—while the collective term for the tribe or the-people-as-a-whole is *Ubantu*. One might therefore say in a Bantu tongue: *Bvakala bantu* as against *Mvakala muntu* —"There were men" as contrasted with, "There was a man." This concord of initial sounds throughout all the associated parts of speech—nouns, adjectives *and* verbs—links together those utterances considered logically connected in a far more precise fashion than can the rather simple-minded (by comparison) three-gender, eight-case system of primitive Indo-European.

In its earliest form the Bantu languages were probably uninfluenced by the so-called *clicks*. (The sounds, common in many "Black African" tongues and reminiscent of the "tsk-tsk" we make in commiseration or the cluck of giddyap encouragement made to horses, presumably originated with the Bushmen.) Somewhere and somewhen among those small, wise and secretive people of the interior—Negroes only by virtue of dark coloring—these phonemes came into being as integral parts of human utterance. But they have spread to the tongues of other peoples. Some conservative Bantu languages—Luganda, for instance—are completely innocent of them to this day, however.[8]

Yet though the Bantu group of tongues is perhaps the most representative, there is one non-Bantu language which is probably the single most widely-spoken language (aside from English, French or Arabic) in all Africa: the tongue known as *Hausa* or *Xosa*. There are perhaps some twenty million of the world's people who know this speech as their own. Its affiliations are obscure; it is spoken by people of unmistakably Negroid or Negro stock, yet there is some evidence to indicate that the language may have come originally from the North; a *Hamitic* language,

---

[8] As illustration of the essentially prefixing nature of the Bantu tongues: the *language* is "Luganda"; the name of the *people* is "Baganda"; a single member of this folk is a "Muganda"; while the name of the country itself is "Buganda." Though the root-form "-ganda" does not normally occur alone (any more than the "Engl-" of "English," "Englishmen," "Englishman," or "England," this kernel form still bears its own full measure of meaning, perhaps roughly equivalent to the notion of "man" or "people." Thus: *Luganda*, "peoplish"; *Baganda*, "people"; *Muganda*, "person," or "one-of-the-people"; and *Buganda*, "the-land-of-the-people," i.e., *Bugandaland*, "land-of-the-Ganda."

perhaps—kin to the speech of the ancient Egyptians, the Coptic church-language of the inhabitants of Upper (Southern) Egypt to this day, and a possible cousin to the tongue of the mysterious Berbers who share the desert country uneasily with the Arabic-speaking Bedouin of the Sahara.

These Berbers are not Arab by any stretch of the imagination. They would probably take to the man who suggested this with knife, rifle, and a vengeance. Among this people, it is the men who wear the veil—proudly and fiercely. Aside from the Berbers themselves, and a handful of French administrative officials and professional philologists, there are few if any who know the ways of their speech. One thing can be said in safety, nevertheless: the Berbers have managed a set of consonant clusters well nigh impossible for strangers to pronounce: thus—*ttss,* "to fall asleep," in which not only the -*ss* is truly a doubled [s] (easy enough to pronounce for the Westerner, given enough practice), but in which the *tt-* is an honestly doubled [t]. Let any tongue not born to it, or accustomed to spectacular muscular acrobatics, try *that* sound.

*   *

We have spoken earlier of some of the oddities (to our way of thinking) implicit in the languages of the Amerind. There are no generalizations possible concerning the languages of this proud people who lived on the broad lands before we came. Some spoke tongues as monosyllabic and as analytic as Chinese; others found the shape of their thoughts in languages as purely "rational" as Latin or Greek. There were other tribes whose way of life was as broad and sternly gay as the horizon, and they used their voice and throat in a completely polysynthetic speech— their word would have been our whole-hearted and whole-thoughted sentences.

Some of them walked through forests, some made a way of life from the view that a man catches from the height of a horse's back. Some saw the Tribe as a sufficiency; others built a nation, or even a Confederacy of nations. Whatever their pride or their achievement, they went by—and the memory of their lives, their languages, is a part of the dust that gathers on the *Handbook of American Indian Languages* or perhaps a single touch of remorseful remembrance toward a past of buffalo and joy in freedom.

Otto Jespersen, a Dane, suggested that the fantastic variety of Amerind tongues might be explained by child-abandonment. Perhaps, he thought, as the ancestors of the present-day Indian emigrated from Asia a millennia ago over what was then a bridge of dry land but is today the Bering Strait, children were lost or left behind along the way. And perhaps, *just* perhaps, some of these children were at a crucial age: old enough somehow to survive alone, but too young to be masters of the languages of their respective tribes.

Jespersen was one of the giants of Linguistics, a scholar whose spirit—an admirable one—shines out clearly from almost every page he wrote. Yet about this theory one must have the strongest reservations. First of all, it is inherently unprovable (though we must remember that Jespersen, born in 1860, belonged to a generation which still had the imaginative generosity to yearn for ultimate explanations). Worse still, even accepted as a possibility, though an unverifiable one, it cannot explain all that it sets out to explain. A child is in some small measure conversant with its parents' tongue by the age of 3 or 4; to reconstruct a completely new variety of tongue, the abandonees would have to have been younger even than that, and such children would not have been likely to have survived as two-year olds in the uncompromising cruelty of a new and empty continent.

Your good Logical Positivist will reject out of hand any sort of speculation which cannot be confirmed by observational data, but if we wish to be heretical about the matter, we might guess that a variety of causes help to shape the Amerind tongues; the scattering of children along the immigrants' route may have played a part, but in all probability, only a small one. First we should admit the possibility that *there may have been others here first*—even before the Indian. The origins of Man are supremely obscure. It seems all but certain that he did not evolve in the New World, but there may well have been incursions of humankind at a relatively low level of culture long before the nearly historical Amerind folk-wanderings of ten to fifteen thousand years ago.

(Thomas Wolfe once asked, rhetorically: What man knows his father? and wrote incessantly of Man's wanderings over the earth to find his identity. The same plight in a literal sense is that of the anthropologist or any student of Man before recorded history. We know pathetically little of ourselves, even as we are today. When we attempt the journey up that long river of Time . . . who can be sure? At most we can be supremely grateful for any small fragments of flint or pottery or bone which tell of our fathers who came before us.)

Then again, in contemplating the dazzling variety of Indian languages, we should remember that the Asian home of these peoples was itself the probable scene of diverse modes of speech. Within the borders of China today there are such little-known tongues as Lo-Lo and Miao; in India itself there is Khoreswashti —as mysterious in its affiliation as is Basque. There is no reason to think that the proto-Amerinds belonged to a single linguistic stock, or even to kindred stocks. Within the last two generations, a single boat would often bring to these shores a collection of peoples bound together by little but the desire to leave their old homes. One and the same ship could carry—often in steerage —Irish, Germans, Yiddish-speaking Jews, Russians and Lithuanians, all speakers of Indo-European tongues (though only a philologist would probably be aware of the fundamental identity), Finns and Hungarians (whose languages are kin to one another, but alien to their fellow-passengers), and perhaps even a Basque sheepherder or two.

Something like this potpourri of languages may have made up the picture of those earlier immigrants—the ones who got here first, and whom we have successfully robbed of their lands and ways of life. We can not be sure that this is the case, and such an explanation only places the problem of ultimate kinship further back in time; but at least such a theory would account for the large number of apparently unrelated tongues spoken on this continent when the White Man came.

*   *

Over a broad expanse of the Pacific are found the Melanesian languages. As we might guess from the name, Malay, that admirably regular tongue (see p. 31), is a member of this family though it should not be taken as the necessarily ancestral or normative dialect. In some respects, however, it does occupy a mediating position.

Tagalog, for instance—one of the better-known Filipino languages, and often suggested as a common tongue for those language-ridden islands—is a member of the Melanesian clan. A tongue of respectable phonemic complexity, it is marked by a wealth of inflectional forms comparable with those of German. As in German, much of the task of indicating case relationships lies with the definite article. With a common noun such as *arao* ("week") one employs *ang, sa* or *nang* in the singular, and one of these three + *manga* in the plural. There is a separate form of the article used with proper names only, as in *si Carlos, ni Carlos, kay Carlos,* where these three forms are roughly equivalent to nominative, genitive, and generalized oblique, respectively. Peculiar to Tagalog is a set of additive forms of the proper-name version of the article; thus: *sina Carlos* (*bukid*)—"Carlos and (his field)"; (*ang bukid*) *nina Carlos*— "(the field) of Carlos and his people"; and *ang kana Carlos* (*bukid*)—"to" or "from" "Carlos and (his field)," or "(the field) of Carlos and his people" as the object of a sentence. Prefixes are freely used, as in *ikalawa* ("second"), *makalawa* ("twice") and *daladalawa* ("by two's" or "two by two") formed from the cardinal number *dalawa* ("two").

At the other end of the spectrum stand Samoan and Hawaiian, whose flexional apparatus is, if possible, even barer than that of Malay, and which exhibit an amazing degree of phonemic (and phonetic) simplification. Case-relational notions are expressed by word-order (as in Chinese and, largely, in English) and a change in position of sentence elements can result in ludicrous misunderstandings: thus, Samoan *ua tiga lou tina* ("His mother is sick") vs. *ua tina lou tiga* ("His pain is a mother"). Perhaps most surprising is the degree of phonemic frugality achieved by these tongues, and reflected in their faithful scripts. Hawaiian has the smallest "alphabet" of any known tongue, twelve units in all: A, E, I, O, and U, plus the seven consonants, H, K, L, M, N, P, and W. Samoan lacks the Hawaiian H, K, and W, but in compensation possesses F, G, S, T, and V.

In spite of this wide gamut of variation, these languages do form one historically related group, as can be seen in a small handful of core words, the number "five," for example: *elima* (Hawaiian), *lima* (Malay), *e lima* (Samoan) and *lima* (Tagalog).

*   *

There is also in the Pacific another cluster of language-families of great potential interest to the student of languages—the native tongues of Australia. Many in the eastern and southern parts of this great island continent apparently form a group, but in the North-West quadrant there seem to exist three totally unrelated stocks. None of these aboriginal Australian languages bears a traceable relationship to any other mode of speech, though there have been suggestions that the "abo's" may have originally come from India, before the invasion of Indo-European-speaking peoples. Unfortunately, these languages still await the intensive sort of study given the Amerind languages. Grammars have been written describing Aranta, Kamilaroi and a few others, but nothing like systematic study of the linguistic situation-as-a-whole has been achieved; and such is the rate at which the "blackfellow"—who in spite of his name has many of the characteristics of white stock, and is most definitely *not* a Negro—is dying off, that it seems unlikely there will be enough time left for thoroughgoing analysis of the native speech.

It was thought at one time that Australian languages might give some clue as to the origins of human language in general. This was back in the bad old days of anthropological evolutionary dogma. The theory then current was that the absolute height of creation was the "civilized" European (preferably of Northern stock). Starting from this apex of culture and wisdom, so the doctrine ran, one worked down a ladder of lesser breeds (generally of increasing swarthiness) until one hit rock bottom with the "abo," supposedly a living fossil unchanged since Neolithic times.

Since then, it has been realized that human history resembles the ribs of a fan more than it does the rungs of a ladder; we all started off at about the same time, and have made appropriate adaptations to the surroundings in which we found ourselves. Each of the varieties of Man apparently has an equally long history behind him. As if in confirmation of this insight, those who actually took the trouble to *learn* Kamilaroi, for instance, found that it had a respectable case-system of its own: *duggaidu*––(nominative); *duggainubba*–(possessive); *duggaida*–(ablative); etc.

It is a pity that we are unable to learn much of the language(s) of the Tasmanians, the inhabitants of that island to the south of Australia. Unfortunately this is impossible since the Tasmanians are dead—killed off to a man by the civilized Europeans who at one point hunted them to be used as dog food. The Tasmanians seem to have been akin to the Australians, and presumably their languages would have reflected the kinship. The question is, however, academic.[9]

It is perhaps unfair to single out the original Tasmanian settlers for especial attention in this matter of premature genocide, however. Double-dealing and slaughter seem unfortunately all too common when one people wishes the land of another, and if the disparity in arms is great—and those with the better weapons decide they can do without slaves—extinction (immediate, or by degrees) appears to be the rule. Whatever became of the Picts, for example? As a people, at least, they were effectively eradicated, though doubtless much of their blood still flows in British veins. It is of interest that the highest concentration of non-Saxon and non-Norman population lies in the hilly country of Wales, while the Basques have been confined to the mountains between Spain and France. It was apparently the ill fortune of the "abo's" to live on a continent with too much flat land. It is difficult to roll boulders down on your enemies when you are both on the same plain.

*   *

Let us hope that Voltaire was being overly-cynical when he wrote that "History is little more than the chronicle of human crimes and disasters." Appearances to the contrary, he may have been wrong. In spite of the growing ferocity of war and diplomacy within the last generation (and let us hope that it is "last" only in the sense of "most recent"), there *have* been green and struggling shoots of what may be an increasing piety towards our surroundings—natural *and* human.

Within the last half-century we have seen the sometimes-uncertain flowering of a conservation movement. For the first time,

[9] Western Civilization was decidedly efficient in its solution of the Tasmanian Problem. The first settlers arrived in 1803; by 1876 they had succeeded in adding the natives to the list of extinct wildlife. The skeleton of the last survivor—a female named Trucanini—is presently in the Hobart museum. The honor is perhaps a consolation.

men have begun to realize that they cannot slash and burn, exploit and slaughter, indefinitely. So far, most stress has been laid on the non-human; the last passenger pigeon—like the last Tasmanian, a female—may have pecked the dust in 1914, but some attention is at least paid to preservation of the redwood, the bison, and the ivory-billed woodpecker.

Among anthropologists at least, there has also been interest in preservation of Man, providing the potential extinctee is sufficiently non-European in orientation and reduced enough in numbers to make his passing a real possibility. But, though making immense strides, Anthropology is still something less than a positive science, and the advice of its followers does not carry as much weight as it might in the councils of the administrators. The dealings of the West with more "backward" folk have improved over the days when native populations were blithely civilized beneath the ground, but there are still improvements to be made in various spots throughout the globe—providing, of course, that Western Man succeeds in preserving *himself* from extinction.

C. S. Lewis—the well-known English moralist, novelist and scholar—pointed out in his *Out of the Silent Planet* the virtues of diversification. In his allegorical picture of the planet Mars, three utterly unlike, yet highly intelligent, species co-exist in friendship: (1) the *hrossa*—otterlike beings who are natural singers, dancers and poets; (2) the *séroni*—vaguely manlike in form, and brilliant theoretical scientists; and (3) the *pfifltriggi*—toadish-insectile folk who love mining, pictorial art and the creation of instruments or machines. Though each is completely alien to the other two in appearance, culture and temperament; a common affection and respect binds all three together, for they are all *hnau*—rational. And they are complementary facets of one unified, and civilized, Society. Each sees a fraction of the universe passed over by the others, and the community of *hnau*dom is infinitely richer for the three varieties of experience.

It is perhaps too much to expect that this sort of wisdom will be found on earth. Both we and the Soviets are certain that our respective systems—sub-varieties of a common technological culture—are just what the underdeveloped nations and territories need. And such is the prestige and might of Communist East and Capitalist West, that many a newly-emergent nation clamors for our techniques and procedures. Such nations generally express a determination to combine the advantages of modern science-and-technology with the traditional values of their societies, but the prospect for success is a dim one. Historically, once the camel gets his foot into the tent, the rest of the beast has been observed to follow soon after.

Perhaps the most that can be hoped for is that the anthropological imagination can make the transition a less deadly procedure than in the past. Certain fragments of non-European life may manage to keep their identity—conceivably even flourish—in the new setting. Who knows? It is even a possibility that all concerned may decide that a diversity of cultural (and linguistic) world-viewpoints (like the stereoptic effect of two-eyed vision) is worth the trouble. The resultant three-dimensional view of the human, and universal, situation may be considered a good bargain even at the cost of certain sacrifices in ideological certainty.

*　　　*

Both the pessimist and the realist would look askance at the remarks expressed above, and they may be right. The lesson of the Maoris of New Zealand is a sad tribute to Man, for the Maoris *have* retained their identity and been accorded the respect of the white settlers. A number of them are authors, scientists, and members of the government; a good many have been knighted. But the Maoris were a well-organized and a warlike people. When the gloss is stripped from their story, the moral is this: be invaded by settlers whose weapons are not *infinitely* superior to yours; have jungle and mountain to retreat to; and kill many, many strangers—for that is the only sure way to gain their respect.

$\mathscr{D}$ I4

A Horatio Alger story: English

> ". . . the English tongue is of small reach, stretching no farther than this island of ours, and not there over all."
>
> —*Richard Mulcaster*, teacher to Edmund Spenser.
> (written in 1582)

In the beginning—an island which shone far off in good weather, for its cliffs were of gleaming chalk. In foul seasons—and the climate was treacherous—a small world of its own wrapped in raw fog. This was Britain.

It was an island which invited invasion from the Channel where the cliffs were comparatively low, and beyond them, mile after mile of rolling plain. We shall never know who the first inhabitants were, or from where they came. Long before the Celts arrived, however, there were the Iberians: that small, dark people whose likeness is found to this day in many a Welshman or Irishman. They were the ones who came down to the shore to trade with the Phoenicians who sailed to the edge of the world in search of tin and anything else which might be bartered or stolen. (The distinction between merchant and raider was dim in those days.) Originally wielders of flint, "the Dark People" mastered in time the uses of bronze; they were far from being savages. Quite likely it was they, or some other obscure folk of the time, who raised Stonehenge in honor of the solstices: a feat we would find respectably difficult even today.

What language or languages they spoke we do not know. It was not the ancestor of Welsh, Irish and Scottish, however. That was brought in (in at least two sharply differentiated dialects) by the Celts, who subdued Britain much, much later—sometime about the 6th century B.C. We know something of this latter people from the documents of the Romans, who conquered them in turn. They were apparently a tallish people with light eyes and a tendency to red hair. Even if all other things had been equal, the Iberian aborigines of Britain might have given way, for the Celts would have had a longer reach—important in swordplay. But these big-boned invaders had an additional advantage, the ultimate weapon of the time: swords made of iron. The littler, bronze-using people had to give way.

A visit to the Welsh countryside will show that obviously the Iberians were not exterminated. Perhaps it was then that the first of those stubborn retreats to the western mountains took place; the Dark People surrendering their beloved territory reluctantly, and taking as many of the red-headed strangers down to the Underworld as they could before a single acre was given up. It *is* true, whatever the historical explanation for it, that the highest concentration of Iberian blood lies in the West Country.

The Celts established their dialects as the speech of the islands (the Irish Channel having been almost immediately crossed), and there seems to exist no word to which we can point and say with certainty that *this* is a surviver of pre-Celtic days. In the course of time the conquerers set up a relatively well-organized society of tribes and confederacies, but a society in which shifting alliances and internecine warfare seem to have been commonplace. Nevertheless, certain tribes of the South had developed a system of money and coinage by 150 B.C. (copied from the golden coins of the kings of Macedonia), and it was at least a *semi*-civilized population of barbarians who dominated Britain when the *next* invaders appeared on the scene: the legions of Caesar.

The Roman occupation of Britain, insofar as it brought the light of a city culture ("civilization" in its most precise sense) to the dark of the island, was a false dawn. For a scant 400 years the Romans managed to hold Britain, but when they left it was almost as if they had never been. Two things only they left behind: the pride of Rome—roads; and the scandal of Rome, pagan Rome—Christianity.

For a while it seemed as though Roman civilization might put down lasting roots in British soil. The comforts and luxuries of town life were attractive, and in the central portions of the island a true Latin-Celtic sub-culture flourished—for a while. The Iberians in the vastness of wild Wales, and the Celtic tribes of the hinterland might preserve the ways of their fathers; but in the towns—Camulodunum ("Colchester"), Glevum ("Gloucester"), Londinium and the rest—the Celtic chieftains and their people began to adopt the dress, the manners, and the language of the Empire. Villas dotted the safer parts of the countryside. In time there came intermarriage and by about 250 A.D. there existed a Celto-Roman culture and a Celto-Roman people. But in the North and West the old dark ways of the tribe hung on. Now *both* dispossessed, tribal Celt and tribal Iberian finally began to learn the art of living in peace, doubtless bitter and enraged at the hybrid society in the South.

But things were happening back on the Continent, even in Rome itself. Decay was slow at first, and this young provincial culture probably thought it was still living at high noon long after its sun had begun the sad fall to the west. Twilight was near. The legions began to fall back as troubles made themselves felt at the heart of the Mediterranean world. On the abandoned island, weeds pushed up among the cobblestones, and the long straight roads which cut across the moors and through the forests fell back into the wild undergrowth that had always been there—waiting. The old, unconverted tribes moved back toward the South, cautiously and by stages. Perhaps they burned an outlying farm or two, the owner and his family (their faces a queer blending of Britain and Italy) stammering fearfully in heavily-accented Brythonic.

Civilization was given up, and often surrendered voluntarily. There were the occasional raids and burnings, but from the little we can still unearth, it appears that the exodus from the towns was frequently a willing flight. With the falling-off in trade and commerce, and the recall of the armies with the attendant loss of security, urban and urbane life became first a luxury and then an impossibility. There must have been many a Roman citizen (born in the island and never having seen Rome) who watched his grandchild scamper through the mud streets of some shabby village, jabbering away in pure Brythonic to his playmates whose fathers dressed in skins and had never heard of wine or letters. It may have been precisely one of those grandchildren who, having heard his gaffer mumble something about writing but never having learned a single letter, devised the *Ogham:* a series of parallel lines cut into stone.

Then, for a century or two, we know nothing.

And it was during this period of which we know so little that the Saxon Conquest took place. Late in the 300's we catch our last glimpses of the Celto-Roman world, and it is falling to pieces before our eyes. Sometime in the 500's the picture clears once more, but now it is a totally different world we gaze on: a world in which the German tribes are ascendant. But lost forever in the centuries between those two moments are a handful of events which shaped what was to become England for all time to come. Vortigern, Hengist, Horsa—we have nothing but their names and scraps of legend. How much of the legend is fact, how much fancy, we can not say.

And this was the time of the greatest English legend of all; a time when there may have existed a man attempting to hold fast to something of the vanished Roman glory, battling against the darkness and losing somewhere in the West. He may have called himself *dux bellorum* (Latin for "war commander"); he may have been nothing more than an unusually powerful chieftain. His name may have been Ambrosius, it may have been Artos. But we remember him as a King whose name was Arthur.

Though the arrival of the Saxon did not signal the extinction of the Celtic tongues, they were restricted to the West and North, along the borders of German-occupied territory. Thoroughly pagan to begin with, the Saxons (as well as their close kin the Angles and Jutes) were soon converted to Christianity and the use of the Roman alphabet. (They had come to the island already in possession of the *Runes,* an angular form seemingly derived from an early Greek or Greek-Italian alphabet of very early times. The Germanic peoples who used this writing—principally for the inscription of incantations and statements of ownership on swords, etc., did not know the collection as an *alphabet,* however. It was to them the *futhark*—called such from the first six letters.)

Though relations with the Romano-Celto-Iberian subject population were probably something less than cordial ("Saesneg" is still the Welsh semi-generic term for foreigner-in-general, used with a touch of opprobrium), the Germans managed to establish a fairly settled way of life. The typical raider was essentially not an irresponsible burner and reaver, after all. Though the first tentative landings at river mouths or channel beachsides may have been for hurried acquisition of loot, once it was found how easily one might move into this disorganized land the next boatloads came with property-rights in view. And in not too long a time, Britain had become England—the Land of the Angles (Saxons, and Jutes).

And later—much to the dismay of the by-this-time-acclimatized Germans—Land of the Danes, as well.

Seen from the long perspective of our day, there seems little to choose from between these two Teutonic folk; but to the typical Saxon franklin, *ealdorman* or *thegn,* thoroughly at home after a century or two or three of residence, these latest comers were a terror. (Almost certainly the pre-German inhabitants of the land—now collectively known as Welsh [*wealsc,* "foreign"]

—sat back in the hills grinning happily. Let the two packs of dogs fight it out among themselves. The fewer there would be left afterwards.)

These new folk were Scandinavian and, if the Anglo-Saxon records are to be trusted, fearsome indeed. It should be remembered, however, that these are the chronicles not of the invader but of the invadee. The Celtic tales and poems of the Saxon incursions of three hundred years before tell of acts fully as bloody and fierce.

There was, however, one important difference. The Dano-English conflict was no matter of savagedom vs. civilization-fallen-into-barbarism. Strange as the customs and language of pre-Norman England may seem to us, the land of the "Angl-ish" was one in which the future—not the past—was bright with possibilities. It was a land in which towns were growing, not falling apart. It was a land which began to see a resurgence of trade and commerce. Towns and villages had their churches and monasteries had begun to dot the countryside. There was even —under Alfred the Great—a growing interest in and patronage of art and education.

The age was a rough one, however, and each side was cruel. Though we may not find it too surprising that the viking Scandinavians of the time had a reputation for brutality, it is rather a shock to realize that the English themselves were not too civilized to forebear the nailing of slaughtered Danes' skins to the door of the local church. Eventually peace was established, even so. The Danes—who, it subsequently appeared, had latent agricultural and domestic ambitions of their own—were allotted part of the island as their own (the *Danelaw*) in which they might follow their native ways and customs. In return, the Danes swore an end to hostilities and their ruler, Guthrum, accepted the Cross. And for roughly a century and a half, England knew something approximating peace.

England was now an island of two peoples—the Saxon[1]

[1] Including Angles, Jutes, Danes and any other non-Celts. And as we have seen, "Celt" is itself a misnomer.

(*Saesneg, Sessenach*) and (outside of Ireland) the Welsh, between whom there would be sporadic fighting for centuries.
They were set against one another in many ways: the natural
hostility of an ousted people for the usurper; difference in religious practice—Celtic vs. Roman rite (the Saxons and Danes
had been converted to the latter version); clan blood loyalty as
against the Germanic system of non-familial war bands and fel-
lowships. And of course there was the barrier erected by the very
words each group spoke: the difference in language.

Most of this chapter will be devoted to a brief résumé of the
English tongue, but it would be both misleading and ungrateful
not to acknowledge the existence of that family of languages
which still share the British Isles with our own, and which long
pre-dated ours. Though we can not go into a detailed account of
the speech of the "Celtic Fringe," we may at least pay it the
honor of recognition.

Even today, probably no one but a student of linguistics is
aware of it—and certainly the first confrontees did not know, or
care—the languages of Saxon and Celt are distant kin, bound
together by the venerable and long-dead Indo-European. This
consanguinity is *not* demonstrated by such resemblances of vocabulary as the Welsh *capel* and Irish *séipéal*, "chapel," or Welsh
stesion and Irish *stáisiún* "(railroad) station." It can easily be
shown that such terms are the result of borrowings made long
after the ancient divergence of the Indo-European tongues from
a common standard.[2]

It is in a meagre store of words, widely changed in pronunciation since Indo-European days, that the essential oneness in language of Cymro, Gael and Saxon can be seen—by the eye sharp

[2] The very similarity of the forms to comparatively recent language forms is
evidence of this: *capel* is obviously modelled on either the Latin *capella* or the
(dialect) French *capelle*; *séipéal* (pronounced with an initial "sh," is in all
likelihood taken directly from the English. *Stesion* and *stáisiún* (both pronounced approximately as is the corresponding English word) show their
origin quite obviously in their pronunciation and their limited meaning. The
word would not be used, for instance, in speaking of "Stations of the Cross,"
or in the general sense of any "place to stand."

enough to see it. Thus, those basic vocables, the numbers, which in the lower range are rarely borrowed—since most peoples can count to five at least—have obviously been forged on a common anvil:

Welsh—*un, dau, tri, pedwar, pump, chwech, saith, wyth, naw, deg*
Irish—*haon, dó, trí, ceathair, cúig, sé, seacht, hocht, naoi, deich*
English—*one, two, three, four, five, six, seven, eight, nine, ten*

And furthermore, these numbers show kinship with other tongues as well. Compare, for instance, the Latin:

ūnus, duo, trēs, quattuor, quinque, sex, septem, octō, novem, decem

and even the Russian (transliterated into our alphabet):

odin, dve, tri, chetyre, p'at', shest', s'em', vos'em', d'evyat' and *d'es'at'.*

The similarity extends even further than to simple numerals. Words obviously primary in any language, and hence almost always preserved, also reveal points of common origin. Thus: Welsh *ŵyr*, Irish *fear*, Latin *vir*, Saxon *wer* all express "man," yet have existed independently as long as their respective tongues have had separate identities.[3] The Welsh *haul* and *hal* ("sun" and "salt") are ultimately one with Latin *sōl* and *sal*, as are the Irish *seasaím* ("I stand") and *ithim* ("I eat") with the corresponding forms of the Latin *stare* and *edere* or Anglo-Saxon *standan* and *etan*.

However, prospective landowners are not generally interested in the linguistic affiliations of those they are in the process of forceably dispossessing, nor are their victims any more predisposed to philological research. Each side is far too busy attempting to kill off the other—at least in the beginning, before there is any attempt made to co-exist in peace. And even when the most virulent forms of warfare had died down, it was tacitly

---

[3] *Wer* survives in modern English only in such terms as *wer(e)wolf*, literally, "man-wolf"; and *wergild*, "man-payment, man-money" which a manslayer was obliged to pay to the blood kin of his victim in lieu of physical punishment.

assumed by the medieval Establishment that the Welsh might be allowed to live in safety—among the mountains; the *decent* land, however, was to go to the victor. The Saxons were quite happy with this arrangement—until the Normans arrived. Unfortunately, by this time there were no mountains left for the Saxons; all those available were already filled by Celts, whose spears were—if possible—even longer than their memories. This probably explains why there is an English language today, rather than an odd form of French—with a hypothetical Welsh-Saxon or Saxon-Welsh spoken by irreconcilables in the West Country.

It is a pity that the speakers of what was to become English never took more trouble with the language of their opponents. It might have led to a reduction in bloodshed—either through a lessening of enmity, or by the principle that the best way to fight your enemy is to know him. If nothing else, it might have gone far to simplify the Anglo-Saxon tongue, if reform-by-contagion is valid in linguistic history.

Even today, the *spoken* languages of Wales and the Gaeltacht (the Irish-speaking portion of Eire) present many attractive features. Cases have worn away—entirely in Welsh, and to a comparative nubbin in Irish. The word-order is straightforward in most instances, and the bane of most learners of a new language—the verb—is relatively simple. Characteristic of the Celtic tongues is a preference for the verb "to be" used together with nouns, adjectives or fossilized verb forms, as against full conjugation of each possible separate verb itself. The phrase meaning literally *I buy* is therefore used by and large as a future—*I shall buy*—while to express the present, Celtic idiom prefers *I am buying;* in like manner, *there is a hope in me* vs. *I hope* or even *I am hoping.*

Now that the passions and hatreds of the last thousand years have abated somewhat, it might be a gesture of friendliness on the part of more English-speakers if they took the trouble to acquaint themselves with the rudiments at least of the Celtic tongues. There are, however, three things which stand in the way of such linguistic conciliation: (1) absence of bread-and-butter need—throughout much of Wales and even more of Ireland one *can* get along in English; (2) the Welsh *w* and *ll*; (3) most forbidding of all—Irish spelling.

Little can be done about (1). It is impossible—and undesirable—to force the English-speaker to bother with a family of languages so unimportant from the so-called practical point of view. Hopefully, this chapter may prompt interest.

Point (2) seems far more formidable than it really is, for the main difficulty in Welsh springs from its superficial appearance —and in Welsh appearances are most deceiving of all. Those innocent of the language may be understandably fazed by such a form as *cwrw* ("beer"), for according to English lights, *W* has no business in a word all of whose other elements are consonants. Yet the spoken word is a rather simple thing—"cooroo"; in Welsh, *W* is an amphibian—either a vowel (close to our *oo* in "tool," "spoon," etc.) or a consonant (pronounced as in English). The Welsh *ll* on the contrary is not a familiar sound expressed by an unusual symbol, but rather an unusual phoneme written in what strikes the English eye as a commonplace way. For one *l* plus one *l*—in Welsh—does not make two *l*'s, nor even a prolonged version of the sound taken once. Rather, *ll* is simply a voiceless *l*, a consonant produced without vibration of the vocal cords. There is nothing intrinsically difficult about the sound— it is only that it does not exist in English as a distinct phoneme.[4]

About Irish spelling—only the authorities of the Ministry of Education and the Translation Branch of the Oireachtas have much chance of improving what is still an almost intolerable situation. Anyone who has even glanced at a modern Irish grammar has probably been frightened silly—and unlike the immediate reaction to Welsh words, *this* response is fully justified. A word such as *buidheachas* ("thanks") is almost as disconcerting

[4] In many persons' enunciation, however, it may occur as a *positional variant* when immediately following another voiceless consonant. Thus there is many an American or Englishman who pronounces *l* without voice in "please," though he gives it the voiced character in "bleed."

as *cwrw*. The brave student, however, after a second look may decide that things are not so bad as they seem—it is merely a matter of unfamiliar orthographic conventions. With the best will in the world, he will attempt something on the order of *bweedhayahkhas* as a hopefully-not-too-far-wrong rendering. Alas! Irish in its written form is a language in which things are even *worse* than they appear at first glance. Every tongue is entitled to its own conventions of spelling, but those of Irish are not merely unusual—to an outsider this is true of every language—what is worse, they bear next to no relationship to the sounds of the words. The author has never been able to decide which spelling is more outrageous: the English or the Irish,[5] but they certainly run a close race for the dubious honor of infidelity to the spoken tongues which they claim to represent. For *buidheachas* is as treacherous a form as is our "through"; it is, in fact, pronounced very roughly as "bekhuhs" (the *kh* like the *ch* in *Loch Ness, uh* reminiscent of the *a* in *sofa*.

It is true that certain reforms in Irish spelling were put into effect in 1948, but though they are improvements, the improvements could be improved upon. *Buidheachas* has now been reincarnated as *buíochas*, but to the unjaundiced eye there still appears to be a superfluity of consonants, and what consonants there are give the impression of being the wrong ones. Thus *cathair* ("city") and *cathaoir* ("chair") are both pronounced roughly as *kaheer*—the second member of the pair having a longer vowel—while *geimhreadh* ("winter") is approximately *gyeeryee*.

Spoken Gaelic is not a difficult tongue to learn, but attempts to learn the written form—and connect this with speech—are likely to remind the student of the Chinese water torture or death-of-a-thousand-cuts; just when one thinks the agony is about to end, something horribly unexpected comes over the orthographic horizon. The spelling of the language has probably discouraged a number of non-Gaelic-speaking Irishmen, and if

[5] He has tentatively awarded the booby prize to English, bending over backward to avoid ethnocentricity. However . . .

the idiosyncrasies of *Gaedhilge* can trouble an Ó Flaithbheartaigh (pronounced "O'Flaherty"), an Ó Séaghdha ("O'Shea") or a Mac Suibhne ("McSweeney"), you can well imagine what it is likely to do to such poor outlanders as Mr. Breathnach ("Walsh") or Ó hAirt ("Hart"—yes, it is the *A* not the *H* which is capitalized). The author can only wonder whether Irish orthography had any influence on the literary development of Séamus Seoigheach ("James Joyce").

Until enough letters of protest are sent to Dublin, however, there is only one *relatively* painless way to acquire the Irish tongue. The student must use a grammar which employs some system of phonetic re-spelling in conjunction with the official renderings. Otherwise he will soon be calling for *théalp*.[6]

*   *

The Danish and non-Danish invaders meanwhile had contrived to understand one another. This was not as difficult as we today—even recognizing the common Teutonism (See chapter 10) of Scandinavian and Germanic—would imagine. Even now, a thousand years later, the bonds between English on the one hand, and Swedo-Dano-Norwego-Islandic on the other are clear and unmistakable. In the 10th Century the North and South Teutonic groups were probably well within the limits of mutual intelligibility. When Saxon spoke to Dane there was in all likelihood a degree of understanding which no non-linguist citizen of London or København could appreciate today. (We might have added Stockholm and Oslo to the list, as well, for just as "Celt" and "Saxon" have become misleadingly generic terms, so "Dane" referred to the entire collection of Scandinavian North-Teutonic-speakers who went a-viking and eventually settled down in Britain.)

If the Saxons and the Celts were cousins, then Dane and Saxon were to all intents and purposes brothers. As Jespersen has pointed out, if we had no written material dating from be-

[6] Pronounced "help."

fore the Danish invasion it would be impossible to say whether such words as *father, mother, folk, come, see, think, stand, sit, good, mine, thine, over* and *under* had come down to modern English directly from Anglo-Saxon or from the common Scandinavian dialects of the more recent invaders. As it is, there are a number of words which we think of as "good old English" which were Danish imports. Examples of these pseudo-Anglo-Saxon immigrants are *ill, want* and (*to*) *die,* which no one but a scholar would guess had ever been absent from our ancestral tongue. (*Die* supplanted the original Anglo-Saxon *steorfan,* which then came to denote only "to die from lack of food" in the more familiar form *starve.* The Dutch and the Germans, however, have kept the South Germanic verb with its primal and extended meaning: *sterben, sterven. Ill* and *want,* in contrast, took their places beside *sēoc* and *willan* ("sick" and "will"), but did not oust the earlier Anglo-Saxon forms.)

Most amazing of all, a set of Norse *pronouns* came into use as dialect equivalents of the Anglo-Saxon, and over the course of centuries completely superseded them. (Pronouns are usually part of that fund of basic words which are discarded only with great rarity.) These are the various forms of the third-person plural—*they, their, them.* The reason for the acceptance of the Scandinavian forms seems to be that there was too much risk of confusion between the Anglo-Saxon *hē, hēo, hit* ("he," "she," "it") on the one hand, and *hīe* ("they" or "them") on the other. Besides, the Norse forms, beginning with *th-* sound, fitted well into the pattern of those native Anglo-Saxon articles and demonstratives which still survive in our *the, this, that.* The Scandinavian imports did not reach acceptance immediately, however, and we find Chaucer still using *hir*(*e*) and *hem* for "their" and "them," although *they* has managed to become the accepted form in the nominative; this was 400 years after the peaceful settlement of the Danes.

In many instances, where the Norse and the Anglo-Saxon forms of language were either identical, or at least highly similar, the Saxons began to use their words with some special connotation which had previously been peculiar to Norse usage alone. Thus, *ploh* in early Anglo-Saxon (before the arrival of the Danes) had referred only to a fixed area of land; *sulh* was the instrument used in tilling it. By contagion from the Norse *plógr*, which *did* refer to the farm tool, *sulh* fell into disuse, and now the only word in English to describe the implement is *plough* (*plow*). Similarly, Anglo-Saxon *dream* had only meant "joy"; in contact with the Norse *draumr*, it acquired its present meaning. *Bread* in the tongue of the early Saxons meant only "a piece, or fragment" of the loaf; while *hlāf* itself meant what we would call "bread." It was again the linguistic usage of the Danes which gave the present significance to these terms.

Thus, though the Saxon and Danish elements of the newly-fused Germanic population in England could speak one another's language, the language which resulted was one with a markedly different cast to it. If the Danes had never made their landings on English shores but the Normans had come later anyway, we should have found something *odd* or *wrong* in the resultant "modern English." It would take considerable *skill* to *root* out the exact nature of the differences; eventually we might seek *haven* in simple *anger* at those *fellows* who simply couldn't get it through their *skulls* that there was something *ugly* about the way they talked. Something about their English-with-a-difference would make our *skins* crawl, perhaps. Then again, it might be that their language would strike us as pleasant, rather than making us *ill;* human beings are pretty much alike, after all, living and *dying* under the same *sky*.

But one way or another, English without the Scandinavian element would have been quite another language indeed. The proof lies in the paragraph immediately preceding, for every italicized word comes not from the Anglo-Saxon, but from the Teutonic dialects of the North.

*   *

We must not imagine that once the Danes had been pacified all was peace and quiet; but at least what bloodshed there was constituted an almost normal part of the life of those days. The combat was between elements *within* a society, rather than the result of outright war. Such periodic clashes—varying in frequency and intensity with the tempers and firmness of King and Noble—were accepted as part of a man's lot in a fierce and decentralized world of village, castle, plain, unconquered forest, poor roads and worse communication. Bad as it might be, intestine strife was still infinitely preferable to War. And England was free of war.

Until the arrival of the Normans.

The story of the Conquest can be found in any decent English history. Our interest in it lies only in the far-reaching changes it wrought on the tongue of the English.

Only 70 years before the Conquest, Aefric, a monk of Dorset, could compose a homily on John the Baptist beginning in these words:

Johannes se godspellere, Cristes dyrling, wearth on thysum daege to heofenan rices myrhthe thurh Godes neosunge genumen.[7]

None today could do more than guess at the meaning, which is:

John the evangelist, Christ's favorite, was on this day taken to the bliss of the kingdom of heaven by the visitation of God.

For the term "Old English" is extremely misleading—"Anglo-Saxon" is at least free of the notion that the language of pre-Conquest England was English in any sense which we would recognize. He who would read *Beowulf* or the *Anglo-Saxon Chronicles* in the original had best resign himself to learning a language at least as foreign as Swedish or Dutch—and somewhat more difficult to learn at that. For Anglo-Saxon was a language whose general cast is strongly reminiscent of modern-day German, and which had even more flexional structure. There was, for instance, a separate group of *dual* personal pronouns that indicated "two of." Thus, the first person pronoun, in all cases and all *three* numbers ran:

[7] The Anglo-Saxon *etha* and *thorn* have been replaced by "th," the texts of the time making no distinction in the use of these obsolete letters.

	Singular	Dual	Plural (three or more)
Nom.	ic	wit	we
Gen.	min	uncer	ure, user
Dat.	me	unc	us
Acc.	mec, me	uncit, unc	usic, us

This tri-partition of grammatical number extended also to the second person, but did not exist in the third.

When the French arrived at a position of unassailable power through military superiority, their language naturally became the channel which gave the ambitious invader any chance of rising in the world and possibly recouping some small fragment of his fortunes. It is generally safe to say that when a ruling class speaks one language and the conquered another, it is the speech of the underdog which changes most profoundly. For what Frenchman—at first—would be interested in learning the barbarous tongue of his serfs? If commands are to be given, they pass down a chain of subordinates in the tongue of France, finally turning to Saxon on the tongue of some sub-sub-bailiff who by force of circumstance or upbringing is bi-lingual.

The Saxon, in contrast, found it all to his advantage to acquire at least the rudiments of French, if he was anything more than a bondsman whose prospects for something other than continued serfdom were poor indeed. There were chances for advancement—perhaps—if one could only learn how to speak the language of those in power. And of course, something of his newly-learned French was bound to rub off on the language which he spoke as his mother tongue.

The French had conquered by force of arms, and for a time ruled England as an occupied country. It was only to be expected that much of the vocabulary of war (itself a French term) should be drawn from the language of those actually in the saddle (and in that age of cavalry, the phrase was no mere metaphor). Thus, *army, armor, assault, battle, chieftain* (literally, "headman," *captain* being a variant), *lieutenant* (a "place-holder" or "deputy"), *officer, siege* and *soldier* are only a small handful of the terms taken in by those whose native language was not French.

As rulers, the French also found themselves charged with administering the law. In matters relating to legality and court procedure the Romance influence was even stronger than in the field of combat; for to obtain justice, one had to plead before judges drawn from the conquering nation. Aside from such elemental words as "right" and "wrong," it is, in fact, difficult to find any terms in jurisprudence which do not stem from the language of France: *jury, judge, justice, session, attorney, plaintiff, accuse, verdict, court, punishment, sentence, felony, traitor, damage, suit, penalty, property, real estate, defend, prove, false, heir, marriage,* and of course *prison.* Though in appearance the word does not seem particularly foreign, *petty* as in "petty larceny" (another French term), is a respelling and Englished pronunciation of *petit.*

Indeed, what had begun as merely a technical vocabulary, in which French terms were borrowed only in specialized contexts, rapidly assumed the proportions of a landslide. Over the succeeding decades and centuries the men who had begun as foreign conquerors lording it over an alien land found themselves growing into the landscape. They were, after all, vastly outnumbered and afloat on the same island with their prisoners, and by the 14th century English was decreed official in Parliament.

But what an English. Alfred the Great would not have known it, nor would any of those who died at Hastings. To all intents and purposes the noun flexions of Anglo-Saxon had perished, leaving only the genitive *s* which has survived to the present day. The strong and weak adjectival declensions had sunk without a trace (Anglo-Saxon had had these forms, reminiscent of the present-day German—see chapter 10). Personal endings of the verb, used in conjunction with subject-pronouns, had been severely eroded, the present-tense forms being identical stems except for the final -(*e*)*st* used with "thou," and the -(*e*)*th* which followed "he," "she," or "it." And it was not long after Chaucer's day that the infinitive lost its final -*n* to join forces with the four uninflected forms of the verb in the present.

By the 14th century, English had completed the greater part of the changes in structure that it has made till the present day.

This is most easily seen when we consider the quotation given from Aelfric's homily on page 299—written some 70 years before the Conquest—and compare it with the famous opening lines of the *Canterbury Tales* (1388):

> *Whan that Aprille with his shoures sote*
> *The droghte of Marche hath perced to the rote,*
> *And bathed every veyne in swich licour,*
> *Of which vertu engendred is the flour . . .*

Something like 400 years lies between the writing of these two sorts of English, and it is six centuries from Chaucer's day to ours. Yet we can read—though haltingly—the language of the *Tales,* while even Chaucer (to say nothing of ourselves) would find the good monk's narrative on John the Baptist completely unintelligible. To borrow a metaphor from Jewish Rabbinical tradition: From the time of Alfred to Chaucer was the Law—all that has come after is Commentary.

*   *

No language stands still, of course. Words, grammar, idiom—these alter yearly, generally so slightly that we do not notice. Though the Norman Conquest truly created English as we think of it, it is obvious that the language of even those so recent as Shakespeare, Addison, Steele, Scott and Dickens differs—though progressively less as we near the present—from the usage of our own day. There have always been and probably always will be additions, deletions, amendments in the history of any spoken language. It is only the dead which is safely beyond change: the Sanskrit of Hindu ritual, the Ge'ez of the Ethiopian and the Coptic of the vanishing Egyptian Christians.

Even so, however, one can attempt to gauge the intensity or rapidity of change—and, allied to that, the degree of "self-confidence" extant at any given time within a particular speech community. We have already seen how the 400 years which lay between Aelfric and Chaucer counted for more in English than have the years between Chaucer and us; the question of self-confidence, however, is something a good deal more intangible. All too often in the past it has been associated with a certain Romantic school of linguistic thought strong in such notions as "folk spirit," "national genius," "the spirit of the times," and so forth. The very idea of such an entity as linguistic self-confidence is easily questioned.

Yet *something* is probably represented by the phrase. It is difficult when reading Shakespeare to avoid an impression of immense vitality and joyful assertiveness. Metaphors are cheerfully mixed—how can one "take arms against a sea of troubles," after all?—and the school-marms' rules about *who* and *whom* or the illegality of "it is *me*" are passed by without a second thought.

Such mournings for the linguistic freedom of a vanished past can be countered by an appeal to the need for *some* sort of "traffic rules" in language. We are not, after all, blazing poets, those whose violations can be excused on the grounds of brilliance and vividity (though in Shakespeare's time there were no grammars to define his usage as violations).

Yet there is another sort of failure of nerve which has also crept in over the centuries—and this one bodes ill for clarity itself. It is the growingly *abstract* nature of English vocabulary. And with the ever-increasing prestige of our language, this abstraction threatens to spread to other tongues as well.

The fault lies ultimately in the amazing reputation enjoyed by Latin over the millennia. English could hardly hope to stand against it in the beginning. Scarcely had the language become half-easy in the possession of numerous French words, than learned men began to infect it with the vaccine of Latin, French's classical sire. Alongside such now-domesticated forms as *sure, frail, chief* and *very* (Old French *verrai*—"true"; compare the modern French *vrai*) there were grafted *secure, fragile, capital* and *veritable,* taken directly from the fossilized corpus[8] of Latinity.

[8] *Corpus* is precisely such a learned form; earlier, the French gave us both *corps*—and *corpse.*

Thus, in addition to the numerous doublets of English—*freedom/liberty*, *wise/sage*, *right/proper*, *go up/ascend*, *near/in the vicinity of*, etc.—there are a number of triads as well: *wise/sage/sapient*, *unbelief/doubt/dubiety*, *high/haughty/altitudinous*, and the like. Often the coordination among these forms is imperfect; that is, the various members of a doublet or triad may be restricted to different syntactic roles. The native Anglo-Saxon *finger* serves as a noun, but we can not say *fingerish*; for the adjective we must employ the Latin *digital*. In like manner we have the following noun-adjective oppositions, largely unknown in other tongues: *breast/pectoral*, *water/aquatic*, *kin/familial*, *ball/spheroidal*, *eye/ocular*. (It is not invariably the case that the native term forms the noun while the imported word is used as an adjective, however. The possibilities are almost endless, as we can see in such instances as *much/quantity*, *above/superiority*, *see/visible*.)

There is no doubt that such widespread importation of terms, even after the infusion of French vocabulary, has given English a peculiar richness of its own. From the simple *hand*, for instance, English is able to generate a multitude of associated terms, most of which stem from un-English sources; and among the lot, very few are true synonyms. *Handle* is not quite the same as *manipulate*, and *handy* is obviously a different creature indeed from *manual*. Perhaps most striking of all, though the Latin roots of the word literally mean to "make by hand," *to manufacture* has in our day almost precisely the opposite connotation.

Yet though English is uniquely rich in this respect, we may wonder to what extent it is an embarrassment of riches. In perhaps no other language is learned vocabulary so divorced from the common roots of speech. Though the term had once existed in Saxon times (dying later), *handbook* was revived only in mid-19th century—and was looked on with suspicion then. It is in fact likely that it owes its existence in the language today only to the fact that a *Handbuch* was a highly respectable outgrowth of German Science. Even so, it was long before the term achieved anything like equality with the established *manual*. (And if we think this strange, let it be noted that *manual* itself was once looked down upon. To an earlier generation of scholars, the Greek-born *enchiridion* was a far more expressive term by which to denote a small and convenient source of data.)

As Jespersen has pointed out, this English passion for coining terms on foreign models is probably useful in technical fields. To speak in scientific parlance of an *acid* (from the Latin *acere*, "to be sour") is preferable to impressment of the native *sourness*; since the Latin-based term carries no associations of taste—an accidental, not essential, feature of acids—it can be defined as a highly specific notion, divorced from irrelevent connotations of sense-data. (The importance of this advantage can be exaggerated, however. The Germans were the best chemists of the 19th century, and their use of the native Germanic *Säure* seems to have impeded them not at all.) In a similar fashion, *rigidity, genus, diabetes, atom, electron,* and so forth, coming as they do from foreign tongues, escape the specific and often misleading overtones of *stiffness, breed, syphon, uncuttability, amber,* which are the root-meanings in their respective tongues-of-origin.

Jespersen had grave doubts, however, about extending this English habit to include the description of everyday phenomena. Why *should* we speak of a "telegram" for instance? The fact that the word is formed from Greek roots meaning "distant writing" is insufficient excuse, since most of those who employ the services of Western Union have little interest in the tongue of Aristophanes. The usage may at least be defended, however, on the grounds that one may safely ask to send a wire throughout all of Western Europe and expect to be understood; those nations which have telegraphy have generally adopted the word as well (*telegramme, telegramma, Telegramm,* etc.).

But how many Americans are likely to wander into a foreigner's living room and ask to look at *television*? Though the institution is an important one—probably too important—the word used to describe it could well have been one which drew upon the individual nation's word stock; German, in fact, has done this. Though the word *Television* is encountered, at least as common is the home-grown *Fernsehen* (literally, "far-seeing").

In an earlier day, this English-language passion for the foreign could reasonably be ascribed to reverence for the Classical Past; Greece and Rome—especially Rome—were the very models of an imagined linguistic excellence. (No matter that the history and structure of English could not be crammed within the circumference of Cicero.) It was such misplaced piety which led Dr. Johnson—witty and incisive in speech—to such written monstrosities as:

The proverbial oracles of our parsimonious ancestors have informed us, that the fatal waste of our fortune is by small expenses, by the profusion of sums too little singly to alarm our caution, and which we never suffer ourselves to consider together. Of the same kind is the prodigality of life; he that hopes to look back hereafter with satisfaction upon past years, must learn to know the value of single minutes and endeavour to let no particle of time fall useless to the ground.

Translation: Take care of the pennies and the pounds take care of themselves.

Unfortunately, the custom has survived without the historical excuse which gave birth to it. It is difficult to believe that a modern sociologist, for example, is driven to use of "reification," "entitivity," "conceptualization" and the like, from motives of historical respect. The psychoanalyst may have what strike him as good and sufficient reasons for employment of "autistic," "affect," "imago," "ego," "id," and "super-ego";[9] but it is doubtful that a reverence for the authoritarian Romans is one of the motives.

[9] *Ego, id,* and *super-ego* are particularly fascinating forms, basic as they are to Freudian psychoanalytic theory. Father-figure Freud himself, writing in German and attempting only to be clear, used the terms *Ich, Es* and *Über-ich*: perfectly clear German for the *I,* the *it* and the *over-I* (or *super-I,* if one wishes to make minimal concession to scientific English). One can only wonder why the translator thought it necessary to impress by translating these key terms into *Latin*—English would have been sufficient. The result is that almost any translation of Freud strikes the reader as turgid, pompous and self-important, while in the original, his work is marked by clarity and a surprising degree of beauty.

George Orwell, who had the disturbing knack of saying exactly what he meant, and saying it extremely well, once wrote a delightfully malicious essay showing just how far the English language could be—and was—mauled at the pens of bureaucrats. As "Washington Choktaw," similar mutilation takes place in the United States. One rarely, if ever, finds anything so clear as "Please follow the enclosed blueprints (or instructions, diagram, outline, etc.) exactly." Good bureaucratese demands instead, "It is desired that the relevant specifications be rigorously adhered to; see attachments MS–2385L–395T–91 . . ."

Please notice that the objection is *not* to the use of a technical vocabulary. Every science, even a social science, is entitled to—demands—a fund of words used in highly particular senses. There can be no demurral to the mathematician's "commutative ring," "Abelian group," or "transfinite cardinality." A physician has something very definite in mind when he writes of "cephalin flocculation"—something which an English translation into "headish tuftedness" would only obscure. It is completely legitimate when both sociologist and anthropologist insist on a distinction between "society" and "culture," and use these terms in senses very different from those of everyday life.

What *is* disturbing is the suspicion that a measurable fraction of time is spent in certain learned disciplines consulting Latin or Greek dictionaries quite unnecessarily. Whatever the virtues of a universal (i.e., European) scientific vocabulary, *within* a given tongue obscurantism can go just so far. If a German social scientist is interested in following the literature written in English, he will take the trouble to learn the language, and the use of such pseudo-universal terms as "entitivity" will prove of little help. Just as his American counterpart might trouble himself to master such hypothetical forms as *Bewesung* or *Seinung* (which capture some of the sense of "is-ishness" that "entitivity" successfully masks); just so, Hans Friedrich Soziolog would find it possible to recognize "being" or "essence," as defined in context with appropriate precision.

*   *

As American readers are doubtless aware, English is no longer confined to the British Isles. In fact, the English of England is quite bluntly in second place. The tail now wags the dog. In the United States alone there are something like four to five times as many speakers of English (or "American," if the reader prefers) as there are in the Old Country. When one adds to this number the population of such nations as Canada, Australia, New Zealand, etc., the voting majority of linguistic stock is seen obviously to have passed out of British hands. In like manner, Spanish is now primarily the language of Latin America (aside from Brazil); Spain is largely an afterthought. Brazil itself—larger than the continental United States—is the nation we think of when we assess the importance of Portuguese. Envy such truly successful colonial nations of the past; these three, at least, have known the joy which is every good parent's. They have produced children greater than themselves.

Just as there are peculiarities which distinguish Brazilian Portuguese from that of Lisbon, and set Latin American Spanish (itself having variations) apart from Castilian; so it would be hard to mistake the speech of Memphis, Chicago, Los Angeles, or New York for that of Glasgow, Manchester, or London.

It has been said that a good Yorkshireman can understand a citizen of Holland more easily than he can a Londoner. This is a gross exaggeration, yet it does give some idea of the sharp differentiation in dialect which exists within national boundaries throughout much of Europe, Britain included. These dialects are the fruit of centuries of relative isolation, when a trip of twenty miles was as much of an undertaking as would be a transcontinental journey today. And of course there was nothing like radio or television which would spread far and wide a given standard of pronunciation, even in the absence of personal travel.

The United States has been fortunate with regard to dialect. Though the evidence is still scanty, there is reason to believe that the "home-dialects" of the original colonists were few in number and did not differ *too* sharply from one another even at the beginning. Given the confusion of groups during the early days of settlement, and the intermixing of populations during expansion to the West, it is not surprising that regional modes of speech never attained the sharp individuality which marked the language across the sea.

Certain features peculiar to American English have been noted by foreign visitors since colonial times. But though references to a "peculiarly drawling manner of speech" recur, it is impossible to be certain of what the phrase meant exactly; the commentators were not, after all, phoneticists. The "drawl" may have been something like the modern-day "southern accent"; it may have resembled the New England "twang"; it may have been some odd sort of mixture of the two. Or again, it may have been a linguistic phenomenon which has completely disappeared from the American form of English spoken today.

Strangely enough, though "American" has been obliged to acquire many a new phrase descriptive of some aspect of reality unknown back in England—*skunk cabbage, succotash, teepee, raccoon, opossum, redwood, painter* (cougar), etc.—a good deal of the difference between English English and the American variety is attributable to widespread changes that have gone on in *Britain*. Of these, the most apparent in conversation is the series of alterations which have produced the "British accent."

It is obviously true that American has not simply marked time for 300 years, but there is a good deal of evidence that if William Shakespeare or Alexander Pope were to return to earth today, they would find it rather easier to understand a cultivated Chicagoan than a B.B.C. announcer. An analysis of their poetry, for instance, seems to show that comparatively full values for the unaccented vowels were assumed, so that "schedule" or "advertisement"—to choose words commonplace today—would have more closely approximated the American *skeh-joo-ul* and *ad-ver-TISE-ment* than the British *shedgl* and *ud-VER-tsmnt*.

Then too, the "silent *r*" was in those days merely a geographical feature of certain South English dialects; it had not received official imprimatur as *the* pronunciation; *cart, bar, bird, worn*—such words were probably pronounced with a clearly audible *r* throughout most of England, since there was as yet no social advantage in acquiring the *r*-less forms. The English "broad *a*"—which American (outside Boston) uses only before -*lm* or -*r*—was also probably rarer two or three centuries ago. Even in such words as "calm," "palm," "bar" and "cart" the vowel may well have rhymed with that found in "hat" and "sad." The resulting flatness of sound would probably have struck our ears as more like the speech of a Nantucket fisherman than that of an Oxford tutor.

However, it is not merely the *sounds* of American that seem to have changed more slowly than those of English; both the vocabulary and the syntactical forms of New World speech also exhibit features which have either died out entirely in Britain, or been confined to local dialect. Thus, "gotten" was once quite common in England—it is often found in earlier printings of the King James Bible in many places where later it was edited out in keeping with changes in British usage. Today it survives principally as a device by which bad writers can immediately indicate the arrival of an American on the fictional scene.[10]

Then too, the *shall/will* distinction—a bugaboo to all those who feel a pressing need to worry about such matters—is, in America, set in proper historical perspective. A quirk of a limited number of South English dialects—and historically unknown in the language of Northern England, Scotland or Ireland—this troublesome pair has never taken strong foothold in the United States, outside of certain specific regions where the settlers' dialect actually possessed it. As in the overwhelmingly greater part of the English-speaking world, the mark of futurity in America is *will*—in conversation, '*ll*—for all three persons, both numbers. *Shall* survives, when it survives at all, as a similarly universalized

---

[10] Though it seems that no English writer—with the honorable exception of Leslie Charteris—can get it through his head that we distinguish between "gotten" and "got" when used after parts of the verb "to have." Though we consistently use "to have gotten" in the sense of "to have received, acquired, become," etc., while "to have got" is merely a synonym for "to have," British authors usually have their "American" characters come up with such howlers as: *I've got sick and tired of it* and *What have you gotten there?*

verb of intense feeling or determination: "I *shall* do it, I tell you!" But even here, *will* steadily gains the ascendancy.

The differences in vocabulary between New World and Old World English have been emphasized so frequently that there seems little purpose to be served in recapitulation. It is doubtful if there is an American living today who does not know that British for "elevator" is "lift," and that "lorry" means "truck." Mencken in his *American Language* took considerable pains to list an impressive number of divergences, but we can only wonder to what extent the list was misleading. Even within the borders of the United States one can find a surprising number of variants for the commonest notions. Thus, the inoffensive creature which we impale on a fishhook to entice the lurking catfish is known as an *angleworm, fishworm, easworm, eastworm,* or *angledog,* depending on one's location. One may carry *crullers* or *dough-nuts* home in a *bag,* a *sack* or a *poke.* If the weather is fair, one can watch the children in the playground playing on the *teeter-totter, teeterboard,* or just plain *see-saw*—whatever the word, the device is the same. On the other hand, if it should be raining, one returns from the store with feet safely dry in *rubbers, gum-shoes,* or *overshoes.*

One can grant the merits of Mencken's half-serious thesis of a distinct "American language" existing earlier in this century. At their most distinct, the differences between the two dialects of English were probably at least as great as those which divide certain forms of Norwegian from Danish (See chapter 10 for a few words on the dialect/language problem). Within recent decades, however, there seems little doubt that the Mother Tongue and its gigantic trans-ocean offspring are beginning to come closer together.

Much of this *rapprochement* is due to the large number of Hollywood productions which have appeared on British movie (the word is now more common than "cinema") screens. From time to time one encounters diatribes in the English press about Americanization of the language. Though one may sympathize with the emotions of an outraged older generation, the trend appears to be irreversible. In return, so great has been the number of English pictures brought to this country that we no longer require sub-titles to understand Peter Sellers or Alec Guinness. (An interesting related phenomenon has been the evolution of a "*Mid*-Atlantic accent." The term describes a compromise form of speech used in many British-made—though usually American-produced—television series intended for showing on both sides of the ocean. To an Englishman, the voice of the titular hero has decidedly American overtones; while an American audience catches something faintly, but definitely, British about the diction employed. Frequently this half-and-half state of linguistic affairs is explained away by making the chief character[s] Canadian).

*   *

And what of the future? What are the prospects for our language in the years, decades and centuries to come? Is ours a tongue with its best times still ahead of it, or has it already seen its Golden Age?

At present, English certainly enjoys favored status. Though Chinese may have a larger number of speakers, we have already seen that in reality that language is essentially a *written* structure: a system of idea-based ideographs which serve to unite *as readers* peoples whose spoken tongues may diverge as much as do English and German, or even English and Russian.

Russian itself enjoys a respectably large number of speakers, and the number to whom it is native is probably comparable with the number speaking English as a mother tongue. Nevertheless, when we add in those who speak English as a second language—for purposes of trade, science, diplomacy, etc.—it seems as though ours is the most widely-known language in the world today.

The temptation is to feel pride in this knowledge—and certainly English has its virtues. The child of repeated invasion and counterblow, English has stripped itself of most of the flexional apparatus it once had. The number of distinct suffixes which must be mastered in the learning of our tongue is smaller than that of any other European language (-s for the third-person singular of the verb in the present; -s' and -s' for genitive singular and plural; -(e)d; and a handful of others).

The historically recent (since Chaucer's time) development of "extended tenses"—*I am walking* and *I do walk* beside the earlier simple *I walk*—has lent our tongue a subtlety in verbal expression which only the Slavic languages with their aspects begin to approach in the European world. And even the Slavic forms lack something in completeness (absence of a perfective aspect in the present tense, for example) and regularity.

The numerous doublets (*folk/people, nightly/nocturnal, go/proceed, well/properly*), triads (*head/chief/capital, walk/march/ambulate, about/concerning/in re*) and still more generalized families of synonym (*answer/respond/reply, say/state/maintain/asseverate/declare, miss/overlook/ignore/aperceive/misconstrue, alive/vital/vivid/lively/vivified, manly/male/virile/human/masculine/mannish*): all of these lend to our language a potential for marvelous precision—or for meaningless hair-splitting and alienation of the non-scholarly segment of the populace.

For it is a poor sword which does not cut both ways. The very virtues of our speech have within them vices.

The comparative absence of flexion in English can make for ambiguity. When Ben Johnson wrote: *But might I of Jove's nectar sip, I would not change for thine,* did he mean that he was willing or unwilling to make the exchange? In *Many a mood my heart is touching sore* is it the heart which touches—or is it being touched? It is true that these examples are from poetic diction in which the word-order is unusual. In prose the author would have taken pains to recast his sentence in unmistakable terms. Even so, English pays for its simplicity in a loss of free arrangement.

The *extended tenses* themselves, although instruments of marvelous flexibility, offer problems of their own. Even a speaker born to English might have trouble deciding which form is preferable: *While I wrote he walked around the room* or *While I was writing he walked around the room* (as well as the insidious possibilities of *While I was writing he was walking around the room* and *While I wrote he was walking around the room*). The choice of any given form often hangs on as many intangibles as selection of a correct aspect in Russian (see chapter 12). And when the hapless foreigner encounters such a construction as *I will have been forced to have been kept waiting here much too long* or *What did you do when he didn't show up? Did you leave, or didn't you?*, he is likely to throw up his hands in horror and leave the room.

And worst of all—totally without excuse for existence, except that it exists—is English spelling.

If, some pages ago, it seemed that we were unnecessarily harsh with Irish spelling, be consoled—the plight of our own language leaves very little room for stone-throwing. Our house is built of an even more fragile glass. There would be no purpose served in citing horrible examples—they lie ready to view on every page of every book that has been printed in the last three centuries. And by horrible examples, the author refers to the "correctly" spelled forms, not typographical blunders. It took, after all, only minor ingenuity for George Bernard Shaw to invent *ghoti* as a legitimate spelling for the word which we normally write as *fish*.[11] In fact, the actual process by which we learn to read our language is a weird mixture of alphabetic interpretation together with something reminiscent of the Chinese pupil's memorization of countless ideographs *en bloc*. We begin with our ABC's, but such visual patterns as *roughage, hiccough* (now almost universally respelled as *hiccup*), *fir tree* and *furlong* must be committed to memory as things-in-themselves. Though approximate cues to pronunciation may be given by isolated characters, such collections of letters are primarily learned as one whole, indigestible *gestalt*. As an object lesson: how many readers have any remote idea of the pronunciation of *sough*—a verb beloved of bad

[11] "gh" as in *tough;* "o" as in *women;* "ti" as in *nation.*

nature-writers when describing the sound of the wind through pine trees? (They are *always* pine trees in the sort of books which stoop to that particular verb.) The answers—there are two of them, utterly different—will be found on page 808 of the Merriam-Webster Collegiate Dictionary, 1960 edition.

*   *

So before we grow too confident of the future of our language, let us at least remember some of its drawbacks. English may be perfect—but it is not *perfectly* perfect, after all. Even the best of us have occasional difficulty with it.

And, on a more serious note, let us remember the sadly human ways in which language is often passed from one people to another. Only a small part of the world concerns itself with literary affairs, after all. The Etruscans learned their Latin at Roman short-sword's point. Welsh bilinguality is the fruit of Glendower's lonely death in snowy mountains, not of good John Wesley's missionary activities, or the Home Service of the B.B.C. We ourselves grew a language in a long two centuries of oppression at the hands of William the Conqueror and his followers, who burned, tore, bled, raped, and finally loved, an occupied country.

There is the English-speaking Union. There are the science-fiction stories which confidently assume that the language of a united future world (and solar system) will be some descendant of present-day English. There are our optimistic time-capsules buried in cornerstones—with instructions and commentary in English, of course.

But let us remember Crete—a great maritime empire, a civilization which made the Greeks of its time seem little more than dirty savages. Crete was mighty, Crete had pride. Crete had culture, religion, government. Crete had plumbing. A land of sophistication and intelligence, a world of subtlety and beauty, Crete might have been expected to survive.

But there are men today who spend their years puzzling over the inscriptions on stone and pottery, tablet and god-offering, found in Knossos, the Cretan capital. And as yet, hardly a word can even be guessed at. For the people and their language are dead, and their bones and their words are dry and empty under the Mediterranean sun.

✍ 15

A shape of things to come

THOUGH Communication Theory is a current vogue (in the specialized sense indicated by the capital C and T above), in all likelihood the first important hint of its eventual development came at least 3,000 years ago—or whenever that unknown Semite devised a truly alphabetic script (See chapter 8). For if nothing else, that nameless inventor understood the concept of *redundancy*. Since the content of a message could largely be specified by a triad (sometimes a pair, sometimes a foursome) of consonants, vowels were omitted. This, of course, was true only because the language committed to papyrus was a Semitic tongue. The Greeks, speaking an Indo-European language, in which vowels make a very big difference indeed—e.g., *raid, red, rid, rod, rude*—found that vocalic elements were not redundant at all; that is, *vowels contributed something absolutely vital to the message*, something which was neither implicit in nor could be deduced from the non-vocalic phonemes, or from the context.[1]

---

[1] We add the qualification of "context" because if all words with entirely different meanings, and distinguished only by a vowel, *belonged to different parts of speech*, vowels *would* be expendable. Thus, since "raid" is solely a noun or verb, "rude" solely an adjective, there would be no ambiguity in: "The r-d was led by the r-d man." In such a case, our minds would reconstruct "raid" and "rude," respectively. Unfortunately, Indo-European languages (to

Even though its basic notion of redundancy is of respectable antiquity, Communication Theory required the rather unlikely combination of problems in (1) telegraphic communication and (2) the aiming of anti-aircraft guns to bring it to full growth. As we shall see shortly, the problem in telegraphy had most obvious relevance to the specifically communicative nature of the theory; but the questions raised in anti-aircraft control have also led to an extremely fruitful concept: *feed-back*.

The notion of feed-back has found applicability in such widely separate fields as automation and neurology, rocketry and mass psychology. Even within the single discipline of Linguistics there are a number of phenomena which it helps to explain with economy and precision. Fine, the reader says, but what *is* feed-back, anyway?

In most general terms, it may be defined roughly as follows: *a closed loop of information, in which data concerning performance is returned ("fed back") to the source of the instructions giving rise to the performance.* One of the most simple, yet elegant and effective, devices employing feed-back is the *governor* used to stabilize the operation of an engine at some pre-determined speed. A classic variety consists of two weights at the end of a pair of pivoted arms which meet at a central shaft with a secondary connecting-link between these arms and the throttle or power control of the engine itself. The more rapidly the engine operates, the more rapidly the central shaft spins, and the further out move the weights (through centrifugal force). The connecting link between pivoted arms and throttle is such that at a certain point the throttle is cut back, thus reducing speed. Speed reduced, the central shaft spins more slowly, the weights lose momentum and fall back toward the shaft, and the throttle opens once more. There is in this action of the governor a sort of see-saw effect, with the speeding-up or slowing-down of the engine beyond pre-arranged limits allowing the device to correct itself.

---

name one family only) *do* have words serving as similar parts of speech and with identical consonants—Spanish *hombre* ("man") and *hambre* ("hunger"), English *vice* and *voice*.

The "closed loop" referred to above might be outlined as follows: engine—central shaft—pivoted arms—weights—pivoted arms
—secondary link—throttle—and back to engine. This type of governor, invented by James Watt, is the simplest—or at least, best-
known—example of feed-back in mechanics, but other forms may
be found elsewhere. A conductor directing an orchestra is a good
example; at any given moment he furnishes a set of instructions
regarding performance and interpretation, while the actual playing of the musicians in turn determines how he will direct them
to play the next passage.

It appears that feed-back is vital in biological activity, as well.
When we reach for a pencil lying on a table, for instance, rather
than willing each individual muscle in the arm to perform incredible feats of precise coordination, it appears that the movement begins as a rough approximation to the task. At this point
our "proprioceptive sense(s)" take over. A series of tiny monitors
which register position and tension relay back to the brain information concerning how far wrong the initial movement has
been. By a series of successive corrections the hand finally makes
contact with the pencil. (This sort of act is, indeed, almost precisely analogous to the problem of the anti-aircraft gunner who
must continually correct the initial direction of his cannon.
When we pick up a pencil which is *rolling across* the table, or
catch one thrown to us, the analogy becomes perfect.)

Dr. Norbert Wiener of M.I.T. was one of those called in by
the United States Government during World War II as a con-
sultant to help resolve this military problem of ballistics control.
A man of wide interests and erudition, Dr. Wiener had long
been fascinated with the idea of finding certain principles which
would be common to, and help bind together, a number of apparently isolated sciences. An interest in computing machines,
the needs of the war effort, and certain rather obscure neurological diseases—together with the imponderable element of personal
genius—finally brought forth the new discipline, *Cybernetics*.[2]

[2] A word invented jointly by Dr. Wiener, and Dr. Arturo Rosenblueth of
Mexico. It was formed from the Greek κυβερνήτης, *steersman,* as appropriate

Cybernetic or quasi-cybernetic processes seem to play a definite part in the functioning of all living creatures, though normally we are not aware of them when healthy. When functioning as it should, that delicate phenomenon called "life" maintains itself by a series of *homeostatic* ("self-standing") mechanisms which preserve the status quo. When our temperature rises above permissible limits we sweat, and evaporation brings the temperature down; if we chill, shivering sets in and the muscular activity evoked helps to raise internal warmth. Life seems to be a precarious tightrope walk between opposed—and fatal—excesses.

Feed-back systems definitely play a role in linguistic behavior, as well. In those who have gone totally deaf, through degeneration or destruction of the auditory nerve, we notice there is great difficulty in enunciation. This is not merely true of those deaf from birth (the so-called "deaf-mutes" who can not speak only because they have never heard anyone and thus have never had the chance to imitate), but it is true even among those lost in a world of total silence long after they have learned the trick of speech. Though such unfortunates generally *can* produce intelligible speech—the proprioceptive mechanisms of tongue and throat sufficing to assure generation of recognizable phonemes—it is, to listeners, a rather odd experience. For the intonations and junctures, the blending of sounds with their successors, the subtle cadences of audible language, are distorted and misplaced. (Presumably, if such a totally deaf person were given a local anesthetic, such as Novocain, which temporarily annulled the proprioceptive sense as well, he would be incapable of any speech whatsoever.)

It is almost certainly true that language at one remove—i.e., the physical act of writing—owes its being to feed-back mechanisms, just as any act of physical coordination does. This can

---

to a field dealing *par excellence* with control processes and mechanisms. Let it be noted that English already had a word derived from this Greek original: *governor* itself, taken at second hand through the Latin mispronunciation of the word. Thus, a "governor" is one who steers, while "government" is the organization which steers or, in the abstract sense, the art of steering.

perhaps be seen most clearly in the first-grader's painstaking attempts to diagram the letters of the alphabet; it is not merely a case of repeating *A, A, A, A, A, A* . . . until Teacher gives her approval. More than that, even in the very act of tracing out a single *A,* the youngster eventually sees where he or she is going wrong and straightens out a crooked line or turns an originally oblique crossbar into a horizontal one.

As we can see by this, feed-back in living creatures is not necessarily an unconscious process. The politician on the platform who notices that his audience is acting rather coolly—if he is an alert politician—swiftly alters the tenor of his remarks: feed-back with a vengeance, and quite conscious. Indeed, insofar as Language presupposes both a Speaker and a Spoken-to, feed-back plays and must play an important role. Each of us modifies his behavior (and language as commonly understood is only one particular mode of behavior) in the light of the response to it— or in light of our idea as to what the response may be.

We have really cheated, though, in using this term, "feed-back," as though in itself it were something valuable and useful. For there are two varieties, and only one—*negative* feed-back— has been the subject of discussion. A re-examination of the definition given on page 318 will show that the closed loop of information can result in either one of two states: the information fed back to the source of the original instructions can act either (1) to reduce or (2) to increase, initial error. When reaching out for that hypothetical pencil, the feed-back process will normally be set up (in the nervous system) so as to *reduce* the errors at each stage of the reaching. Yet this is not inevitable; it is conceivable that the information returned to the source may act so as to *exaggerate* the original mistake in aiming—and, in fact, precisely this state of affairs is found in certain neurological disorders.

"Intention tremor" is a good instance of *positive* feed-back. As long as the patient makes no attempt to move a limb purposefully, the tremor is absent or negligible; but when arm, leg, foot or hand is deliberately moved toward a certain goal, trembling begins which increases in intensity. The arm (for instance) swings in larger and larger arcs until any hope of picking up a pencil—or reaching *any* object—becomes obviously out of the question.

Such cases seem quite definitely to involve positive feed-back. Both muscles and proprioceptive mechanisms are functioning properly; but there appears to be some type of short circuit which *adds* the amount of error reported, rather than *subtracting* it. Something analogous to this, and perhaps like in origin as well, may be seen in the social and linguistic phenomenon of Rumor. Here positive feed-back seems to operate with unbelievable effectiveness. What began as "Mr. Jones just bought a new car," is likely to end—after enough stages of transferral—as, "Mr. Jones just cornered 51% of the _____ Motor Company!"

At a more personal level of linguistic action, the phenomenon of *stuttering* would appear to be connected with reversed (i.e., positive) feed-back. Though the situation is a complex one, and is apparently associated with certain psychological difficulties in the life history of the stutterer, it seems that a possible explanation of stutter lies in an ever-exaggerated attempt to produce the desired vocable. Many a stutterer begins with, for instance, an [s]. Unselfconscious, he may succeed in producing the sound and may even be able to join it to its followers. But it has often been observed that the agony of stuttering lies precisely in the fact that the more intent the speaker is on producing a given sound, the more difficult he finds it. Thus, [s] may slip out easily in such a word as "accessible," where it is merely an easily-overlooked central utterance; but if [s] is an initial form (e.g., in "Superiority is important") both psychologically and phonetically located where attention focuses on it, then difficulties are liable to appear.

Of course, like all insights into the nature of things, any so-called natural law always runs the risk of over-application. In the 19th century, Herbert Spencer fell wildly in love with the central notions of Darwinian natural selection and Newtonian mechanics. In sublime ignorance of both biology and mathematics, he extended what he conceived to be the principles of both theories to human society. One can not say that he was absolutely and completely wrong, but all the same very little was gained. At most, he had devised a handful of metaphors—nothing more significant. For his theories were at best hopeful guesses which might or might not (may or may not) prove ultimately justifiable. They were metaphors only, because there was never any attempt on Spencer's part to *quantify* them—never any attempt to see how well they might live up to reality in terms of intensity, frequency, *number*. "How much?" "How many?" are supposed to be elemental parts of the newspaperman's credo: they are equally essential to the scientist.

In this demand for quantification lies the one real defense of feed-back as a concept to be employed in a diversity of disciplines. For within limits, the conditions of feed-back can be expressed in mathematics. And if the solutions to such predictive equations jibe with the data actually observed, one may tentatively believe that feed-back is the underlying mechanism involved. Unless (or until) some new piece of data is found which upsets the postulated apple-cart entirely. In that case, the feed-back explanation goes out the conceptual window.

At this stage of history, it is rather difficult to predict just how widely and successfully elements of cybernetic theory will find application in linguistics. So much depends on advances in other fields. Certainly, however, we can hope for much from a discipline which has proved so fruitful in the interpretation and elucidation of control processes, and which has been invaluable in the development of machines which possess at least some of the attributes of thought.

*   *

Feed-back deals with a special case in the transmission of information: that in which at least a portion of the information returns to its source, to form a loop. But this is only a special case, and there are many instances which come to mind of information being transmitted in one direction only, with no thought of a round-trip, much less of using returning data to control output of information-to-come.

Yet through all of this we have been begging the question, for what *is* Information? We have mentioned its transmission along closed loops or in a non-return direction, but what is it that we are transmitting?

This question became of more than academic interest when men devised means of transmitting messages over long distances almost instantaneously. The invention of the telegraph and later of the wireless introduced problems. So long as messages were sent as written letters there were few obvious difficulties; the pattern which represented the language consisted of wedge-shaped marks pressed into the surface of a clay tablet (Babylonian cuneiform); groups of straight lines incised on the corners of blocks of stone (the Celtic ogham characters); or various symbols delineated in a wide variety of inks on papyrus, parchment, palm leaves, and rag or wood-pulp paper. In all of these cases the transformation was from a spoken reality to a visual pattern *arranged in space*.

With the introduction of telegraphy, however, a new dimension entered the picture, for with the clicks and clatters of Mr. Morse's new device, messages became series of signals *arranged in time*. (Eventually they ended as written words, to be sure, transcribed by the operator at the receiving end—but as a message in transit one had a series of yes-and-no decisions succeeding one another in temporal sequence.) And of course the primary interest in such a system is the insurance of intelligibility.

One may skip a word in a letter, true; but there is the comforting knowledge that the letter is *there* and can be re-read. There is no such reassuring permanence in the messages sent by telegraph or radio; these are essentially events in time, not space, and if the time be out of joint—a loose connection, sun-spot interference, the natural static of the atmosphere, sea water leaking through the sheath of a transoceanic cable—any of the thousand natural shocks that wire is heir to may cause that message to be lost forever.

Since the earliest days of telegraphy these hazards have been recognized, and in a rough, rule-of-thumb fashion, men developed means to cope with them. One method, still used today, was *simple reconstruction* of the message. If there is garbling en route and one receives such a message as: "I woll bu at thx raol-road stztion tlmorrow," our knowledge of the language used enables us to re-cast it as: "I will be at the rail-road station tomorrow." We may be neither mathematicians nor cryptographers, but years of using a particular tongue have given us an empirical knowledge of the *transitional* and *contextual probabilities* of our language.

We know that, 99 times out of 100, the word (written or spoken) "I" will be followed by some verb or another; there is no such verb form as "woll" in English, nor is there a "wull." Under certain circumstances "wall" or "well" might fit, as in "I wall up the prisoner in his cell," or "I well over with gratitude at the thought of your kindness"; but in the total context of the message (especially that "bu" which must be, also on probability grounds, "be"), and in light of the relative frequency with which we encounter *w-ll* verb forms in English, we are on safe territory when we assert with confidence that the ungarbled original must have been "will."

At this relatively elementary level of garbling, we carry out the process of deciphering with little, if any, conscious thought. So well are we acquainted with the statistical probabilities of our native tongue that the quite incredibly complex operations required to make sense of the imperfect text given above are carried out without a second thought.

Much of this process is based on our intuitive (a misleading word—the knowledge is learned, not inborn, but acquired so unself-consciously that we rarely know we possess it) understanding of *Markov chains*. A Markov chain can be defined as any sequence of elements in which any one element has a definite probability of preceding (or following) another element. It is easy to see that any coherent language must exhibit features of a Markov chain, in that a specified word or phoneme is more or less likely to occur in a given environment. As we saw in chapter 8, an initial [p] in English is aspirated, but when this [p] follows an [s] it loses aspiration. We might rephrase this situation in statistical terms by saying that "the transition probability of passing from the terminal phoneme of one word to a succeeding [p] which lacks aspiration is 0" (i.e., such a transition *never* occurs); and that "the transition probability of moving from an initial [s] to an immediately following unaspirate [p] is 1" (i.e., it is *certain* that a [p] following an initial [s] will lack aspiration).[3]

Such Markov-chain interpretations of language can be applied to words as well as individual phonemes. As we mentioned earlier, there is a very strong likelihood that the word which follows "I" will be a verb form. In like fashion, the probability is almost overwhelming that the word which follows another word ending in "-'s" or "-s' " will be a noun or noun-like form—for both these clusters are marks of the possessive. One may speak in our language of the "brother's (brothers') hats" or the "brother's (brothers') going"; but it is quite simply not in the rule-book for us to speak of the "brother's (brothers') *is.*"

The lower rungs of the ladder of Markov chains are easy enough to climb; if word (or phoneme) Y has a 50% probability of following X, and if Z, in turn, follows Y 50% of the time, then there is a 25% chance that Z will be found two places after X (with Y intervening). Simple addition and multiplication are enough to determine the odds associated with any given sequence of elements, *once the probability of occurrence for each single element is known.*

This little proviso, however, is one which can break the back of any ambitious young mathematically or statistically-inclined student of linguistics. Markov himself, the man for whom such chains of linked probabilities are named, set about the task of

[3] These transition probabilities only apply, of course, to English spoken without a foreign accent (a Frenchman would speak in blithe disregard of them) and spoken without those occasional and generally overlooked slips of the tongue which even the native-speaker makes. This is an idealization of reality, but mathematical analysis is based on the ideal case, not the clumsily everyday.

analyzing the word *digrams* (pairs of words) to be found in Pushkin's *Yevgeny Onyegyin* (Eugene Onegin), and the labor involved testifies to his perseverance if nothing else. To construct such a table of word-digram frequencies, one must note the occurrence of every single word at each and every repetition, together with the word immediately following.

We can gain some idea of the complexity of the task if we imagine a make-believe language which has only ten words in its entire vocabulary. If there were no preferential ordering of terms, then each of these ten words might be followed by any one of the ten—ten, because since there *is* no preference, a word may be repeated. Considering only pairs of words (the word digrams originally analyzed by Markov), one would have a total of 100 possibilities. But of course, no language has in fact such an absurdly limited vocabulary—and furthermore, we have spoken of "ten words" without bothering to define precisely what we mean by a "word." In Markov's case, the analysis was applied to Russian, a highly inflected language, as we have already seen in chapter 12. In Russian there are a number of forms which cluster about a central core of meaning: if we regard *on* ("he") as primary, there exist such derived entities as *yevo* ("his" or "him"), *yemoo* ("to him"), *yeem* ("(with) him"), etc. How many of these do we count as separate words? Translated into the corresponding problem in English—a far simpler problem, since English is less inflected—do we consider such forms as *they, their* and *them* as three words or as one?

Any answer to this question is bound to displease some student of linguistics, for there *is* no one answer. In terms of Markov-type analyses, however, it is perhaps best to regard each variant form as a separate word, since it is often the case that the given form determines the type of word which follows. Thus, though "he" and "his" are ultimately referable to a central notion of "person spoken-about, one individual, a male," the probabilities are very strong that the word after "he" will be a verb of some sort, while the sequel to "his" will normally be a noun. Since Russian does *not* have a vocabulary of only ten words, and since it is highly inflected to boot, one can then begin to appreciate the sheer brute labor involved in determining the actual digram probabilities of an existing language. And let us remember that when Markov carried out this labor of mathematical love, he was unearthing only the *digram* probabilities for a *single written* work.

Though what he learned doubtless had some relevance to the Russian language as a whole, he was working only with the somewhat artificial and stylized artistic production of one man at one stage of his life within a single decade in the entire history of a language. And Markov was considering only *pairs* of words. As we can well imagine, the problem of determining the probabilities of *trigrams* (trios of phonemes or words as the case may be) is much harder; each time one adds a new element the difficulties encountered mount in a pyramiding fashion, until one reaches the literally unimaginable complexity of *n-grams* where one considers the longest possible chain of elements—that is, all the possible combinations which may exist among the total vocabulary of any given language. (We may gain some idea of the drudgery involved if we consider once again our hypothetical ten-word language. The number of possible digrams is 10 times 10 = 100; trigrams will number 10 times 10 times 10 = 1,000, and so forth. The total number of combinations, with any degree of repetition accepted, will be 10 multiplied by itself 10 times— 1 followed by 10 zeroes, or 10,000,000,000 [ten billion]. If we assume that Russian [or English, or German, or French, etc.] has a vocabulary of only 50,000 words—an *extremely* conservative figure—we can see how quickly any calculations must very rapidly grow beyond the bounds of practicality.)

But even if practicality makes a complete analysis of the internal probabilities of any real language impossible, the principle is illuminating, nevertheless. In the light of such approaches we begin to see how there is a destiny which shapes our words—in combination, at least—misuse them how we may. There *does* appear to be some way in which we can speak of "nonsense," whatever our opinion of the sense being stated. It seems that we are *not* perfectly free to say anything we wish, save at the level of infant-babbling where the young learner-of-language dabbles with magnificent impartiality in all the combinations of speech which may strike his fancy.

A pioneer in the use of language may make the rules over to suit his purpose. James Joyce in *Finnegans Wake* could alter the transition probabilities between digrams (and even trigrams); but even he was not liberated from all constraint. Except in those spots where he deliberately employs terms from a foreign language, or where he makes up radically non-English "bribble and brabble," even he sings proudly (and unknowingly) in the chains of a structure not of his own making.

Seen in this probabilistic light, one might well guess that information itself will be associated with notions of likelihood, and this is in fact the case. Information is—in modern Information (Communication) Theory—defined in terms of statistical probability, but *negated* probability. That which is *least* to be expected is defined as that which bears the greatest cargo of information.

Such a reversed view of things should not surprise us upon mature consideration. A deck of cards, all 52 of which are the four of clubs, will be useless for any readily conceivable game; in reality one is merely presented with a single card, repeated 52 times. A letter which read: "Tomorrow . . . tomorrow . . . tomorrow . . . tomorrow . . . tomorrow," would tell us very little new. Tomorrow *what?* In a system all of whose members are identical, the transition probabilities are all equal.[4]

It is when we are presented with an assemblage of elements—in linguistics, such elements as phonemes, words, grammatical flexions, or sequences of any of these—with *differing* probabilities of occurrence, that the possibility of transmitting information becomes manifest. Information in such a context may be defined as the element of novelty introduced into a scattered and dis-

---

[4] And, incidentally, all equal to one specific figure: *1*, i.e., absolute certainty. In the deck of 52 fours of clubs, it is a foregone conclusion that any hand dealt out will consist of fours of clubs. It makes no difference, even, what the number of cards dealt is; two ("digrams"), three ("trigrams") . . . up to, and including the entire pack, the *n-gram* (in this case, a 52-gram).

orderly situation. (By "disorderly" let us mean simply that there is no discernible pattern; a deck of 52 identical cards—though in everyday parlance seemingly very "orderly" indeed, would possess a kind of disorder for our purposes, since there would be no possible structure which we might give to the deck. Simple repetition is essentially a matter of self-identity, and a *single* item can not form a pattern.)

Though Information Theory—as distinct from Cybernetics, with which it shares many points of interest and concern—may be said to have begun with R. V. L. Hartley in 1928, it has since spread its range of applicability and involvement incredibly. Hartley, writing for a technical journal published by a large telephone company, was quite properly concerned with the problems attendant on transmission of messages through electrical channels. Essentially he focussed on the problem of what "quantity of information" might be sent over a system possessing certain specified characteristics.

The details of his investigation may be ignored here—though the reader is referred to them at second hand in Colin Cherry's *On Human Communication,* Science Editions, Inc., 1961 (p. 42 and *passim*)—but one feature is of particular interest: Hartley, in the course of his investigation, was obliged to evolve definitions for both "Information" and "quantity of Information." Though the expressions used to represent these elements have changed somewhat since his original formulation, and though the very notions underlying them have undergone amplification, nevertheless the central ideas behind them are still valid and useful.

In the Hartleian view of things, *Information is essentially selection.* Given an assemblage of elements which constitutes our "universe" of possibility—e.g., phonemes, words, contact or lack-of-contact in a telegraph key, the "on" or "off" positions of an electrical circuit—Information is defined as the result of selecting certain elements at the expense of others which are not chosen. Within the context of this definition, Hartley then gave a lucid mathematical measure of the amount of Information sent as a result of any given selection of elements from this universe.[5]

The *arithmetic* of Information Theory can be deceptively simple: a mere question of addition and multiplication. (It is precisely these operations which characterize Probability Theory, and the similarity is no coincidence.) It is the *application* of these rather simple-minded procedures which makes for subtlety and finesse. And the most elementary varieties of mathematical relationship are likely to show themselves in the oddest places.

Zipf's Law, for instance. A student of linguistics at least as industrious as Markov, G. K. Zipf spent much hard-earned time studying the ways of a man with a word—and came to the conclusion that Man is incurably lazy. Zipf did not put it that way, of course; he was more polite about the matter, dignifying Man's sloth by the phrase, "The Principle of Least Effort," but when the flattering impersonality of science is stripped away, we find the eternal shirker beneath our collective skin trying, as always, to do as little as is absolutely necessary. After examination of a wide variety of linguistic material—from the babblings of infants to tabloid headlines—Zipf found that there was an uncannily regular correlation between the *commonness* of an utterance (or written form) and its *length*. The forms constantly in use—the everyday terms without which we can not make do—are without exception short and/or easy to pronounce: *the, a, of, in, where, mama, dad, home, come, go, run, ride, faith, God, good, friend, en-em-y, food, old, new,* etc., etc. If we rank vocabulary from first (most common) to last (most infrequent) we will find that the rule is quite regular: the odder or less-often-used the term, the longer it is.

The words italicized above are on our tongues every day of our lives, and their equivalents are correspondingly short in all

---

[5] Briefly: a message of N elements chosen from a total universe ("vocabulary," "alphabet") of C characters has C^N possible states. Example: 2-character messages chosen from a 3-character alphabet can be arranged in 9 (3^2) different ways. From a total alphabet of A, B and C one may select the following 2-character messages: AA, AB, AC, BA, BB, BC, CA, CB and CC. By a logarithmic transformation, Quantity of Information = N log C.

other languages. But once-in-a-lifetime vocables such as *anti-disestablishmentarianism, sesquipedalian, aborigine* or *desoxyribonucleic acid* tend to flourish luxuriantly in clusters of syllables. They are so seldom used—and when used, of such specific import —that they can afford the arrogance of difficulty. Yet even these proud and unwieldy rarities are not exempt from the lackadaisical cussedness of Adam and his children.

When such a notion as may be expressed by one of these Goliaths becomes central to a given human community, it is either trimmed to convenient size, or a new—and shorter—term is coined to foot the bill. Thus, when it was discovered that a certain compound was of amazing significance in chemical genetics, even the scientists cut the original word down to size; DNA is now universal—and even in technical articles "desoxyribonucleic acid" is likely to appear only once in the essay, with "DNA" after it in parentheses. Subsequently, the three letters alone are used to represent the serpentine original.

Upon reflection, such an inverse relationship between length and frequency-of-use seems to be preëminently natural. We are such innately lazy creatures that this sort of linguistic parsimony strikes us as a truism. Yet it is a truism that very few people ever bothered to notice before; everyone has been swayed by it— for the regularity of Zipf's Law in all sorts of contexts is one of the most amazing things about it—but few of us have ever been conscious of our self-riveted chains.

One exception to this chronicle of human unawareness is Mr. Samuel F. B. Morse, the gentleman whose invention of the telegraph was indirectly responsible for the development of Information Theory in the first place. Anyone who has ever attempted to learn Morse Code—and some have succeeded—has probably noticed that certain characters in this dot-and-dash system are shorter than others. "E," for example, consists of only a single dot, while "Z" is represented by dash-dash-dot-dot.[6] It is no co-

---

[6] In point of fact, Morse's original version of the Code differed in detail from the current international form. The principle of "character economy" is, however, common to both varieties.

incidence that "E" is the most common character in English (Morse's native tongue) and that "Z" is the rarest. Morse understood that. When devising a code suitable for telegraphic transmission, he deliberately attempted to make sure that the elements which appeared most often would be the easiest to send, and in this sense he was perhaps the earliest practitioner of scientific Communication Theory. With surprisingly few modifications his system is still in use today, more than a century after its invention. (*How* Morse determined the relative frequencies of the various characters used in English spelling was simplicity itself— yet a kind of brilliant simplicity it is all too easy to overlook. He simply walked into a print shop, and obtained a count of the varying number of *A*'s, *B*'s, *C*'s, etc. held in the print case; this, in the days before monotype and linotype, when printed material was still universally composed by hand. The printers, in turn, had learned how many of each character to stock through the wearying yet ultimately effective process of trial-and-error. They had had a good number of centuries since the days of Gutenberg to discover how often they ran out of the various letters of the alphabet while trying to make a deadline.)

*   *

One can only wish that the inventors of numerous artificial languages had shown as much humility in the face of fact as did Morse; but human pride being what it is, this was perhaps too much to expect. The notion of universal understanding, of man confronting man with no impediment between the two, has always exercised its charm, and it is all too understandable that most men who have come upon the problem have perhaps seen themselves as somewhat larger than life-size. The very notion of correcting the linguistic follies of all Mankind—and such an idea has certainly been behind a good deal of language invention— implies a generous quantity of pride on the part of the inventor. Something seems to have been learned over the centuries,

however. The vogue for *a priori* artificial languages seems to have
fallen off in the last hundred years or so. Such languages (some
meant only to exist in written form, others also designed so as to
be spoken) were essentially made of "whole cloth," owing structure and vocabulary to their authors' notions of what was logical,
sensible and *right*. The "Universal Character" (1661) of the
Scot George Dalgarno was a comparatively virtuous example of
this essentially wrong-headed breed. The Universal Character,
like Bishop Wilkins' "Real Character," and many others of the
sort, was based on a carefully schematized ordering of the world—
according to a detailed arrangement which was the creator's very
own invention. Major categories within the Universal Character
were represented by consonants, so that, for example, "natural
objects" all had names beginning with "N." Within each category there were sub-categories; within *these*, sub-sub-categories,
and so forth, down to any degree of precision that one might
care to achieve.

Dalgarno had at least hit upon one ingenious device: his
nesting sets of categories began alternately with a consonant and
a vowel, so as to produce a sequence of pronounceable syllables.
In this scheme, "N" might represent "natural objects," while
each of the immediate subdivisions within "N" had a vowel
assigned to it. Within each of these vocalic sub-categories in
turn, a sub-subdivision began with a consonant. The pattern of a
typical word, therefore, was *CVCVCV* . . . out to as many
syllables as one desired.

Such artificial tongues—artificial not only in their origins, but
handmade in their very logic as well—have one deadly fallacy
implicit in their structure; possibly the reader has already
guessed it: such languages assume that *everything is essentially
known about the universe,* so that all conceivable phenomena
may safely be pigeonholed. Unfortunately, the universe keeps
surprising us, and it takes only one new fact, properly placed, to
blow all such "rational" languages sky-high. To give but a single
example: most of these *a priori* languages were developed when

it was still generally supposed that the whale was a fish (rather than the warm-blooded mammal he is). Presumably then, "whale" would have been assigned to some sub-category within the class denoting "fish," with subsidiary modifications to indicate the numerous types of whale afloat.

What happens to this lovely scheme of things, however, on the black day when it is learned that Moby Dick is closer kin to *us* than he is to the tuna? Answer: Woe and General Consternation. And when a new body of knowledge is unearthed which really upsets the fundamental categories of such a tongue, one will be left with a structure and vocabulary which are not merely inadequate but are rigorously and consistantly misleading.

Another school of linguistic creation—more recent, and far more preferable—is the *a posteriori* group. Examples of languages which have been constructed according to this general principle are the world-famous Esperanto, the Interlingua often employed for summaries of articles in a number of medical journals, and a host of lesser-known relatives: Ido, Novial, Idiom Neutral, Latino Sine Flexione, etc. These tongues are basically regularized "natural" languages. Sometimes the connection is quite obvious as in Peano's Latino Sine Flexione, which was, as its name stated, "Latin Without Inflexions"; or Jespersen's Anglic which was little more than English with all its verbs made regular and its spelling reformed. At other times the relationship is rather more tenuous, since the new creation is modelled on a supposed consensus of European languages; thus, Esperanto, Esperantido, Ido, and the like, are essentially regularized versions of a hypothetical pan-European, with vocabulary and—sometimes—grammatical devices borrowed from a number of recognized languages.

These *a posteriori* languages have a number of advantages over their *a priori* cousins; two stand out immediately: (1) since their vocabularies are primarily reflections of actual speech *somewhere*, these tongues lack that charming (but fatal) system of categorization which strait-jackets the "logically" planned tongues; (2) the vocabularies of these *a posteriori* tongues are human, they follow to a greater or lesser extent the actual practices of human speech. In sum, this class of artificial language actually obeys Zipf's Law, displaying such forms as *bono* (or something similar) for "good," and *amplificatione* for amplification." *A priori* languages, on the contrary, are superbly indifferent to the exigencies of conversation or writing. Such languages, in fact, have a very definite tendency to violate Zipf's Law at every turn; the more general logical categories are usually short, while concrete or specific phenomena within the encompassing class are generally derived by a succession of added syllables. Unfortunately, human beings have a tendency to speak—and even write—of specifics rather than universals; so that a language in which "roundness" is *Ga*, but a "dish" may be *Ga-do-la-si*, is a tongue which runs against the fundamental grain of Language itself.

These two categories of artificial language—*a priori* and *a posteriori*—are not pure types. Though the line of demarcation between the two classes is usually quite sharp, there are occasional examples of hybridization. This is perhaps most clearly seen in the best-known of all modern artificial languages, Esperanto itself, which exhibits a number of quite regrettable lapses from sensible linguistic behavior—all for the sake of a specious logic. The most notorious example of such wrong-headedness lies in the "mal-" formations peculiar to Esperanto. Thus, whereas "good" is *bona*, "full" *plena* and "large" *granda*, "bad," "empty" and "small" are *malbona*, *malplena* and *malgranda*. With the general signification of "the contrary of," *mal-* helps to breed such oddities as *malfermi* ("to 'dis-close,'" i.e., "to open") and *malamiko* ("an 'un-friend'" or "enemy").[7]

There is nothing immoral about *ignoring* Zipf's Law, of course; it is merely descriptive, not prescriptive. But indifference to this Law can cause trouble for the haughty artificial *parvenu* who

[7] In the case of *malamiko*, however, Esperanto does only what Latin itself did long before: "enemy" is ultimately traceable back to *inimicus* ("hostile") from *in-amicus*, literally, a "not-friend." However, since Latin was a tongue once actually spoken in everyday life, such forms were kept within bounds by the human desire to have often-used words as short and direct as possible.

scorns it; for, in turn, the language will suffer—or at least change, which is what languages have always done, anyway.

*   *

What can we really say of these creations which have generally reflected their inventors' desire to see logic prevail or insure world-wide understanding? It is sad, but probably true, that at worst they are harmless, at best poignantly futile. It may be true that Man *will* learn how to take the logical step, the sensible course. It may be that he will decide to accept some created language which is no one's native tongue, and steer clear of the overtones of superiority and dominance which "natural" international languages have often lent to its original speakers. Perhaps he will do these things, but let us not be bitterly disappointed if events turn out otherwise.

Greek, Latin, French and now English—each of these languages has had its fierce partisans who saw in the spread of a pet tongue, outward and visible proof of an inward invisible virtue. Invariably there are the claims for a unique degree of beauty, strength, logic, clarity, power . . . what-you-will. Who knows? There may even be certain elements of truth in these assertions, though all such fervencies are open to the strongest doubt, colored as they always are by ulterior motivation of one sort or another. The reasons for growth were darker.

There are good and sufficient reasons why English is presently in a heyday of expansion, and though it is a bonus that Shakespeare and Keats used the language, literary merit alone is incapable of explaining the widening circle of English acceptance. It may well be that English will become the *lingua franca* of a world community, but History has never drawn up an agreement with the speakers of our tongue guaranteeing us a bright and uninterrupted ascendancy. English may, after all, find itself only one among a handful of regional languages: Russian, Arabic, Spanish, Malay and (some dialect of) Chinese. Or there may be a world language after all—but one which *we* shall have to learn as foreigners.

Within the last two to three decades, the science of Language has made immense strides, and in directions which it would have been almost impossible to foresee. Mathematics has joined hands with biology and electronic theory to provide the groundwork for a discipline of symbols which we can do little but guess at. Already on the horizon is the hint of machines which will be able to translate from one human language into another. In a certain sense, the computers already have a language of their own—one which men are obliged to learn when they have some request to make of their mechanical servants. The day may be closer than we imagine when these children of our technology can speak unequivocally to the world with the tongues of men—if not of angels.

There is the promise of a new day dawning in the field of Language. But what the light will show as it falls over that now dimly-lit landscape can only be conjectured.

Epilogue

We have come a long way since that time when our ancestors huddled together around smoky fires, pathetically needful of company, a sense of community, to keep them from the surrounding dark and the things which lay in it. The soft and yearning voices of those learning-to-be-people died away long, long ago.

Now we can whisper, and our words circle the world. We look forward, afraid, perhaps, of what we shall see; there is dark weather. And in spite of a rather pathetic cocksure pride in our mastery of Nature, we are as frightened as any of those long-gone cave people were. But now it is ourselves we fear.

To C. S. Lewis, Man is still "the ape in trousers." He may be right, but if so, Man is a very strange ape indeed: one who fell out of the tree of Innocence and must now learn how to survive on the rocky ground of Experience. It may be that this is impossible. Whatever that odd and subtle trick was that occurred in the human nervous system making Speech possible—it may not be enough. The great lizards of 100 million years ago placed their faith in size and strength and yet the most flourishing survivor of the clan is the box turtle who moves sedately among the rocks of a garden.

It may be that being human is simply not enough. To have been given the privilege of Language, taking tumbled thought and ordering it to make better thought possible in turn, may not have been sufficient; it may be that something better was needed.

And then again, it may be that Man stands at the very beginning of the road. We do not know. But for better or worse, we have lived our lives always with the sound of words in our ear, the gift of words nesting in our throats.

Before we came, the world did not even know that it was. We became the consciousness of Earth, touching it with awareness. And in us, Life has achieved a complexity of being and action which will leave our planet very much changed for our having lived upon it.

We began with the blurred and groping voices of creatures just beginning to be something quite amazing: Men. And for the past million years, perhaps, the world has been touched by their sound—the sound of human voices.

Index

NOTE TO THE READER: This Index is not complete, since certain entries—*word, verb, grammar, language,* etc.—would have to be listed for almost every page. In addition, names of specific languages occur so frequently as to preclude mention in the Index, save where text or footnote goes into considerable detail. The asterisk (*) is used to indicate that reference is made to a footnote only.

About the Author

MICHAEL GIRSDANSKY, poet, technical writer, professional translator and interpreter grew up in a home full of books and where four languages were spoken. Today he has a fluent knowledge of many more languages including German, French, English, Russian, Biblical and modern Hebrew, and a good knowledge of all the Romance languages, as well as Greek, Polish, and related Slavic languages. At the age of 17 he was winner of the Fiske-Billings Poetry Award at The University of Chicago. Mr. Girsdansky's poetry and fiction have been published in the *Chicago Review* and in *Dial,* and he has done free-lance science articles for medical journals, and journals in the fields of biology, mathematics and physics.